Returning Son

From Bagdad, Kentucky to Baghdad, Iraq (and back)

By

Dennis W. Shepherd

authorHOUSE

1663 LIBERTY DRIVE, SUITE 200
BLOOMINGTON, INDIANA 47403
(800) 839-8640
www.authorhouse.com

First published by AuthorHouse 09/13/04

ISBN: 1-4184-2459-5 (e)
ISBN: 1-4184-2458-7 (sc)
ISBN: 1-4184-2460-9 (dj)

Library of Congress Control Number: 2004093838

Printed in the United States of America
Bloomington, Indiana

This book is printed on acid-free paper.

Order this book for a friend or loved one from your favorite bookstore, through ReturningSon.com, or AuthorHouse.com.

Table of Contents

Dedication

This book is dedicated to two little boys named Kyle and Jared. It is written in the hope that the world will quiet down before they reach adulthood.

Acknowledgments

Though this is the story of Private Sean Cassedy, it is also very much his family's story. The author offers his sincere appreciation for the selfless contributions of Sean's parents, Linn and Carol Cassedy, and his big sister, Heather, and for some wonderful memories supplied by Sean's younger brothers, Joshua and Stephen, and his younger sisters, Hannah, Sarah, and Rebekah. Heather's husband, Brian, also provided video footage of Sean's homecoming that proved to be invaluable. Phyllis Bailey has chronicled the history of small Kentucky communities including Bald Knob and Bridgeport. Her pictorial history of Sean's hometown of Bagdad was very helpful. In the many years I spent on active duty in the Air Force, I never met a Marine I did not respect. Captain Jason Grose is no exception. He was my cross-check for several areas that only a true Marine could tell me about.

Returning Son is written for anyone who seeks a better understanding of the arduous challenges faced by military men and women, and of the emotional roller coaster parents and loved ones must experience. I consciously omitted anything that might give it the look of an academic exercise. But to ensure the accuracy of the many historical facts I used, I retained the services of Mr. Antonio S. Thompson, a Ph.D. candidate in history from my alma mater, the University of Kentucky, to verify my own research. Mr. Thompson's areas of expertise include military history and American foreign policy.

The photographs in this book include pictures taken by Sean Cassedy as he served in Iraq and by Linn Cassedy when he served in Vietnam. They also include many family snapshots. They are by no means professional quality, but they accurately show the different generations of the family and two wars two Cassedy sons returned from.

Author's Note

Every story contains filters to the truth. No matter how hard we try to accurately tell others what happened, there are barriers between the storyteller and the actual event that remove us, sometimes only slightly, from reality. This story is no different. It is Private Sean Cassedy's story, but the filter is me. I am retelling what Sean told me. I am ordering the events in the way I believe effectively conveys his message. Every effort has been made to accurately portray what happened. No factual event presented here has been embellished. In a few instances, the identification of the actual people involved has been generalized to protect privacy interests. Every photograph from Kuwait or Iraq was either taken by Sean or one of his Marine buddies. Every photograph of Vietnam came from Sean's father or one of his Marine buddies. This is a simple story about those men and women we've all seen in the stores, in the classrooms, pumping gas, or selling computers or insurance, who somehow wind up shooting a weapon at an enemy they do not know. Above all, this is Sean's story.

Preface

This book is not about heroes. It is not about one particularly courageous Marine. It is really about one of over one hundred thousand American military men and women ordered to face death in Iraq. It's a book about how. How a young American barely out of his teens living on a very unique farm in Kentucky woke up one day fighting for his life in Iraq. How the Marine Corps hammers its young fighters inside a crucible of yelling, training, and personal deprivation. How that same Corps can sometimes be unfair, inflexible, and unforgiving. How Sean Cassedy of Bagdad, Kentucky, became Private Cassedy on the road to Baghdad, Iraq. How men kill other men. How a warrior learns the face of death. How a hometown boy returns from war.

This is where Private Cassedy was headed (Baghdad).

This is where Private Cassedy was from (Bagdad).

Prologue

In March 2003, Sean Cassedy stood alone. Just twenty-one years old and thousands of miles away from his Bagdad, Kentucky, home, he had been thrown into the caldron known as the United States Marine Corps and the chaos of Operation Iraqi Freedom. Like Sean, America also seemed to stand alone, fighting a war many countries felt was unnecessary and some thought was unjust. Both Sean and his country would have to search hard to find precisely the same thing—the justice in it all.

Chapter 1

The Face of Death

TO EVERYTHING THERE IS A SEASON,
AND A TIME TO EVERY PURPOSE UNDER THE HEAVEN.
A TIME TO BE BORN AND A TIME TO DIE ...

Ecclesiastes 3:1

You never really know that death is a teacher until you see it face to face. You never truly appreciate the preciousness of life until the teacher shows you the ugly permanence of death. Life lets you change. It lets your skin change, your hair change, your eyes, and your mind. It is being able to feel that change that is life. It is going through life's processes—growing, maturing, thinking, and loving—that allows life to explode before us. It explodes with feeling and change. It is feeling the growth of a family. It is feeling even pain, like the pain of being court-martialed by the very military service you love so dearly. It is learning to suffer the insults of boot camp. It is falling in love and feeling so completely immersed in that love only to have to live with the loneliness of a forced separation from your lover. Life is the entire gamut of human emotions. It is all of the processes. It is both winning and losing; it is pain and pleasure. It is even just barely making it.

Death is no change forever. It is no feeling ever. It is never finishing the family you were well on your way to creating. It is never seeing the baby your wife was pregnant with when you went to Kuwait to prepare for war and your eventual death. Death is all of the potential for change and feeling built up inside the shell of a man or woman and never released because it is stopped instead by another kind of shell. When death explodes before us, it is always for the last time.

Sean Cassedy learned about death from two great teachers. The first one spoke from a makeshift podium in nature. The second one lectured him from the battlefield. When he was younger, when he was a small boy, Sean Cassedy learned about death the same way most people do. Someone in the family died. Someone close to him. He would go to the funeral. He stood a few feet away from a well-preserved, well-dressed body. The body lay in a nice casket adorned with bouquets of flowers. The casket was in a clean room filled with the odor of the funeral flowers, and soft, doleful music played quietly. It was this way when his grandfather died. He also learned

1

about death through life on the farm. From a very young age he knew how to shoot. Sean's father taught him how to hunt. By the time he went off to war in Iraq, Sean was both an accomplished farmer and hunter. He knew how to prepare the game he killed. He could skin an animal and do what was necessary to convert its carcass into something fit for the family meal. He also learned about death when the family slaughtered farm animals as part of growing up in Bagdad, Kentucky. Sean was a sensitive child. When he discovered a bird that was injured, he cared for it. The bird was out of the competitive cycle. Its wound had made it easy prey to both its natural enemies and the natural elements. But with Sean's help it remained immune from attack until the injury healed and Sean released it. Back to nature. Back to its own war front.

When he was a teenager, Sean liked to play online video games—so-called massive, multiplayer, online, role-playing games, or MMORPG for short. Sean formed a team with his two younger brothers, Joshua and Stephen, and played a game where thousands of other players who subscribed for server time played both with the Cassedy team and against them. But the death he learned here was something called virtual death. The characters killed in the medieval world of this game did not die a permanent death. To provide an incentive for subscribers to die but come back, and to keep paying their monthly subscription, the rules of the game permitted reinstatement with blue crystals known as lifestones.

There was another teacher for Sean. Not from nature's landscape but from the unnatural landscape of war. Where he really learned about death—or, more precisely, the first time Sean Cassedy learned about the ugly reality of death— he learned in Iraq in 2003 when he faced his own death each minute of each hour of each day, when he saw the dead bodies of others, when he *felt* the bodies, when he went on a slow-motion ride through a corner of hell watching a Marine directly in front of him die a horrible and bloody death, and when Sean felt his own life threatening to pass out of his body. That's where Sean learned about death. That's how he came to know the face of death and its very permanence. Something neither dressed up to look good nor connected to the family supper table. It was not virtual. It was not temporary. It was in Iraq, beginning in March 2003, and when it came, there was no crystalline lifestone to revive it. He learned a simple but penetrating truth: Life is not permanent; death is.

When it happened, when Sean got his most striking lesson about that face, he was already educated in the look. The news media never report it, but there is a grim duty that troops, in particular Marines have during combat. It is corpse duty. Members of Sean's platoon, including Sean, were assigned to this gruesome task. Marines who really screwed up—the ones who were late, or who slept too long, or, worst of all, those who fell asleep when they were supposed to be guarding their fellow Marines—these Marines were the lucky ones ordered to police up the bodies. Sean did not screw up, but he still took his turn at the death detail. All in a day's work for Marines.

As the Marines of 1st Marine Expeditionary Force shot north from Kuwait toward Baghdad, bodies littered the highway, towns, and barren desert lands all along the way. Bodies from tank battles. Bodies from coalition bombing. Bodies from helicopter gunship attacks. Bodies from artillery and mortar shelling. And bodies from infantry attacks, from riflemen like Sean. The coalition forces had the sharp eyes of technology to pinpoint the enemy and destroy them. Those same forces had prepared the battlefield by virtually blinding their enemy. The result was that Iraqi bodies were always there. Everywhere.

So when it happened, Sean had quite literally several days of hands-on experience with dead bodies. He picked up decomposing corpses. The idea was to eliminate the horrible sights and smells from the Iraqi landscape, as well as to give back some small measure of human dignity to the dead Iraqi soldiers. International law required this.

The smell of death Sean recalled was as horrible as death's face. It's a smell that would never leave him. It would always be in his memory. He would have flashbacks to it triggered by virtually anything that he ever saw that once lived, whose deathly odor reminded him of Iraq. It wouldn't leave him until he joined the very dead he helped gather up. Sean helped collect the most awful array of once-living troops. Troops who were flattened beyond belief, crushed to death by some unknown coalition machine. Maybe a tank. Maybe a truck. Maybe the kind of gargantuan, seventy-ton behemoth of a vehicle that would crush Sean. He picked up the stiff, the rotting, and the limp. Sean saw all varieties of dead faces. Some had been shot, their faces twisted in awful and deadly distortion. Others had been burned as black as charcoal. Still others were mangled and bent out of human form altogether.

Sean and his comrades took these bodies and placed them in bags. Even in the middle of ferocious combat, American victors sought to treat their defeated enemy with respect, even the dead. They did not throw them, and they did not drag them. They placed them in body bags, placed the body bags onto stretchers, and took the remains to a large hole that had been dug for the mass burial. This was not the sort of mass grave that tyrants like Saddam Hussein or Slobodan Milosevic had dug to hide war crimes or, probably more accurately, peace crimes. It was an efficient way of providing a final resting place for enemy troops who, like Sean, were ordered to kill other troops they did not know. These were the troops who lost their fight and lost it with extreme prejudice. As Sean helped carry the bags that held the corpses to the gravesite, he could not help but thank his God that he was a carrier and not one of those being carried. The dead Iraqis were buried with as much honor as the fast-paced war permitted. Under international law, cremation could only be used for imperative reasons of hygiene. Sean did not have to contend with this. He only had to contend with his own stomach and conscience.

When Sean's final episode in the combat of Iraq finally happened, he already had a very bad feeling, the kind a military man gets as a premonition of his own death or of the death of one of his friends. He felt something in the air. He had seen a lot in the day or two leading up to that final day of April 3, 2003. Choppers nearly landed on top of his unit. A C-130 cargo plane landed on a makeshift coalition airstrip that Sean's outfit was charged with defending and barely missed hitting one of the trucks in Sean's convoy. The seven-ton truck that Sean and his squad of fourteen called home during the war nearly overturned in a swampy patch near that same runway. That same truck's tire blew out riding across metal joints sticking up on the airstrip like spikes. Luckily, it was a self-inflating tire. Things just weren't going right. When Sean's unit was told to move on north toward Baghdad, now a mere seventy miles away, one of the most elite Marine units, Marine Force Reconnaissance, took over airstrip security. Force Recon almost never relieved a grunt unit. It was as if the grunts had been given a sensitive assignment, and no one told them about it—a place to guard with more danger than anyone was willing to warn them about. A very expensive Predator drone, an unmanned aerial vehicle, crashed on take-off before Sean's eyes, smashing into the bridge Sean's truck was using for cover.

No one was hurt, but when Sean and his squad left the [
disconcerting feeling traveled toward Baghdad with hi[

On the road north, dust and smoke obscured his
as the convoy got started. Something about the villa[
and something about the townspeople on the side of tne [
right. He could barely see through the dust, and what he did see [
suspicious. Just before it happened, Sean felt physical things but no real
emotion. He felt the desert air as one hot blast against his dry, chapped
skin. He smelled it, the unique smell of desert Iraq, as his seven-ton headed
toward disaster. He could feel the cold steel of his light machine gun resting
in his lap.

So when it happened—the ambush or whatever it was that caused
the collision between Sean's truck and a truck five times as large—Sean
had a premonition about the face of the driver whose huge vehicle headed
for Sean's truck. He had that look. In Vietnam and in other wars, combat
veterans developed the thousand-yard stare: a wide-eyed, hollow face that
belonged to the shell-shocked and war weary. The constant pressure of
battle aged the fighter years in a matter of months and left him just going
through the motions. When Sean looked into the eyes of the driver about
to crash into Sean, he had the hollow gaze of the thousand-yard stare. It
was similar but not exactly the same. The driver's face looked as if life was
draining out of it. It was the look Sean had learned so very quickly, in just
two weeks inside the *intentional* zone of Iraq. The enemy inside this zone
fully intended to kill Sean and his fellow Marines.

The driver of the huge logistics vehicle system, or LVS, was on
an unstoppable course heading straight for Sean. His vehicle was truly a
"system" all its own. It was the gigantic workhorse of the convoy of vehicles
heading north, an oversized truck, an eight-wheeler used to transport other
large vehicles and massive amounts of cargo. It could even be configured
to become the world's largest winch truck, able to pull huge vehicles out
of trouble. By itself it weighed over twenty tons and could stretch nearly
forty feet long. The LVS that changed Sean's life weighed closer to seventy
tons because two huge trailers were connected to it. On April 3, 2003, the
driver and this monstrous machine were moving quickly toward Sean's
corner of his seven-ton truck, a truck that was dwarfed by the giant metal
object crashing toward it. The driver's face seemed to be screwed to his
instruments, and then it seemed to be frozen. Frozen out of life. It was the

...eath bearing down on Sean, and there was absolutely nothing he ...do to stop the disaster that was about to happen.

It was a face Sean had seen over and over again as he moved from ...uwait to this fateful spot within easy reach of Baghdad. The Combat Service Support Battalion-10 unit he was a part of helped relieve elements of the 1st Marine Division on its push toward Baghdad. Often Sean could hear the battle raging north of his own unit's position. Sometimes he could hear the bombing going on not too far away. Then it would happen. The bodies began to appear. Iraqis in twos and threes. Solo Iraqi troops blown out of their fighting holes. Holes Sean and his fellow Marines would sometimes then use. Out go the dead; in come the living. One constant recycling of fighters. Sean became accustomed to the faces of men who were no longer.

When it happened to him, despite the uneasy feeling that Sean was having that day, Sean thought he was going to make it out of this war alive. Maybe even unscathed. His unit had just finished duty guarding an airfield converted from a strip of highway. Then a strange series of events began to pile up until Sean began to wonder what was happening. When a soldier in a combat environment begins to lose confidence, bad things can happen. That's when it happened. That's when the vehicles collided. Sean would eventually take his K-bar, or Marine utility knife, and try to pry his legs out of the mangled mess of metal, flesh, and bone.

Strangely, as it happened, and despite the fact that it happened so quickly, Sean saw everything around him in slow motion. He remembered the face of the driver of the LVS. He could see him up close because the LVS struck Sean as he sat at the rear of his seven-ton truck, machine gun on his lap. He recalled the entire episode as an ambush but had no idea how he was shot. The Marine Corps' preliminary investigation would later label it a non-hostile vehicle accident. His mind worked like a camera, literally freeze-framing the various grimaces of the LVS driver, until that final horrible face occurred. The face eventually froze, still looking at the dials of his control panel. It was the face of death. Both the driver and Sean were very young Marines. Both came from small towns of rural America. He looked into the windshield of the LVS and watched the expression on the driver, an expression that said this was the end of his life in Iraq and in this world. It was as if Sean was looking in the mirror.

Sean heard the distinctive noise of metal colliding with metal. He heard brakes squealing as if the huge machines were great prehistoric beasts trapped in a tar pit, going through their final death throes. He heard the sound of several huge engines, the engines of the many vehicles caught up in the collision, wheels stopped in their tracks, but whose motors purred on. But most of all, through the blinding dust kicked up by the crash, he remembered the driver's face. It was looking down, distorted against the glass windshield. On the driver's right was a Marine in the passenger side of the big cab. He was the driver's assistant. Sean remembered the assistant holding both of his arms out in front of him, bracing for impact. Sean recalled the driver literally exploding before him, with his blood reaching Sean as the LVS struck the very corner where Sean was sitting.

None of what he experienced over there was like the sterile funeral parlors of his boyhood. No music. No flowers. No immaculate cleanliness or constant comfortable temperature. Real death was unexpected and messy. Real killing meant meanness directed at other meanness. In 2003, Sean learned firsthand—up close and personal—that classic warfare still went on, and there was nothing pretty about it.

The world would see a largely sanitized version of this war. The news media broadcast the shock-and-awe bombing campaign. Killing was reduced to computer terminology, to the application of a menu of lethal options, and a conscious effort was made to avoid body counts. Killing was taking out targets with cruise missiles fired from ships miles and miles away in the Persian Gulf, or with bombs dropped from stealth platforms. But neither Iraqi military or civilian deaths would be specifically reported during the taking of Baghdad.

But at the ground level where Sean was, killing and the results of killing were every day, even every hour realities. Despite all of the different kinds of high-tech, ultra-precise weaponry available for this war, Sean was part of the biggest fighting machine in this war, taking enemy territory mile after mile, day by day, battle after battle, using weapons a Marine grasped, loaded, and fired. Death at the ground level could be seen. Sean saw it almost every day of the fifteen days he spent inside of Iraq as one of his squad's two machine gunners. There was nothing sterile about it. There was nothing distant about it. It was ugly and shocking and could arrive without warning. It was final. Men and women rushed at one another with locked and loaded weapons, and, in the case of Sean and his fellow Marines, the training that made them Marines was supposed to get them out of there alive. But the driver of the LVS did not get out alive. He died in Iraq. Sean eventually pulled his own crushed legs out of the wreck and found himself on the side of the road about to pass out. His premonition was frightening because something really happened. His bad feeling ended with a Marine dying before his eyes and with his own life in jeopardy.

He also learned about death when the family slaughtered farm animals...

When he discovered a bird that was wounded he cared for it.

The seven-ton truck that Sean and his squad of fourteen called home during the war nearly overturned in a swampy patch...

A very expensive Predator drone, an unmanned aerial vehicle, crashed on take-off before Sean's eyes, smashing into the bridge Sean's truck was using for cover.

He could feel the cold steel of his light machine gun resting in his lap.

The driver of the huge logistics vehicle system, or LVS, was on an unstoppable course heading straight for Sean.

Solo Iraqi troops blown out of their fighting holes. Holes Sean and his fellow Marines would sometimes use.

Chapter 2

A Family from America's Heartland

So it's home again, and home again, America for me!
My heart is turning home again and there I long to be,
In the land of youth and freedom, beyond the ocean bars,
Where the air is full of sunlight and the flag is full of stars.
Henry van Dyke, "America for Me"

The midsection of the country has always been a ready source of young men and women serving in the nation's military. Sean Cassedy grew up in different parts of the country, but when he left for Parris Island and Marine Corps boot camp in the fateful month of September 2001, he had been living in the tiny town of Bagdad, Kentucky, for several years. It was his home. He was one of thousands of American troops sent to fight who came from small-town America.

Sean was part of a new generation of American war fighters, one that was not just computer literate, it was computer dependent. The coming of Sean's generation coincided with radical changes in the rules of war and peace. Peace no longer meant peace. War was no longer fought according to the traditional rules. Outlawed weapons loomed on the horizon of Sean's battlefield. Forbidden military tactics were practiced during the war he would take part in. Sean arrived at Marine boot camp exactly one week after September 11, 2001. He was in the new wave of modern, cyberspace-age warriors completely changed by the tragedy of that day, shocked into the defense of their country. His was a time when thousands of average men and women from all over the country formed the heart of the coalition force to take Baghdad, Iraq. Sean of little Bagdad, Kentucky, was one of the first American troops to step across the border from Kuwait and start the invasion.

His hometown of Bagdad, Kentucky, has nothing whatsoever to do with Baghdad—with an *h*—Iraq. The name does not come from settlers passing through who, in recalling some exotic Arabian story, decided to name the town in honor of a precious story-time memory. It is not named after someone named or nicknamed Bagdad. Bagdad is in Shelby County, Kentucky, a county sandwiched between Jefferson County to the west, with its Kentucky Derby city of Louisville, and Franklin County to the east, home of the state capital city of Frankfort. There are conflicting stories about how the town got its unusual name. One version suggests that men working on the trains passing through the Shelby County depot began calling the community around the depot Bagdad as a shortened form of "daddy's bag," a phrase used to affectionately refer to a youth who worked at the train depot and was loved by all. Another explanation is more widespread and is tied to the heart and soul of the town itself. The town mill has always been at the center of life in Bagdad. So, the second explanation for the town's name is that it came from the way the son of the local miller would signal his father when a customer had dropped off an order to grind in the mill: "Another bag, Dad."

Before Sean's family moved to Kentucky, the Cassedys lived near Chicago and then moved to San Diego, California. San Diego was Sean's early childhood home. It was later during his early manhood that he would train for war at nearby Camp Pendleton. The family's move from California to Bagdad, Kentucky, was like moving to the moon. They went from a nice, middle-class neighborhood in a city of over a million people to a patch of totally undeveloped land located near a tiny rural community known principally for its grain and feed mill. But the family had roots in Bagdad that went back for over fifty years on Sean's father's side.

Linn Cassedy is Sean's father. He too served with the United States Marine Corps. He is a former Marine. He is not an ex-Marine, a term Marines themselves hate and regard as meaning a dead Marine. One legendary quote sums up the relationship: "Once a Marine, always a Marine." It is that simple. Linn served during another war, during the Vietnam War. Linn is descended from Cassedys from back east, primarily from New Jersey. His grandfather had been a schooner boat captain. His father played semi-professional baseball during the Babe Ruth era in Camden, New Jersey. Linn grew up thirsting for knowledge and devoted to his religious faith. After a couple of years of college in the United States, he traveled to Switzerland to study at the renowned Christian academy, L'Abri Fellowship Foundation, located in the Alpine village of Huemoz, Switzerland. He was drafted into the military during the heyday of the Vietnam War. He served a full ten-month tour in Nam, returning to March Air Force Base, California in 1971, and eventually receiving an honorable discharge with the rank of sergeant.

Linn is the epitome of the rugged individualist. But the rugged side is offset by a gentler part. He grew up loving hiking, hunting, and fishing.

He also enjoyed playing the piano. His classical training in music seemed a little odd for a Marine serving in Vietnam. But Linn preferred classical music over the music of his day, Beethoven or Mozart over Rod Stewart and Janis Joplin. His son would inherit Linn's passion for classical music, sometimes donning his Walkman headsets to listen to a symphony as his convoy passed through the Iraqi countryside.

Linn became a highly skilled expert in a field that would help him provide for his family, a family that would grow to include seven children. He developed a very specialized knowledge of water treatment. He created his own treatment software. He obtained patents on tablet granulation and on the dispersible tablet. Another patent is pending for Klystron water treatment. He published an article in his field entitled *SCHRA: A Method for Mass Rearing of Hydra.*

Beginning in 1976 and continuing for the next ten years, he operated a water treatment company, the Hydrow Systems Company of Roselle, Illinois. During this period, Sean Cassedy was born. Linn's company was eventually bought out by a larger concern, so he took his expertise to San Diego in 1986. The Cassedys lived there until 1992. Sean was five when the family moved to California and eleven when they left for Bagdad, Kentucky.

Carol Smith Cassedy, Sean's mother, traces her roots to the mountainous west. Her grandfather was a Montana cattle rancher and part-time lawman. Her father, William Albert Smith, was from Oklahoma City. He was the first generation of United States Marines in Sean's family. He took part in the Marine landing force during the 1945 battle of Iwo Jima, a battle that saw 30,000 Marines storm ashore in the first wave. The landing was particularly treacherous because the water remained over six feet deep right up to the shore. Gaining a toehold was almost suicidal. Of over 26,000 casualties at Iwo Jima—counting dead and wounded—over 23,000 were Marines.

Carol's father also served during the Korean War. Her mother worked for the Department of Defense during this time. As a young bride and expectant mother, her job was to write letters to the families of the GIs who died in the Korean War. Carol was born in 1951 at Bethesda Naval Hospital. When Carol was a child, her father showed her some of his personal papers from World War II. These included leaflets dropped in the Japanese war zone, leaflets he called mama-san pamphlets. They were intended to counter the Japanese propaganda that Americans were coming to kill them all. Psychological warfare had not changed much in over a half a century. In Sean's war, Iraqi television broadcast almost nonstop allegations that coalition bombers were targeting purely civilian centers.

Carol's father also showed her his "death letters" from the war. These were the letters he wrote that were never sent. He wrote them to his family, fully expecting to die in battle. He hung on to them wherever he went. The modern equivalent was what Sean would do in Operation Iraqi Freedom. He wrote e-mails to his family and to the woman he loved, right up to the moment his Marine unit headed into combat. He composed them in Kuwait as he trained feverishly for the invasion. He never actually wrote a letter in anticipation of his own death as his grandfather had, but the sense of urgency and foreboding found in his e-mails was the same. He also did something his grandfather could never do: Sean spoke to his family in real time from a foxhole during combat operations.

The two families, the Cassedys from the east and the Smiths from the west, united through Linn and Carol's marriage. The couple eventually settled down to raise their growing family roughly halfway between Camden, New Jersey, and Oklahoma City, in the small town of Bagdad, Kentucky. Like many other areas of Kentucky, Shelby County was originally populated by veterans of the Revolutionary War. Veterans of the country's first international war were given land grants for service to their nation. It was a very special kind of military service offered for the very founding of their nation. Grants of land were parceled out according to rank. Sean's family farm can be traced to the opening of Kentucky by Daniel Boone and his brother, Squire Boone. Squire Boone founded Painted Stone Station in 1779 in Shelby County between the towns of Shelbyville and Eminence. The Cassedys' fifty-acre tract, known as the Whitestone Organic Farm and Bakery, was once a part of Squire Boone's land holdings.

A trip to Bagdad, Kentucky, is a journey back in time to a simpler life. It is a daydream about church-going people breathing clean country air, but the dream always comes true in Bagdad. It is leaving the big cities and fast interstates and traveling on small rural routes back into the beautiful hills and valleys of Shelby County. The land around Bagdad is not mountainous. It is several miles from the Kentucky River on high ground, so floods do not threaten the town during heavy rains.

Bagdad is a small country community tucked away from it all. It is fourteen miles west of Frankfort, down Interstate 64 to the Waddy/Peytona exit, past the Flying J truck stop, then another eight miles north on Highway 395. A road sign at the truck stop says Bagdad is just eight miles further, but in truth, it is a million miles away from city dwellers and crime centers. Small farms, old barns, and silos abound all along the way to Bagdad. During the summertime, the fields are full of tobacco and corn. Louisville lies forty-five miles to the west, Lexington forty-five miles to the east, and Cincinnati is almost due north of Bagdad, ninety miles away. But the region around Sean's hometown isn't defined by any of these big cities. The world of Bagdad includes places like Hatton, Consolation, Christiansburg, Jacksonville, and Cedarmore. Shelby County is not that large, but towns too far away from Bagdad yet still in the county aren't really considered part of the Bagdad community. Finchville, Simpsonville, Cropper, and Waddy are too far away.

The approach to Bagdad down State Highway 395 is relatively unspectacular. Less than a mile away from town, a long, white board fence appears on the left, reminiscent of the fence surrounding the famous horse farms of the Bluegrass. At about the same time the white fence becomes visible, the Bagdad water tower rises in the distance. Bagdad Cemetery is located on the left side of 395, just past the last row of white board fence. The cemetery was founded in 1876. Lots once sold for twenty-five dollars.

Entering Bagdad from the south, or the cemetery end of town, the first two streets past the green and white Bagdad city sign are Ralph Roberts Road and Kessler Mills Road. A Ruritan building is on the right, just past Kessler Mills Road. Ruritan is a community service organization prevalent among rural communities throughout America. The name comes from a combination of two Latin phrases: open land and small community. Across the street from the Ruritan building is a large sign that went up in 2003: "Bagdad Supports Our Troops and Our President." It was erected by one Bagdad family but seems to describe the feelings of the entire town. Until recently, the town had a long history of voting Democrat, but party loyalty is secondary to loyalty to the country. Across the street from the sign is the Bagdad Roller Mills.

Bagdad, Kentucky, is small. There are just over 750 rural route mail deliveries. The public schools have been closed, and the children of Bagdad are bused to schools in Shelbyville and other locations in Shelby County.

It takes just a couple of minutes to completely drive through town from one end to the other. Highway 395 cuts through the town at a right angle, starting from the green and white Bagdad sign at the south end of the town, past Bagdad Roller Mills, the Baptist church, the post office, and the fire station, to the one bank in town. Here the road bends sharply to the right, cut off by the railroad tracks to the north. Highway 395 darts to the left, and State Route 12 continues around the turn another five hundred feet or so until another highway sign appears: JACKSONVILLE 3 CEDARMORE 6. From one end to the other, Bagdad is one long, lazy, sweeping right turn.

Bagdad is defined by the beliefs of its residents. The town has one Baptist church, just past the mill. The marquee out front contains the message of the day—messages like: "Forbidden Fruits Lead to Many Jams." Between the church and nearby fire station are old, white, frame houses. A two-story, white, frame building was once a place of dance until the citizens of Bagdad stepped in. The name on the sign above the front entrance is faded, but the words can still be made out: *Karen's Place—Kentucky Hillbilly Cloggers and Line Dancers.* Clogging, also called hillbilly tap dancing, is a rousing dance movement with Irish and Scottish roots. Dancers are dressed like square dancers, and everyone taps and stomps their feet in unison at the call of a "cuer." The house of dance replaced a two-pump gas station and garage. A young couple took it over, renovating it so the wife could give line dance lessons. Everything went according to plan, and Karen's Place kicked off with a bang. After three or four Saturdays of dancing, the people of Bagdad had had enough. It wasn't the kind of dancing that suited Bagdad, and cloggers and line dancers ended their dancing in Bagdad forever.

One of the main town meeting places is located across the street from the bank, just south of the railroad tracks at an establishment called B & N Market. A combination Marathon gas station and food mart, B & N is the modern successor of Bagdad's original general store. Ben D. Estes established the B.D. Estes & Son general store over a hundred years before the war in Iraq began, during the horse-and-buggy days. The B & N store carries on the tradition of bringing townspeople together to talk about the events of the day. Sometimes they gather just to listen to Newt, one of the town's great storytellers. Bagdad has two main meeting places, and that sets it apart from the typical small country town in Kentucky. Down the street from the B & N Market is Young's Market, another combination gas station and grocery store. The people of Bagdad eat lunch at one of the two markets. They stay close to one another through this simple tradition of eating a bite and talking about the kids, the crops, and the other news of the day. All things Bagdad, including fact or fiction, will be discussed in B & N or in Young's Market.

The Bagdad Roller Mills started turning out flour and cornmeal in 1884. The name refers to the three huge cylinders, or rollers, which ground corn into finer and finer meal. It is the oldest operating mill in Shelby County. It has served as the town's principal employer for most of its existence. Townspeople simply refer to it as the mill. Over the years, it has evolved into primarily a feed mill, producing several varieties of feeds sold locally and in neighboring counties. Today's staple products include horse, cattle, hog, and chicken feed. But the mill also makes feed for rabbits, ostriches, and emus. The mill's nutritionist custom mixes the feed according to the needs of a farm's livestock. Old horses require different nutrients than young ones; dairy cattle differ from beef cattle, etc. It all makes sense to the farmers and to the people at the mill who serve their needs. Red-cabbed trucks indistinguishable from tanker fuel trucks come to pick up hundreds of pounds of feed at a time. Their tanks are divided into several compartments so they can deliver several different orders without mixing the feeds together. Today the mill employs nineteen Bagdad citizens.

Bagdad Roller Mills has been the lifeblood of Bagdad since its start. The name Bagdad is believed to have come from a miller's son. When typhoid devastated the town in 1915, the mill was there to provide foodstuffs for the area. During the early days of the twentieth century, the mill even lit up the town at night. Each evening, after the last work orders were filled, the huge belt on the electric generator that powered the mill's machinery was taken off and installed on another generator located just outside. This generator supplied electricity to light the street lamps of the town.

The mill is Bagdad's oldest industry, and directly behind it, almost hidden from view, is the town's new industry. A large, brown, steel building houses the RPS Barge Company. Founded in 1990, the company builds sectional barges that can reach ninety feet in length. Steel is brought in from Louisville and Cincinnati. Residents marvel when one of these huge, river-going structures is loaded onto a tractor-trailer truck. The truck then crawls slowly down Elmburg Road on Highway 395 toward Interstate 64. Tiny, landlocked Bagdad is the birthplace of barges destined for rivers, lakes, and even the Gulf of Mexico.

Bagdad has its share of small-town history. It is not monumental history, just the kind of news stories that connect Bagdad with halcyon days and to the heartland of the country. Just a few miles north of Bagdad, a small group of ex-slaves formed their own small community called Stringtown. In 1872, a party of the Ku Klux Klan raided the community; this story has been passed down through the generations and is known as the Stringtown Massacre. One Stringtown resident was murdered, and several others were injured. Only one Stringtown house is left standing today.

In 1941, the local paper, the *Sentinel-News*, reported an amazing and deadly coincidence: the deaths of three prominent citizens in Bagdad, all by heart attack and all within a three-week period. In 1946, the same paper reported that the wedding ring of Mrs. James Whitman had been found after being lost for twenty-five years. Bagdad's main claim to fame occurred in November 1983, when Kentucky elected its first ever woman governor, Martha Layne Collins, a Bagdad native.

There is another history in Bagdad. It is the unofficial history of the town as recorded by a long-time employee of the mill. Henry Lewis was a black miller for Bagdad Roller Mills during the 1940s and 1950s. No one remembers why he began the history, but his work is still there for all to see. He began to record it on a wall located on the second floor of the mill where he would grind corn into cornmeal. On the wall, he wrote down the births of brand-new Bagdad residents. He also wrote down the town deaths. He even recorded accidents and weddings. No one keeps up the history wall any longer. The wood is darkening as it ages, making the miller's writings hard to read. The history wall will probably last as long as the mill. The town owes its name and decades of employment to the mill. When the heart of the town stops pumping, when Bagdad Roller Mills shuts down, the history wall may die with it. Bagdad will never be the same.

Bagdad is one of many farm communities that once fed the city dwellers. It is one of the thousands of small towns dotting the national landscape that used to provide corn and wheat products for everyone. Sean had fallen out of the sky into a patch of the national heartland, from his birth near Chicago, to formative years in San Diego, and finally to the Bluegrass and Bagdad. His young life's journey took him from the Midwest to the West Coast, and finally back to the rural roots of Middle America. Bagdad is a place where children and elders of the city alike receive the utmost respect. A local pictorial history of Bagdad is filled with photographs of schoolchildren, senior townsfolk, and local characters. Characters like Pop Morse, who lived during the time of the nightriders and died in 1980 at the age of eighty-nine. Adventuresome men like Daniel Boone Gray, who moved to Oklahoma during the land-rush years.

The farming days of Bagdad are numbered. Like in so many communities across the country, the number of big dairy farms and crop farms that once surrounded Bagdad has been reduced to a handful. Large tracts are subdivided into five-acre baby farms. The smaller parcels of land attract buyers from all over. Bagdad is now a mix of long-time residents and those who came from other parts of Kentucky and the United States seeking little pieces of beautiful Kentucky acreage.

Bagdad has become a town of full-time workers and weekend farmers. There are still a few large farms raising cattle and horses. Tobacco is still a popular cash crop, along with corn and soybeans. There are three green storage tanks situated in the center of town. They are rusting with age. They speak of another day when farming was Bagdad's main business. The nearby train tracks were built to allow a railroad car to offload farm feed directly into these tanks, which would then fill local trucks. Now these old symbols of Bagdad's past are to be torn down.

Bagdad is a deeply religious community. Several churches with proud local traditions surround the territory in and around Bagdad— churches like Christiansburg Baptist Church, dating back to 1799. A couple of miles outside of Bagdad, down Highway 395, south of the cemetery, is Buffalo Lick Baptist Church. It was founded in 1805. Bagdad Baptist Church, founded in 1889, is located inside the city limits next to the mill. It is also the town's daycare center for Bagdad's children.

It was Bagdad's simplicity that inspired Linn Cassedy. He had enough of the dog-eat-dog world of big cities. He watched as a big company swallowed up the water treatment company he created. He suffered through tough financial times in San Diego. He did not like what public schools taught his children. In Bagdad, people believe in a strong work ethic. One of the most respected citizens in town goes around with a hammer and nails fixing things. Linn was also moved by the small-town togetherness he found in Bagdad. Toss a stone into a farm pond, and the entire pond is affected. Send a son of a Bagdad family off to war, and the whole town feels it. Even with its several churches and different religious denominations, Linn saw Bagdad as a refuge of rock-solid Christian values. Bagdad was also attractive to him for what it did not have. It had no crime to speak of. A county sheriff and constable took care of all criminal matters. So Linn Cassedy moved his family away from Chicago and away from San Diego to a place most Americans and many Kentuckians have never heard of.

Like so many rural communities in Kentucky and in the nation, Bagdad has always prided itself for its patriotism. Sean and his father became part of a pantheon of Bagdad residents who went off to serve their country in time of war. Despite its size, Bagdad has its own unique ties with the country's military tradition. In 1871, George Armstrong Custer was sent to Elizabethtown, Kentucky, eighty miles from Bagdad, to provide protection against threats from the Ku Klux Klan, then in its fifth year of existence. One contingent of Custer's 7th Cavalry was sent to Bagdad and lodged in the Bagdad Christian Church. Local Bagdad lore holds that one of the men who fell at Custer's Last Stand in 1876 came from the nearby town of Jacksonville, Kentucky. The 7th Cavalry would rise again, most recently in Operation Iraqi Freedom. As Sean's Marine unit pushed north toward the other Baghdad, the Army's 7th Calvary fought to the west of the Marines, eventually destroying a major Iraqi army stronghold.

Sean and his father join a long list of Bagdad veterans who served their country. That service has spanned all major conflicts of the twentieth century to Operation Iraqi Freedom. J.W. Miles, Ullman Waits, and Hazel Weakley served in World War II. George Busey was a pilot in the same war. Several members of the Bagdad chapter of the Future Farmers of America joined up during World War II, including Sam Bryant, Charles Cook, Paul Neel, Leland Perkins, Earl Young, Chester Black, Tommie Clark, and more. Leland Bland and Lonnie Quire were navy veterans.

When GIs began to return to the farms in droves after World War II, Bagdad was among the first communities in the nation to provide transition training to help the veterans adjust back into the peace-time economy. Military service in this small Kentucky town simply fuels the town's own pride. The American flag is raised high and proudly. Folks in Bagdad trust in the glory of America and in the glory of God.

The Cassedy family farm is located five miles down the road from Bagdad, near the even smaller town of Jacksonville, Kentucky. Leaving Bagdad out the back door, where the Jacksonville/Cedarmore sign appears, means following Kentucky State Route 12. Highway 395 brings visitors into town from Interstate 64, and Route 12 takes them out the back door.

Route 12 begins where the huge, rusting, green tanks are located, adjacent to the railway tracks, and continues past the Keystop gas station next to Young's Market and out of town. Across the street from the Keystop, train tracks appear on the left, but disappear behind a line of fully grown trees. Just beyond the Keystop, heading out of town on Route 12, is the Bagdad Bargain Barn. Past the Bargain Barn are a few old frame houses, and then the beautiful open countryside takes over.

Within a mile of leaving Bagdad, a large cornfield appears on the right, and a few hundred yards past this, the road comes to a T intersection that ends in another giant cornfield. The original settlement of people in this area was located near this T, in a small community called Consolation. During the 1840s, when the Louisville and Nashville Railroad built a depot one mile west of Consolation, the whole town moved toward the depot. Bagdad as it now exists was born. The railroad once figured prominently in the lives of its citizens. It took the grain harvest to larger markets. It brought feed in. A passenger train took Bagdad residents into the "big" city of Frankfort for the day and returned them home by the evening.

Turning left at the T where Consolation once stood leads to Jacksonville. The road becomes a narrow, twisting rural route that knifes its way through tunnel-like chutes of trees. A mile or so from the turn is Indian Fork Baptist Church. After another mile, Jacksonville, Kentucky, appears. Upon entering this little town, a highway sign for Cedarmore appears. A mile toward Cedarmore is Cedarmore Road, and Sean's farm can be reached by a dirt and gravel road that connects to Cedarmore Road.

Sean grew up performing chores on a very unique Kentucky farm. The farm animals included the usual cows, pigs, and chickens, but in Sean's time there were also geese, rabbits, and llamas. The family also kept bees on the farm, occasionally harvesting honey but primarily to help in the pollination of the crops. All able-bodied family members helped. This meant helping to raise several kinds of herbs. It meant growing sorghum cane and later processing the juice of the harvested cane into different cooking products. Part of the unique nature of this farm is its bakery, run by chief baker and mom, Carol Cassedy. It produces artisan breads and European-style pastries. Bakery items include such delectable-sounding things as apple pie bread, orange blossom pound cake, oatmeal and honey bread, and Sean's favorite bakery item, gingersnap cookies. The most popular of all from the Whitestone oven is lemon tea bread. Handmade quilts and a full assortment of jellies and jams are also part of the farm operation. The farm where Sean learned so much was an old-fashioned farm renovated by a very high-tech family. Virtually everything the farm produces is offered for sale through the family's Internet Web site.

Complementing the farm business is Cassedy Company, a small water treatment consulting company run by Linn. He added a computer division to offer Web design and related services, a division run by Sean when he was only sixteen. Cassedy Company and Whitestone Organic are by no means giants. They do not always turn a large profit. But over the years, they have allowed Linn and Carol Cassedy to raise their children in a very special way, according to the values the parents felt were so important.

In addition to running the family farm, Sean's parents also assumed the role of the educators of the family. Linn became headmaster of Whitestone Christian Academy, the home school for his children, including Sean. Sean's mother, once a computer programmer, also became an integral part of their home-schooling process. Home schooling was not a decision that Linn and Carol made without great thought and preparation. They began to educate their children in this manner in 1993, while still in San Diego. Before accepting such a challenge, they spent a great deal of time trying to understand how great teachers taught and how an effective home-school curriculum for their children should look. They read about some of the recognized best teachers of their day. They tried to identify what it was that made these teachers stand out. They looked at various programs offered in both private and public schools. They examined textbooks. They studied the state laws that governed home schooling. They set out to create a program for each child that was tailored to that child's unique personality. Their goals were simple but profound. They wanted to develop each child's potential and focus on the development of human character in all of their children. After Sean finished Marine boot camp, he told his parents that he thought finishing his home-schooling program was much harder than getting through boot camp.

Heather was the first to be educated this way. After the fourth grade, Sean was home schooled until he entered the Marine Corps. The rest of the children, Sean's two younger brothers and three younger sisters, all have been educated by their parents all the way. As their home-schooling program evolved, Linn and Carol asked each child to always focus their studies and their lives on answering three questions:

Where will you spend eternity?
What will be your life's work?
Who will be your life's partner?

As he stood on the edge of war, Sean drew strength from his own belief in God. For such a young military man, he showed an uncommon peace of mind in the face of war because he felt strongly that he knew where he would spend eternity. The second question was the one he constantly wrestled with. If there was a painful side to his personal search for answers, it came with the third question. When the invasion of Iraq began, Sean had just come to an important conclusion regarding his life's partner. She was back there, and he was heading toward Baghdad. She did not know about his resolve to marry her, and the war stood in the way of Sean's hopes and dreams.

When Sean went off to war, he was a lucky man. He was lucky to be a part of a large military family of fellow Marines who would fight alongside of him. He was also blessed to be a part of a large family of brothers and sisters who loved him so dearly. His younger siblings have five distinct personalities. Each one looked up to Sean, their big brother serving the United States Marine Corps. Closest in age to Sean is seventeen-year-old Stephen. He is described by his mother as a quiet adventurer. Where Sean moved head first at full speed on the river of risk, Stephen took a slower, wait-and-see approach. He assesses and looks at what others are doing before jumping into the water. He did that quite literally when he was five. Stephen watched as other kids splashed in a pool, obviously enjoying themselves. Stephen decided he could do the same, even though he didn't know how to swim. He jumped in, and his father had to pull him out. Stephen is also much more of a skeptic than Sean with his naturally trusting nature.

Fifteen-year-old Joshua is labeled the student and thinker. He is definitely not subtle. He takes after his mother in that regard. Ask him a simple question and expect a detailed lecture for an answer. When Sean went overseas to fight, his mother gave an interview with the British Broadcasting Corporation. She was asked her opinion of the French. She held nothing back. It was an interview heard around the world. Joshua could have given that interview. Thirteen-year-old Sarah is the family's equine expert. Despite her own petite size, she can handle large, English show horses with ease. She bubbles with confidence in all she does. Sarah loves computer games and doesn't let the boys shut her out of competition. A couple of years younger is Hannah the Interrogator. Hannah has a natural tendency to get to the heart of the matter. She has a bulldog's tenacity. Her parents think she'll grow up to be a journalist. Rebekah is the baby of the family at eight, but like Sarah she doesn't lack confidence. When she noticed her father wasn't paying attention to his driving the way he should have, she blurted out, "Daddy, empty your mind of everything except for driving." He did.

Sean would need the support of his family not only during his time in Iraq, but through other tough times in the Corps. Boot camp would be challenging. One particular exercise, known simply as the Crucible, would test his survival skills. Before he ever stepped foot in a war zone, he would be fighting for his life, his name, and his family's honor in another war, inside a different crucible at a military court-martial. He constantly drew strength from his parents, from his four sisters and two brothers, and from his family's proud Marine tradition. It was a family that helped each other. His were parents who cared. He would need them all during the times when he was under fire in Iraq and under attack by the Corps itself.

By the time the war in Iraq had begun in 2003, Whitestone Organic Farm and Bakery experienced the same slump that businesses and farms across the country were going through. Its products still sold at a local farmer's market and on the Internet, but the profits were getting smaller and smaller. Cassedy Company also suffered a severe drop in business. Its main business, water treatment consulting, had fewer and fewer clients. Carol had to take a job at a department store to help make ends meet for the five children still living at home.

In early 2001, Sean decided to join the Marine Corps. It was a decision related to his family's situation and to his own desire to follow the family's proud Marine heritage. He entered through the delayed-enlistment program, signing up in February but not being required to report for duty for another six months. He left for Marine boot camp on September 18, 2001. With the tragedy of September 11th so fresh in his mind, his reasons for joining were undergoing a radical change. In answer to that second crucial question—*What will be your life's work?*—Sean's mind became preoccupied with a desire to fight back and protect his country against such catastrophic attacks. More life-changing events lay ahead.

Linn Cassedy's grandfather, schooner boat captain.

Linn's father played semi-professional baseball during the Babe Ruth era in Camden, New Jersey.

Her father, William Albert Smith, was from Oklahoma City. He was the first generation of the United States Marines in Sean's family. Carol is standing directly in front of her father.

The Cassedy fifty-acre tract, known as the Whitestone Organic Farm and
Bakery, was once part of Squire Boone's land holdings.

The B & N store carries on the tradition of bringing townspeople together
to talk about the events of the day.

Down the street from the B & N Market is Young's Market, another combination gas station and grocery store.

Bagdad Roller Mills has been the lifeblood of Bagdad since its start.

George Busey

Hazel Weakley

J.W. Miles

Ullman Waits

Veterans of Bagdad, Kentucky.

Four generations.
Front row: Rebekah, Hannah, Sarah, Brian (Heather's husband),
Heather holding Brooke, Carol, Linn.
Back row: Dutch, Joshua, Stephen, Jean (Carol's mother and Dutch's
wife).

Future warrior.

<u>Chapter 3</u>

Sean Cassedy: An Atypical Typical American Boy

E-MAIL; DEFAULT SETTING; REBOOT; FLOPPY;
PROGRAMS; ONLINE; INTERNET; CYBERSPACE;
COMPUTER VIRUS; CDS; DVDS; MULTIMEDIA;
SERVERS; SPAM; INSTANT MESSAGING; GIGABYTE;
RAM; ROM; BROWSER; CACHE; CRASH.
Language from Sean's Generation

Like so many Americans, Sean was a transplant to his eventual home state. He was not a native-born Kentuckian. He lived where his parents needed to live to earn a living. He was born in the Chicago area, in Arlington Heights, Illinois. The Cassedys lived in a working-class neighborhood of Roselle, Illinois, just fifteen miles from Arlington Heights. Linn ran the Hydrow Systems Company. Sean lived in Illinois for just over five years. His childhood memories there include going to his father's plant and running a forklift as a four-year-old to the great surprise of the other employees. At about the same age, he figured out how to release the parking brake on the family van. The van coasted out of control down a hill. Fortunately, no one was hurt, and nothing was damaged. In a local department store, while his pregnant mother tried on clothes in a dressing room, Sean pulled down all of the clothes racks surrounding the dressing room, leaving his mother exposed to the world.

They were ordinary and fairly normal times that saw Sean grow and develop, and learn through trial and error. He enjoyed all of the usual fun of childhood. He learned to bike and skate. He liked gymnastics and swimming at a very young age. And he seemed to always be in the thick of it when kids in his daycare, kindergarten, or elementary school got into trouble. Sean had a tendency for blind if not literal obedience. During first grade, his teacher told him to go straight back to his seat. To her dismay, Sean marched back using a line-of-sight method that saw him climb over desk after desk, stepping clumsily over the poor children occupying those desks. To Sean, he had obeyed the teacher to the letter. During another such episode in elementary school, a school bell inadvertently went off very early in the school day. Young Sean responded like a robot, leaving school immediately. His mother was shocked to find him home from school several hours ahead of schedule with the principal calling to ask where he was.

After Illinois, the family moved on to California. The six years Sean spent in Southern California were happy ones. He did the sorts of things any boy would do growing up in Southern California and a few that were unique. He played soccer and took to skateboarding. In and out of school, he continued to build on his reputation as a different kind of child. Someone put Sean up to painting his next-door neighbor's house with a can of spray paint. Sean remembered his older sister, Heather, had something to do with it. Heather denies the charge to this day. Seven-year-old Sean emptied the can, decorating the neighbor's outside walls, drawing things only a young Renoir would understand. He spent several hours on the clean-up crew. It was also during his California years that Sean learned a critical survival skill. He learned to shoot a gun.

Linn and Carol Cassedy decided to make a remarkable change in both the way the children were being raised and the environment they were to be raised in. A couple of things pushed them in this direction. During the early 1990s, California was suffering one of its worst recessions in history. San Diego was not exempt. Linn's business was failing. In addition, the children of his growing family had never even met the relatives on Linn's side of the family. That family included a sister, a cousin, and nephews and nieces, all residing in little Bagdad, Kentucky. The time seemed right to make a radical change. Linn and Carol purchased about fifty acres of raw, undeveloped land a few miles outside of Bagdad. They left the big city behind. They abandoned the public school system for good. They traveled east and went back, back, back to the basics.

Clearing the land to make room for a log home, which they also had to build, definitely got them back to the basics. They cut down all the trees on a couple of acres to clear enough space for their house and a garden. The area they cleared overlooked a beautiful valley on one side and deep woods on the other. They constructed a unique log house built deep into the soil, so that a large part of the living space was sunk into the earth to conserve heat in the wintertime and to keep the house cool during hot Kentucky summers. The true rough part about roughing it as they prepared their home had to do with water. The nearest water source was over a thousand feet from the house. They went for three months without running water while they ran the water line. After the house was finished, they began the job of converting the land into a real farm. They began with a herd of Jersey cows. They added two hundred chickens. They even had a llama. This was not the average everyday Bluegrass farm. It would be stamped "Cassedy" through and through.

Besides Linn's desire to have his children know his family, he and Carol wanted the right setting in which to teach their children. If others thought the rural Kentucky countryside was remote, the Cassedys saw it as insulated from many of the problems associated with big-city living. If others thought Bagdad had nothing for the children to do, the Cassedys viewed the town as a haven for hard-working people and a good place to teach the kids that hard work was a gift, not something to avoid. They also thought that Bagdad was the right place to teach Christian values in a way that their children would understand them and cling to them no matter what career path they chose later in life.

That is how Sean found himself a Kentuckian growing up in tiny Bagdad. As he grew up, he joined a generation of young men and women shaped by national tragedy and exploding technology. He was eleven when terrorists detonated explosives beneath Tower One of New York's World Trade Center. Six died and over a thousand were injured in this first major terrorist attack on the American homeland. Two years later in 1995, one hundred and sixty-eight people died when homegrown terrorist Tim McVeigh blew up the Murrah Federal Building in Oklahoma City. Six years after this, he experienced the horror of September 11th with millions of other Americans. Peace no longer meant peace. Civilians were no longer immune from attacks by terrorists no matter how innocent they were. Even children had to die in this new age. Nineteen of the most beautiful angels on this earth perished in the Oklahoma City bombing. In the span of just eight years, as Sean grew from a boy to a man, he lived through the most shocking assaults on his country imaginable.

Both of Sean's parents had extensive computer knowledge. His mother, Carol, worked as a programmer for years. She knew several computer languages. His father helped Sean found his own computer company, Computer Technologies. The world was rapidly changing, and Sean was a part of a space-age generation that grew up glued to computers. At the time of the first attack on the World Trade Center in 1993, personal computers were already a popular phenomenon. At about the same time, the World Wide Web, or Internet, was being launched. E-mail was fast replacing cork bulletin boards all over the country. Cell phones were beginning to catch on in large numbers.

Just before turning sixteen, Sean went on a saving spree. He decided that he had to have his own computer. His dad had a better idea. He told Sean to build his own computer. By building one, he told his son, he would learn all about computers. Sean bought the components and constructed a completely operable machine. He saw how right his father was. Computers were not nearly as intimidating if you understood what made them tick. His interest in computers led to a related interest in Web programming. After only a few months of building computers and experimenting with the programming end, he felt he was ready to sell his expertise. Sean designed his own business, building customized computers. Computer Technologies, Inc. was born.

Sean's father was born in 1947. He is considered a part of the baby boomer generation. Baby boomers had no idea how unlucky they were. Their large numbers were in part due to fathers returning from one of the bloodiest wars in history. Living through the experience of World War II motivated the survivors to come home and sew seeds. They started families at a record pace. But large numbers of these returning sons would mean that many of their own sons would go to war. Baby boomers came of military age when the war in Vietnam needed lots of young men over a very long period of time. Boomers would fall into the widest possible crack for going to war. Linn Cassedy reached adulthood when the Vietnam War still had years to run. In 1969, the first ever draft lottery was held to determine the order of induction for men born between 1944 and 1950. Linn's birthday drew a very low draft number, guaranteeing his induction.

Nixon began to implement a policy called "Vietnamization." It meant that U.S. troops would try to turn over more and more of the fighting to South Vietnamese troops. In the aftermath of the assault on Baghdad in 2003, some would call for the "Iraqi-ization" of the fighting in that occupied country. By the end of 1968, Vietnamization had to address an American troop strength that neared 540,000. This was approximately four hundred thousand more than would head to Iraq in 2003. In addition to the sheer number of men chosen, Linn's war was an extraordinarily long one. It began in the early 1960s and did not officially end until the spring of 1975. It ended with a bang, and the bang was the fall of Saigon captured in frantic scenes of video news coverage broadcast worldwide. Marines were in the thick of the final desperate evacuations of U.S. and pro-U.S. Vietnamese from the U.S. Embassy in Saigon. In the last hours of the evacuation, the embassy compound swelled with nearly ten thousand people seeking safe passage out as North Vietnamese forces seized control of Saigon. It was a compressed, frantic version of *Casablanca*, with everyone begging for an exit visa. That was Linn's war—long, bloody, indecisive, and with no endgame ever revealed.

Linn lived in an entirely different universe than his son. It was a different time, and he fought in a radically different type of war. Linn grew up in the age of typewriters and pinball machines. He was born the very year the Gottleib pinball company added a striking new feature to its Humpty Dumpty pinball game: flippers! Linn's game vocabulary was short and simple: push, pull, flipper, free ball, free game, and tilt. When he went through Marine boot camp, physical strength and dexterity ruled.

Sean was part of Generation X plus. Born on January 24, 1982, he was too young to be a part of Generation X, roughly defined by being born between 1965 and 1977. Sean grew up in the age of computers and video games. In the year he was born, a company called Silicon Graphics was founded, a company that made high productivity servers and supercomputers using shared-memory system architecture. Sean was a part of the Playstation Generation and, even more specifically, of the Playstation 2 species of that generation. He was never a latchkey child. He passed right through the Nintendo (pre-GameCube) generation. When he went through Marine boot camp, physical strength and dexterity—*combined with lightning-speed-*

45

absorption-of-high-tech-weapons-dependent-on-computers—ruled. Sean was headed toward a three-week-long fierce battle more than a long war. It was his fate to reach adulthood, train as a Marine, and be fully prepared for combat precisely when a tiny window defined by a twenty-one-day march to Baghdad, Iraq, needed him. While his father was sucked into a huge vortex of young men headed for combat, Sean dropped through the eye of a needle and landed on the battlefield just in time to fight.

In 1999, when Sean was just seventeen, a local Louisville television station ran a story about how computer-smart teens were garnering the attention of big companies. The news anchorwoman introduced the story: "With the right certifications, you can now earn a top salary as a teenager." The beat reporter took over: "The wave is the World Wide Web, and Sean Cassedy is riding high on it with his own company called Computer Technologies." After a few video shots of Sean busily working on his computers, the reporter continued: "Cassedy does everything from building computers to developing Web sites." Less than four years later, the same station again featured Sean, but this time as a returning war veteran who had gone to hell and back.

Until he left for Parris Island in 2001, Sean successfully managed his little company as a teenager. More than one news crew featured him. His company attracted the attention of local newspapers, radio stations, and other television reports like the one from the Louisville station. Sean built computers from scratch for a living. He accepted broken computers and used his skills to troubleshoot and repair them. He also re-programmed units, constructed office network layouts, and designed Web pages. At the very young age of sixteen, Sean assumed control of this company. He even had a company credit card, so he could surf the Internet for the best bargains for components and buy them on the spot. Sean's business left him with many of his own computers, including a handful of laptops. The Marine Corps would tap into this expertise, sending Sean to a small computer specialist school. Sean would graduate near the top of his class, and the Corps would take his valuable skills and then pour them down the drain. As incredible as it now seems, someone in command circles would accuse Sean of taking another Marine's computer. It would never click with the Marines who accused him that not only did he never steal, but Sean owned his own computer company and never needed or wanted a commercial version of a machine he liked to build from the ground up. When Sean left for boot camp in 2001, he passed on Computer Technologies, Inc. to his father and two younger brothers to run.

In addition to inheriting the family treasure trove of computer expertise, Sean was an avid online gaming fan. He was light years away from his dad's pinball generation. Sean loved role-playing games where thousands of players tried their thousands of hands at outmaneuvering one another on a virtual battlefield in cyberspace. His favorite online game was Asheron's Call. A game company review described it: "Asheron's Call is a massively multiplayer role-playing game that draws together thousands of players within a dynamic, 3-D online world. Players can create truly unique characters by choosing between extensive combinations of visual appearance, attributes, and skill sets. Asheron's Call immerses players in an intense role-playing fantasy environment where they must compete or cooperate with thousands of other online players. An extensive system of allegiance and influence greatly enhances social interaction."

Asheron's Call is vastly different from the average 2-D video game. As the review suggests, it is a game about social interaction. Players pay a monthly subscription fee. When Sean and his brothers played, it cost ten dollars a month to play. It is not merely a shooting gallery that focuses on blood and gore. Asheron's Call is a game where the thousands of players are asked to pit their minds against one another. The game is set in medieval times. It involves swords, archery, and Merlin-like magic. The namesake character, Asheron, is a powerful magician. The basic premise is simple: kill monsters and keep advancing without being killed. The levels of the game go from level one to level 126. To keep players playing and paying, the game contains lifestones, blue crystals embedded in the graphics of the game architecture that can restore a dead character to life. Death in the online game world is merely virtual death, not permanent death.

Sean played the game with Joshua and Stephen. The three of them created unique virtual characters, each one with specialized survival skills. Stephen was the Phantom, adroit in hit-and-run raids and who used his archery skills to defeat the enemy. Joshua chose a very different route, as Eclipse, the unarmed fighter. Sean created a reverse character of Mr. Rogers of *Mister Rogers' Neighborhood* fame. Sean became Mr. Dark Rogerz, a mage or magician who could resort to any of four separate schools of magic, depending upon the situation. A mage had unbelievable powers, including the wonderful power to save lives.

The entire Cassedy team—Phantom, Eclipse, and Mr. Dark Rogerz—played on both of the servers available to subscribers. On one server were players swearing allegiance to one another. Players on this cooperative server could only be killed by monsters and designated PKs, or Player Killers. The other server was probably the more realistic one that was closer to the times in which Sean lived. It was the Player Killer server. Rules meant very little. Players on this server recognized allegiance to no one. The sinister forces on the PK server were the RPKs, or Random Player Killers. Sean and his brothers were always on the lookout for these.

The nerve center of the game for Sean and his two brothers was located in an old, double-wide mobile home that had been converted into a work area and kitchen. It was just twenty yards from their log home. To maximize their chances of surviving the game, the three Cassedy brothers connected three personal computers to form their own local area network. This allowed all three to control their individual characters at the same time.

But Sean's computer business and computer games had to fit within a rigorous home-school curriculum. In addition to the traditional subjects he was expected to master, work on the farm was an integral part of learning to be responsible. Sean was in charge of running the tractor. During planting season, this meant attaching a cultivating disc to help prepare the ground. The primary source of heat on the farm was firewood, so Sean joined the rest of the family in cutting, splitting, and stacking wood. He also fed the farm's two hundred chickens. His pet rooster, Roy, received special care. Sean also took turns hand-milking the Jersey cows. The milk produced drinking milk, yogurt, and ice cream. The three Cassedy brothers—Sean, Stephen, and Joshua—were in charge of harvesting the sorghum canes, then sending them through the press and cooking the juice. Linn even assigned Sean a home-school project involving carpentry. He told Sean he needed several small sheds built for the farm. He needed some as shelters for farm equipment and a few to house animals. Sean was responsible for designing each shed according to specifications, then purchasing the material so that there would be no cost overruns.

Linn and Carol chose Bagdad, Kentucky, for a number of reasons. They left California and the business downturn that had made it impossible for them to eke out a living and raise a large family at the same time. But they also chose a small town in a rural setting because they believed it was the ideal setting for teaching their children about faith in God. They were far from narrow-minded in this regard. Teaching faith to the Cassedys meant teaching their children to freely discuss anything at any time. It also meant stressing sincere personal belief over the outward trappings of the morally righteous. Linn and Carol taught Sean that belief in God begins in one's own heart.

Just a few months before the attacks of September 11, 2001, the Billy Graham Crusade spent four days at Papa John's Cardinal Stadium in Louisville, Kentucky. Sean applied to work as a counselor. Counselors assisted those attending with the various materials given out before speakers took to the podium. The crowds were enormous, with nearly 58,000 attending any given night. Counselors often dealt with ten to fifteen people at once, guiding them through the material. Applicants for these positions had to fill out an extensive questionnaire and be interviewed to get the job. Question number 17 of the questionnaire asked how and when the applicant accepted Jesus Christ as Lord and Savior. Sean answered simply and from the heart as his parents had taught him: "Christ has always played a large role in my life. Being raised in a Christian family, I accepted Jesus Christ when I was very young. Christ still plays and will continue to play a large role in my life." Sean became a counselor.

When Sean turned nineteen in January 2001, the future looked promising. He had completed his home-schooling program. He had already tasted the business world and had gained important confidence even at a very young age. Like his father over thirty years earlier, Sean wanted a journey. He wanted to leave his home and the Bagdad community and find something. He did not think in the same terms as his father did when he traveled to the ends of the earth, up the Swiss Alps to the L'Abri Fellowship Foundation. Sean made up his mind that the best path for him was one taken by two other generations of his family. He decided to enlist in the United States Marine Corps.

In February 2001, he signed up for the delayed enlistment program. While he waited for a boot camp reporting date, he attended meetings with his Marine recruiting team. He also worked out with them, showing them that he had the physical ability and mental desire to be a Marine. He also went with his recruiters to various schools in Kentucky to spread the Marine gospel. Sean took the aptitude and qualifying tests that all enlistees are required to take before entering the service. To no one's surprise, he scored high on the electronics exam. Because of this, he was able to sign an enlistment contract that guaranteed him a job with computers.

Sean Cassedy entered at one of the single most critical times in the history of the country. He began boot camp on September 18, 2001, precisely one week after the ultimate national tragedy. Some of his friends tried to talk him out of going. When the Twin Towers collapsed and the country was thrown into an indescribable chaos of fear and suspicion, his friends encouraged him to wait as long as he could. But the terrorist attack affected him much like it must have affected a lot of young men and women who had dreamed of becoming Marines. It was like the patriotic fervor in the country after Pearl Harbor. Somebody played dirty. They killed our folks on our territory in a cowardly sneak attack. Pearl Harbor and 9/11 were sixty years apart, but the revulsion was the same. The different reasons that led Sean to choose the Corps came together in an instant, an instant captured on television. He wanted to continue a proud family tradition. He wanted to earn his own daily bread instead of depending on his folks. He wanted just to be on his own. Then, after four plane crashes, he wanted to be a Marine because the country needed Marines. All of his reasons merged into the last one.

The Japanese military had struck Pearl Harbor without warning and killed unsuspecting Americans when there was no official war with Japan. It was an unforgivable and most despicable thing in the eyes of all Americans. The ranks of the American military swelled overnight with young men wanting to do something about it. That's how Sean felt. He was devastated by 9/11 and wanted more than ever to help. He wanted to aid in the defense of his country against an insidious enemy.

This was like no enemy ever imagined. It was a sinister force that targeted the unarmed, the non-military, and just everyday men, women, and children. Throughout the history of warfare, the trend has been to minimize death and injury among non-combatants, not to blow them up as the principal target. The treaties and customs of war strictly forbid attacks on unarmed men, women, and children. On September 11, 2001, decades of rules changed in a couple of hours. Terrorism has always been outlawed, but terrorists up to this point had not struck with such deadly results during peacetime at ordinary people who were just doing everyday things like earning a living or dropping children off at a daycare center. This attack was so radically different in terms of its lethality and in terms of the pure innocence of its victims that the world simply had no way to describe it.

Nearly 3,000 people were killed in a single day. The Final Report of the 9/11 Commission investigating the terrorist attacks put the final death toll at 2,981, with 2600 perishing in the World Trade Center, 125 dying when the Pentagon was struck, and 256 victims inside the four airplanes made instruments of death by the terrorists. On December 7, 1941, approximately 2,400 were killed, with only about sixty of these being civilians. Even though the overwhelming majority of those killed in 1941 were military, that doesn't make the Pearl Harbor attack any more civil or justified than 9/11. The Japanese forces were attacking a country that was technically neutral, so even the military casualties represented innocents. But in terms of the size of the tragedy and the target of purely innocent people, the events of 9/11 represent an equally dark day of infamy, if not the single most tragic one in U.S. history. The memory of Pearl Harbor Day had been fading as more and more generations separated that event in 1941 from the present day. The memory of the national revulsion over such an attack and of the national resolve to strike back was also fading away until a new national day of mourning revived the same feelings.

Sean did not need a history lesson to understand that volunteering for the military now had a cause of something up close and personal. The danger normally associated with military service all of the sudden was multiplied by a factor of nearly 3,000. He watched with millions as American Airlines Flight 11 crashed into the north tower of the World Trade Center at 8:46 in the morning. His confusion was mixed with fear and utter disbelief when just seventeen minutes later, the television cameras recorded the second crash as United Airlines Flight 175 slammed into the south tower. At 9:37, American Airlines Flight 77 crashed into the Pentagon. At 10:03, United Airlines Flight 93 crashed in Somerset County, Pennsylvania, near Pittsburgh. Heroic passengers aboard Flight 93 tried to regain control from the hijackers, their collective courage epitomized by Todd Beamer's now famous line, "Let's roll." All of this happened within a day, and most shocking of all, it all happened within just ninety minutes of that day. Though he had decided to enter military service several months before the tragedy, Sean quickly realized that he was preparing his mind and body for the very real likelihood of going into combat sooner rather than later. Boot camp would be hard, but it had to be to serve the purpose of preparing him for any battles that lay ahead.

Sean had a tendency for blind, if not literal obedience.

California boy.

It was during his California years that Sean learned a critical survival skill. He learned to shoot a gun.

They constructed a unique log house built deep into the soil…

Future Asheron's Call Three. Joshua (Eclipse), Sean (the mage, Mr. Dark Rogerz), and Stephen (Phantom).

Sean also took turns milking the Jersey cows.

Sean and the sorghum harvest.

Hunting with dad.

<u>Chapter 4</u>

Preparing for War

The conversion from civilian to Marine is more than just putting on a uniform. It is wearing along with that uniform the tradition itself. And it means conveying to the public a certain image. It also involves the most challenging military training of any of the four services. What is it about that image? What makes our hearts yearn? What makes our voices choke with emotion when a young man in a Marine uniform gets off a plane? What is it about the Marines? Is it the storied history of battles fought for this country that causes us to crumble? Do we so closely associate Marines with patriotism that our very knees buckle when Marines come our way? What is it about the myth and mystique that makes it so hard to get the words out, that fills our eyes so embarrassingly with tears—when that famous music about the halls of Montezuma and the shores of Tripoli plays? What is it?

How has it crept so deeply into this society's fabric? When we take our young men and hammer them into fighting machines—young men from all segments of our population, young men of all races, young men with problems, fresh-faced teens with the Walkman-cool strut, knifing through airports to a beat only they understand—they go quickly from boys to men and leave sweethearts behind, sweethearts who are waiting for them, or so they hope. And increasingly, joining these transformed men who sometimes must march off to war, there are similarly transformed women converted from the traditional mold of American women into warriors.

Is it the fear and sadness we collectively feel when the farm boy, or the future banker, elementary school teacher, or scientist—when these young men and more frequently now women, all filled with promise, are sent to face their mortality prematurely? Before their time? Before arthritis? Before cancer? Before they've had time to marry and have kids? Before the future farmer or businessman can ever reach that future? Fear and sadness are joined by a measure of overflowing pride—pride from the legend, the folklore, that these Marines with their history of war fought for the homeland are the world's most lethal fighting force and will protect us.

Parris Island, South Carolina, is one of two recruit depots for training Marines. The other one is located in San Diego, California. Boot camp is the starting point for the process of conversion in which anybody from anyplace, U.S.A., goes to become a United States Marine. Parris Island is located on the extreme southern coast of South Carolina, just a little north of the South Carolina-Georgia border. The small cities of Beaufort and Port Royal are a few miles north of the Island. The Island does not really look like an island, just an ugly hunk of land jutting out into Port Royal Sound. It has the shape of a small caliber bullet.

Due south of the training depot on the other side of the Sound is Hilton Head Island, creating one of the starkest contrasts in the world. One island is devoted to pain, the other to pleasure. Palm trees greet visitors at the main entrance to the Parris Island Marine Corps Recruit Depot. Everything generally associated with the Deep South, with the antebellum south, and with the coastal south is found either on or very near Parris Island. Sandy beaches. Marshy swamplands. Pine trees galore. Magnolia trees. Just across the Sound, happy vacationers bask in the luxury of tennis and golf, beaches and plush restaurants, harbors and historic mansions—all of the creature comforts one of the country's premier resort spots can offer.

For the recruit going through boot camp, none of the nice things are within reach. On Parris Island, the word is humping. Recruits enjoy a three-month-long vacation dedicated to humping. Humping is marching. Humping means suffering through heat and cold under circumstances of severe deprivation. Humping is marching so much that blisters form on blisters. The memory etched on a recruit's inner eye is the memory of humping. Sean began his Island training during the absolute best time of the year, when the weather down south wasn't too hot, and winter was still a long way off. Immediately upon arrival, he understood what his task would be. The nice weather made no difference at all. Humping was the only reality he would come to know on his Island.

Parris Island is where Marines go so that drill instructors, or DIs, quite literally drill survival skills into their recruits. This is where Marines are hammered into rock-hard troops able to survive the elements and outlast formidable foes. Many Americans know Parris Island by name, but the details of its screams, grunts, and groans are locked inside of the approximately 85 percent who succeed there. For those who fail, the secrets are safe. They failed. Why on earth would they tell anybody about the site of their failure? Sean himself had a slightly better picture of this legendary place than the average incoming recruit. His father was an Island grad. But no one can truly know what goes on there without actually experiencing the chaos and madness. Drill instructors yelling at you, playing mind games with your pride. Every field exercise is designed to press the mind and body to their limits, *and a little beyond*. No one can really pierce through the mist that hangs over Parris Island like fog over a swamp. There will always be mystery and wonder about the place and the idea of Parris Island.

There's an old saying found in every military service, including the Marine Corps: "If you haven't been there, shut the [expletive deleted] up!" It's one thing to imagine Marines loaded down with gear marching on the sandy and sometimes swampy soil of South Carolina. It's entirely another thing to feel the pain they feel, the pain of a ten-mile march in the rain, a pain that convinces you that your feet cannot possibly last any longer. It's one thing to see a photograph of Marines fighting each other with long wooden pugil sticks, but entirely another to get inside their heads and feel the fear of losing, and how overwhelming the fear of losing must guide them to victory.

In boot camp, Marines learn to forget. They learn to forget about hunger. They must survive long periods of severe deprivation. They learn to forget pain. Pain to some degree or another will be there constantly. It's a given in combat. It comes in different forms, but no matter what form it takes, the mind has to tell the body to forget about it. So they block it out. They forget about whining and about wishing they had it better. Marines do not complain. They forget how to complain. Complaining means you want something more. Marines make do. They constantly adapt to the environment. They forget about creature comforts and just assume things could be a whole lot worse.

And they forget about the other person's pain. They forget about the enemy's pain. It is the pain the Marines inflict. The Island teaches them to kill or be killed. To win, you can never be concerned about the deadly force you send the other way and the pain it causes. You can't dwell on the force of a bullet from an M-16 rifle. The bullet flies toward its human target like a perfectly thrown football spiral but at warp speed. It initially penetrates a few inches into the body with its sharp point. Then it degrades, bending or breaking in half or into little pieces. There is a midpoint groove on the M-16 bullet known as the cannelure, a groove that allows the bullet to either bend at that point or disintegrate. In the process of breaking down in the flesh, part of the bullet behind the cannelure fragments into several lead and copper mini-projectiles, all doing their own individual damage to the enemy's flesh. The lethality and the pain of what they do are better left to the scientists, the doctors, and the coroners. The Marine simply and efficiently takes out the target so the mission can be achieved. Cleanly. Surgically. Deadly.

Sean arrived for processing at Parris Island on September 18th. But he was actually an unformed mass of a pre-Marine from the time he put his signature on the enlistment papers. From February 2001 until he put his foot on the Island in September, he was regarded as a poolie. Once he began training, he became an even more worthless piece of human waste matter known as a recruit. A recruit is still a pre-Marine. It would only be when he passed successfully the boot camp test known as the Crucible that he could claim the full title: Marine. That was a long way off.

Boot camp is thirteen weeks long. One week of this is just processing. But just processing Marine-boot-camp-style comes at a price. Two principles are key toward an understanding of Parris Island. First, recruits are never supposed to be happy. Second, recruits can never make a DI happy. No matter what. Sean, like most of his fellow recruits, only saw the part of the iceberg sticking out of the water. This was the part of the Corps he had heard about. The vast hidden territory below was about to crash into his reality. His way of thinking would have to be seriously altered. His notion of right and wrong had to go. His American sense of fairness and justice was useless to him now. Maybe most out of place on this Island was his own family's belief regarding the importance of the individual. That definitely had to go.

All of this garbage he arrived with was about to be eaten up by him and his fellow maggots under the careful direction of the maggot gods, the DIs. For there was no right or wrong on Parris Island, just the Marine way of doing things. And life was never fair or just when DIs ran the show. Most important of all, there were no individuals in boot camp. Or to put it another way: All individuals were created equal—totally, absolutely, and absurdly meaningless. The individual had to always give way to the entire whole. The whole meant the team, beginning with the most basic of Marine Corps teams, the four-person fire team. The fire team supports its squad, the squad supports the platoon, and a platoon forms part of a company. Companies join to create a battalion, and battalions make up a regiment. Regiments lead to divisions, so that, finally, four divisions create the ultimate Team and the mother of all fighting forces that ever visited God's green earth, the United States Marine Corps! To become one tiny little maggot with a claim to this venerable Team, Sean Cassedy had to lose himself completely at Parris Island.

Parris Island is devoted to letting the maggot gods rip holes in the maggots, and to the maggots ripping to shreds the baggage they arrived with. During every phase of training, DIs tear down the bright-eyed, bushy-tailed notions that twelve years of public education and all of the sweet mothers in the world tried to instill in their rosy-cheeked babies. From hour one of day one, the demolition process begins. There is the right way, and there is the Marine way. Of course, the Marine way is always the real right way, and if the right way is not the Marine way, it follows logically that it must be the real wrong way.

Words are used in boot camp in an entirely different way to promote the Marine way. High school graduates and college kids alike are now maggots, the lowest form of life on the planet. DIs are the highest life form in boot camp. They are, without question, the most effective public speakers the world has ever known. They are this country's most perfect linguists. They have to be in order to get around silly rules that forbid them from making physical contact with a recruit. Word blows take the place of physical blows. Technically speaking, a DI is not even supposed to use the "f" word, or any profanity. These rules are merely the official policy. They do not necessarily coincide with the reality of Parris Island. But even if they are obeyed, DIs still have ways of getting around them. They yell so loudly that you think your head will split completely open. Physical assaults may be welcome after a recruit feels his DI's face within a half-inch of his own, spitting out words that cut the recruit in half and nearly bust his eardrums. This is merely wall-to-wall counseling, or Marine Corps mentoring.

Drill instructors use a very specialized form of English, re-tooled to be lethally effective. A recruit may not be referred to as an "asshole," but the word *ass* is a legitimate, non-profane word in any number of other ways. For example, ass-breath, ass-soaked brain, ass-sucking idiot, etc., are all fair game. Power substitutes for profane phrases abound:

"You are a suck."

"You are a maggot-sucking slime bag."

"Listen up, suck head."

"Shut that ugly sucking pie hole."

A mouth is a *pie hole*, or your *suck*, or your *sewer*. Probably most emphatic of all, it is your *dick holster*. Hands, of course, are your *dick skinners*.

Sean soon learned that you didn't need to physically assault someone or use four-letter words to effectively communicate. He got the message loud and clear. The DIs actually could refrain from using the "f" word, yet be just as effective when every other word was preceded by "freaking" or "frigging," or, even more gently, "mother-frigging" or "mother-freaking." DIs are true wordsmiths. They are venerable geniuses despite their abbreviated vocabularies and one-yell-fits-all voices.

In his first days with his class of recruits, Sean recognized one overriding emotion: fear. True, they were *just processing*, but still they felt the fear. Fear became their very first lesson in the ways of the Marine, and it guided them toward the proposition that the individual does not matter. Forget the individual. Individuals are singled out by the DI for individual torture. Better to blend in. Not make waves. Cooperate and graduate, but don't stand out. There is strength in numbers. Individuals do wrong things.

Individuals face the wrath of an escaped hyena. Fear taught Sean and the rest.

The most telling sign that the individual was on his way out came with the haircut. Military haircuts without any service affiliation at all denote off with the sideburns, off with facial hair of all kind, and wear it short. But in the Marine Corps, it means something more. Short hair in the Air Force generally lasts about as long as basic training, which is seven weeks shorter than Marine boot camp. After that, many airmen do the natural thing and let their basic training haircuts fade away, as they once again become individuals. Not Marines. That first close haircut, part of the *just processing* phase of training, is really the start of the enlistment-long, and sometimes a career-long, habit. It's the habit of not standing out, of not rejoining the civilian world. It's the mark of a Marine, of someone who wants to be known, not for himself or herself, not for vanity, not for looks, but as someone who is part of the Corps.

Sean arrived at Parris Island with a lot of hair. It took all of ten seconds and less than six strokes of the clippers, and it was gone. All gone. Soon he and his fellow recruits were one with each other. Black recruits were bald. White recruits were bald. The haircut reduced them all to the lowest common denominator. They went into the barber shop as somebody from Council Bluffs, Nebraska, or from Bagdad, Kentucky, and they came out simply as a recruit in training.

Each recruit answers to three masters. They are trained by a three-person DI team. Sean's platoon had a Staff Sergeant and two Sergeants. It is the ranking DI, called the Senior Drill Instructor, or SDI, that a recruit must watch out for. The senior barks out most of the orders and is the one person in all of boot camp who must not be angered. Like some schizophrenic god from Roman mythology, the SDI has both the power to destroy and the power to save. He can tap the second or third hat on the shoulder and in one look or with one word issue a pardon for a recruit who is about to be sent to DI hell. The SDI is the mage and the maniac of boot camp. A recruit who crosses the SDI is committing suicide. Sean would find that out.

The second DI, called the second hat, specializes in chewing out recruits, but more than that, he is also a teacher. His job is to indoctrinate recruits in the history and lore of the Corps. He also shows each recruit how to properly wear the various uniforms and gear.

The third DI team member, the third hat, is also called the heavy. The name is deadly accurate. The heavy provides motivation and incentive to correct errors. The third hat usually doles out IPT, or incentive physical training.

Incentive PT in Sean's platoon was referred to as taking a trip to the pit. When a recruit makes a mistake, the pit allows him to be rehabilitated with endless sit-ups, pushups, or any of a number of diabolically hard exercises made that way by the Marine Corps. One of the most dreaded exercises is a four-count muscle throbber called bends and thrust. The recruit begins in the standing position, bends his knees, and places his palms on the deck. Then he throws his feet back and assumes a pushup position. No sooner is he in this muscle-aching position than he must reverse the process back into the standing position. The exercise is repeated over and over until the pain becomes unbearable. When a recruit is motivated back to the right path with bends, he is said to have "gotten bent." Bends and mountain climbers are the motivational tools of the DI trade in the pit. Sean would have this honor soon enough.

The second and third hats also like to tag team. After a real screw up, one hat would give the recruit a facial, meaning yelling at the poor soul nose-to-nose. Before the victim knew what hit him, the other hat would join in. Pretty soon, the recruit would be trying to separate the woofer DI from the tweeter DI, listening to the surround sound yelling. Marines know this as "DI stereo." It could become very confusing very quickly, and no recruit wanted to be double teamed. One Tasmanian Devil let out of his cage was normally enough.

Sean's heavy hat was a bitch and pig man. Recruits were one or the other. The lowest of the low was a little bitch. But none of the name calling and none of the DI hellfire ever really got to Sean. He was used to the system. He had enough forewarning from his own father to make the yelling and the name calling nearly benign.

It would take him several months of reflection to figure it out, but Sean came to the realization that his father, Linn Cassedy, had always played the heavy hat in raising him. Many times he sent Sean to the pit, the woodshed, or whatever the civilian equivalent was for IPT. As a former enlisted Marine himself, this made perfect sense. Sean realized that his mother was his Senior Drill Instructor. She could place her hand on Linn's shoulder and in an instant save Sean from the heavy. Sean received many pardons from his mother over the years.

Sean learned quickly the Parris Island Book of Sins. During his first couple of weeks in boot camp, Sean committed what seemed like just a harmless accident. In the middle of an intense training exercise, Recruit Cassedy kicked some dirt on the senior DIs ultra-polished corfam shoes. He didn't mean to do it. But that didn't matter. He had tarnished the look of a maggot god. He had committed an assault against a DI. It was not just a crime; his actions shook the entire boot camp universe.

The DI stopped everyone immediately in their tracks. He addressed Sean by the impersonal title that all trainees learned to love. "Recruit," he yelled, looking directly at Sean's pie-hole, "did you kick sand on my corfams?" Sean was required to answer not by his name, but in the same depersonalized way, speaking of himself in the third person. More training to tear down the self. "Sir, this recruit wasn't aware that this recruit did, Sir!" In a fair world where right and wrong are well understood, this might have been deemed just an accident. But Sean had committed a Marine wrong, not a real-world wrong. The senior called over the third hat and gave the orders. "He's yours."

Sean spent the next several hours island hopping. Island hopping means going from one pit to another doing every conceivable incentive exercise known. He also was given some bonus incentive training. He had to bury himself completely in sand. Periodically, the third hat would ask:

"Are you destroyed yet?"

Sean's answer was always the same:

"Sir, no, sir!"

The exercises and torture continued. The same question followed each set:

"Are you destroyed?"

Sean, now covered from head to toe with sand, kept giving the same response. More exercises. More self-burial. More questions. The same answer. After several hours of island hopping, the third hat said something different. He told Sean all he had to do to end IPT was to say he was destroyed. No questions asked. Admit he was finished and his trip to the pits would end instantly. Sean refused to admit any such thing.

The punishment continued until the schedule called for chow. Sean went through what seemed an eternity of crunching and pushing and bending, until his joints and muscles couldn't muster any more energy for lack of oxygen. He got bent. He was smoked. Then it finally ended. Sean was allowed to go eat. His third hat warned him as he left his grave in the pit that if he got one grain of sand anywhere in the chow hall, he would be heading back to IPT.

Sean went to the chow hall looking like an overgrown baby who had spent the day playing in sand and mud at the beach. Word spread quickly of his day of torture. His fellow recruits didn't need Marine training to see he was hurting very badly. They saw it on his face. They saw it on a body completely covered in sand. They closed ranks for one of their own, for a recruit brother. Not for a Marine brother. Recruits cannot think in terms of being a Marine until they earn the title. At this stage in Sean's training, he had not earned it and would not until he faced something even more frightening than being buried in sand: the Crucible. They took turns sneaking extra food onto Sean's plate. Sean remembered that meal as one of the best of his life.

He also remembered that his little shoe accident led him to one of the primary rules of being a Marine: never, ever give up! One year after his visit to the pit, Sean would stand convicted of something he would always maintain he was innocent of. He would be disgraced in front of his fellow Marines. He would be stripped of his rank. He would go from a highly skilled computer specialist to a fabric repairman. Lesser men might have given up, but Sean would never admit that he was destroyed. Eighteen months after his boot camp island hopping, Sean would sit in a field about to pass out with both legs crushed. Nearly in shock and on the verge of passing out, he had to pry his mangled legs from a mammoth-sized wreck with his own Marine knife. One man close by would be dead. Several others would be badly injured. Sean would completely recover from his injuries.

From the day of his best meal ever, from that day forward, no drill instructor attempted to break his spirit ever again. He still had the toughest part of boot camp ahead of him. He had many tests of strength, endurance, and mental challenges to survive. But it became very clear that by standing his ground in the pit, the DIs knew they had a winner in Sean. Their time was better spent on the others.

Sean trained according to schedule. He was not overweight, so he never ran the risk of being sent to PCP, or the Physical Conditioning Platoon. The fat boys went to that platoon. PCP is also affectionately known as the Pork Chop Platoon. As his physical training continued, he also learned the customs and history of the Corps. But first and foremost, he learned how to fight. Marines are this country's most highly skilled close-in combat fighters. They learn to destroy an enemy in hand-to-hand encounters.

Before Sean went to Parris Island, the program in boot camp that trained recruits in close-in combat was the LINE program, or Linear Infighting Neural override Engagement. This was a fancy title for "kick ass." When Sean entered training, LINE was replaced by MCMAP, or Marine Corps Martial Arts Program. The new program improved on the old LINE program by increasing the offensive moves. It also included a martial arts belt system of progress so that Marines would be encouraged to maintain their skills after boot camp by improving to higher and higher skill levels. Within his first two full weeks of training, Sean was saturated with combat lessons. He went through two phases of MCMAP, two phases of pugil stick training, a separate course in upper body strikes, bayonet training, and weapons training.

Sean's weapons training included mastering the essential weapon for all military services, the M-16A2 service rifle. His own family upbringing made weapons training all the easier for Sean. He learned to shoot at an early age. He had been around guns all his life. His sister, Heather, seven years older than Sean, began competitive shooting when she was fourteen. She shot the .22 competition rifle in California in the junior Olympics. In Escondido, California, she won in her age category during a Memorial Day shoot-out. In Kentucky, she was a gold medal winner in the Bluegrass Games, a competition held for amateurs every summer and winter. Having been taught by his Marine father and having been around a highly skilled shooter in his own sister, Sean had no trouble adapting to weapons training in the Corps.

Throughout boot camp, Sean operated under a handicap. Sean was part of the four horsemen crew. The four horsemen were four recruits assigned by the DI to atone for the sins of the screw-ups. The crew had to always be on the lookout for the recruits who would slow up the entire platoon. Sean and his horsemen not only learned their own boot camp lessons, but they had to work behind the scenes with the slow learners to make sure they got through boot camp. If one of their students still screwed up, the horsemen were given extra pushups.

One day after finishing M-16 practice at the range, Sean was out front leading his platoon back to the barracks at a fast clip. A senior drill instructor from another platoon decided to dog him. He told Sean his pace was too slow for a Marine. He picked on the wrong recruit. The daily physical training had turned Sean into a highly efficient physical specimen. Sean accepted the challenge. Despite being loaded down with fifty pounds of gear, he opened up the throttle. He let his legs fly into an open sprint. He left the SDI in his dust. When the SDI caught up with Sean, he told him to slow down, a compliment to Sean if there ever was one in boot camp.

The Marine Corps is all about killing. The heart and soul of the trained Marine killer is his rifle, the M-16. An M-16 is just a little heavier than a laptop computer and costs about six hundred dollars. It fires a round that travels at approximately 3,000 feet per second. This was Sean's new best friend. This was the weapon that would make or break him and all other Marine infantrymen. Learning to shoot it, break it down, and keep it clean become solemn rituals for every Marine. All recruits are required to memorize the United States Marine Corps Rifleman's Creed. Sean went to bed with the creed. He woke up with it. Once he learned it, it never left him. *This is my rifle. There are many like it, but this one is mine.*

The words guided him. They gave him a simple philosophy of life aimed at warding off death: *My rifle is my best friend. It is my life. I must master it as I must master my life.* Sean and his rifle were one: *Without me, my rifle is useless. Without my rifle, I am useless.* No Zen philosopher could say it any better. The creed was short and simple; it was perfect. The consequences of error were obvious and deadly: *I must fire my rifle true. I must shoot straighter than my enemy who is trying to kill me. I must shoot him before he shoots me.*

Some recruits memorize the creed as ordered and leave it at that. They can spit it out word-for-word on demand. But they don't really believe in it. They do not look at the creed as a true survival philosophy. Sean did. He knew that when he went to war, it would become his ticket out. His father had learned to depend on the creed in Vietnam. The creed was written after Pearl Harbor was attacked, and it was just as important to Sean's generation if not more so after 9/11. So he memorized it, and he lived the creed. There would be reports of weapon jams during the march to Baghdad. During his two weeks as part of that assault force, Sean, assigned a machine gun, would never experience a jammed weapon. He cleaned his gun over and over again like his life depended upon it, as the creed taught him.

There are three categories of M-16 qualifications. Scoring is done according to a point system, with a bull's-eye awarded five points. In a fifty-round qualification, it takes fifty bull's-eyes to attain the maximum score of 250. The marksman category is the lowest of the qualifiers, and requires a score of between 190 and 209. After this category is the sharpshooter, required to score between 210 and 219. The top category is the expert rifleman, able to score between 220 and 250. Sean qualified at Parris Island in the top category.

Sean's weapons training included firing in four different positions and at various distances from the target. He learned to fire accurately from sitting, standing, kneeling, and prone position, firing at targets. Targets were located 200, 300, and 500 yards away. His weapons training was not limited to the M-16 rifle. It also included qualifying with the nine millimeter side arm and with two light machine guns. One of these machine guns, the M249 Squad Automatic Weapon, or SAW, would become Sean's primary weapon in Operation Iraqi Freedom.

Marine Corps boot camp includes both an obstacle course and a confidence course. The obstacle course is a challenging series of obstacles geared toward testing a recruit's physical strength. Skill areas include scaling walls and rope climbing. Mastery of the obstacle course depends on daily physical conditioning and constant repetition. Key objectives of the course are improving a recruit's speed, strength, and coordination. The first time through, many recruits have a tough time. Repeat performances lead to faster times. The obstacles found in the Parris Island layout are fairly standard at any Marine base. By the end of boot camp, recruits should reach a peak level of fitness so that the final trip or two through the course that at first seemed difficult is a breeze.

There is also an eleven-station confidence course at Parris Island. This course is designed as the name suggests for gaining confidence and overcoming fear in areas that naturally scare people. It also helps each recruit to develop upper body strength. The station called the Slide for Life is one of the more challenging. Recruits must climb a log ladder to the top of a high platform, and then navigate a rope across water, sliding on top of the rope until approximately halfway down. When the DI gives the order "switch," the real Slide for Life begins. From the switch point on, recruits dangle beneath the rope trying to move hand over hand. Diabolical drill instructors like to have fun by trying to swing the rope to throw struggling recruits into Alligator Bay. Other stations include Dirty Name, Monkey Bridge, Skyscraper, and Tough One.

Many of the basic skills learned in the first four weeks of boot camp help prepare recruits for combat water survival training of week five. Skills mastered in the water course continue to increase confidence. Sean learned how to fight in a water environment loaded down with full battle gear. Basic swimming is supplemented with "drown proofing." Each week of the three months of boot camp adds another piece to the combat puzzle. Weeks six and seven stress more weapons training with recruits practicing against both static and pop-up targets. Sean would appreciate the value of being able to quickly take out pop-up targets when he reached Iraq and Iraqi silhouettes would appear out of nowhere. At the end of week six and again at the end of week seven, recruits hump a six-mile march.

The halfway point in boot camp is called Team Week. Sean got to take a breather. No major training is scheduled during Team Week. But it is not as wonderful as it sounds. Sean had to pull his share of menial duties including mess hall duty. By virtue of his boot camp seniority, he was also expected to mentor brand-new recruits. No additional training did not mean there was no humping. Team Week ended with a ten-mile march.

Sean was becoming a complete Marine. The individual training components were starting to come together. They were starting to translate into the ability to go out and fight effectively. Sean was learning routines the combat troop and, in particular, the Marine infantryman learned to carry on the fight. He learned how to conduct patrols during combat. He could set up and break down camp. He trained in the gas chamber exercise and learned the basics of fighting and surviving during a chemical weapons attack. In another day and age, this training would have been just a block that needed to be checked. When he got his orders to join the fight in the desert, chemical weapons training became deadly serious.

Sean practiced daylight shooting and nighttime exercises. He also practiced rappelling, one of the more dangerous maneuvers required of a Marine inside enemy territory. Marines have to be able to scale cliffs and mountains and even buildings with full gear in tow. During each phase of training, Sean and the recruits of his platoon continued to exercise, build muscle, and lose body fat. They weren't all bodybuilders, but they were all moving toward an extremely high level of physical fitness.

All of these skills led to the ultimate test in boot camp, to something called the Crucible. The name alone says it all. It lasts fifty-four hours. It is from exercises like the Crucible that Marines get a reputation as bug- and snake-eaters. Sean recalled his eleventh week, training days 61 and 62, spent inside the Crucible. It was a time of physical torment, sleep deprivation, constant humping, and problem solving.

Sleep deprivation did not mean recruits were forced to go the entire fifty-four hours without any sleep. They got eight. Eight total hours allotted during fifty-four hours of constant humping. When Sean began his journey in Iraq, sleep was hard to come by. The fighting was going on. The fighting was too close to his position. Sometimes the conditions were so incredibly bad with cold rain and howling wind that Sean preferred to stay awake and stay busy. After the great sandstorm of March 25th and 26th, Sean went for two or three days at a time without any meaningful sleep whatsoever. He did not fully appreciate the significance of his trial run inside the Crucible. But the total experience of the Crucible became one of his most defining moments as a Marine.

The Crucible begins with a six-mile road march at three in the morning. During the course of the entire Crucible exercise, recruits cover forty miles of marching. They move from warrior station to warrior station performing some of the most grueling physical problem solving that the human mind can concoct. Through it all, each recruit is responsible for his own food portions. Each person is given two and one-half meals ready to eat. A Meal Ready to Eat, or MRE, is today's modern version of field rations. Three MREs provide approximately 4,000 calories, or three square meals a day from three weather-proofed plastic containers. For the Crucible, recruits dined on two and a half over two and a half days. Eight hours of sleep, two and one-half MREs, and forty miles of field hiking.

Sean's platoon was divided into problem-solving teams. He drew a team headed by a heavy hat and including some of the weakest recruits of his platoon. It was not exactly the crack team he formed with his brothers when they played Asheron's Call. The way a recruit responds to the various problems or missions helps the drill instructor identify that recruit's leadership potential. Each team starts out with a recruit team leader … until the DI fires him. Sean was never named team leader and so he was never fired. But he still solved many of the problems for his platoon. Each team has to cross a rope bridge over mined enemy territory. It has to survive a barrage of pop-up targets with a very limited supply of ammunition. Crucible teams also battle one another with pugil sticks.

Sean passed through the various warrior stations of the Crucible suffering only the normal mental and physical fatigue that comes from constant stress and deprivation. But there was one episode toward the end where he lost it. He was going through the walls-and-crawls exercise. The goal was to make it through an obstacle course of walls and tight holes using squeeze-through crawling maneuvers. He had already logged thirty of the forty miles of humping required in the Crucible. It had been constant humping with full gear. By the time he reached the walls-and-crawls exercise, he had a grand total of four hours of sleep and just one meal in his belly. That's when it happened. One of his team's weak recruits got to him. This recruit had been a major pain in the butt throughout the Crucible and very nearly failed every test up to this point. For the life of him, the weak recruit could not get over one of the walls. So, he did what true Marines are never supposed to do. In his case, it was something good recruits must never do, because he had not yet made the transition to Marine. He began to cry. That's when Sean lost it. First, he screamed at the whimpering recruit at the top of his lungs, calling him his own DI's favorite term, a little bitch. Exhausted and now seeing the progress of the entire team halted by one whimpering man, Sean picked him up and physically tossed him over the wall. When Sean went over the wall, he landed on the man he had tossed. He grabbed him by his helmet and was about to throttle him when the DI broke it up.

In other worlds, what Sean did might have been looked upon as harsh. In a different setting, he might have looked like a bully. But in the Crucible, men did what they had to so they could keep moving forward. In a combat setting, those Crucible walls might be targets in the crosshairs of the enemy's guns. After his recruit-tossing incident, Sean's drill instructor regarded Sean as the unofficial team leader. During his very next mission in the Crucible, the bayonet course, Sean was still seething over the man he had had to motivate over the wall. He lunged so hard at one of the dummies with his bayonet that he lopped off his head.

The Crucible ended the way it began, with a long hump back to the parade ground. But something was very different about this return trip. The conversion from civilian to Marine was nearly complete. As they headed out of the Crucible, each recruit wore camouflage uniforms with names now affixed. They were making the switch from subhuman and pre-Marine to human beings with the official status of Marine. Sean remembered the pride that was bursting inside of him as he marched back from the Crucible. He was fatigued beyond belief. Then it was suddenly over, and the only thing left was marching back. The simple awareness that he was about to become a Marine began to sink in as he marched. He picked up the pace, marching out front as a road guard. He was marching side by side with the company First Sergeant. There wasn't much to think about except that this was it. Boot camp was coming to an end. For Sean, it was a pleasant memory. He and the first shirt were the first two to reach the deck of the parade ground. It was the moment when the feet struck that deck that the transformation took place. In that brief instant. All of the training up to that point culminated in the boots striking the ground. Poolie status was a distant memory. Recruit status was about to end. When Sean hit that deck, he knew. The first shirt he ran with knew it, too. No more the impersonal recruit. No more, "Sir, *this recruit* did not mean to …" He could say who he was now. He was a human being after all. He was now Private Sean S. Cassedy, United States Marine Corps.

There would be another seven days of training. But for all intents and purposes, he had graduated from boot camp. He passed every test the diabolical masters of the Corps could put to him. As he ate the post-Crucible meal known as the Warriors Breakfast, he had that look that comes from surviving a truly harrowing experience. It was a look of overwhelming self-assurance, self-assurance that the combat world could not throw anything at him that he could not handle. He shared a smile with the other recruits eating breakfast, a smile that said, "We did it." It was a smile that communicated an unspoken confidence and pride: "Damned right." It gave way suddenly to another look and emotion. The smile stopped and a look of fright started, as if the recruit remembered something awful back there in the Crucible. It didn't last long, and then the smile returned.

Sean's grandfather, William A. Smith, was one of over 200,000 Marines who made it out of boot camp and into World War II after Pearl Harbor. Sean's was one of the first boot camp graduating classes where virtually every Marine felt the impact of 9/11 from his first day of training on. He was now forever linked to a special fighting force established in 1775. He was now officially a jarhead, a leatherneck, and a gyrene. He was a part of the military service that stood for "first in, last out" for any war it ever fought. From this day forward, he would end his letters and e-mails with Semper Fi, the shortened version of the vaunted Marine Corps motto, Semper Fidelis—always faithful. As a Parris Island grad, he became not a soldier, not a sailor, not an airman, not a seaman. He was now a Marine. He was connected by Corps tradition and through his family's own bloodline to the blood of all of those Marines who had fallen in combat. He was now a descendant of the devil dogs of Belleau Wood of World War I, of nearly 20,000 leathernecks who died in the Second World War, of over 4,500 Marines who fell in Korea, and of the over 14,000 Marines who died following their country's orders in Vietnam. But to succeed completely as a proud, brand-new Marine, Sean would soon learn that he would have to fight the very Corps he was so newly a part of.

A proud family tradition.

Dad at Parris Island.

Dressing like dad.

<u>Chapter 5</u>

Like Father, Like Son: The Court-Martial of PFC Sean Cassedy

WHICH OF US HAS KNOWN HIS BROTHER? WHICH OF US HAS LOOKED INTO HIS FATHER'S HEART?
Thomas Wolfe, Look Homeward Angel

Things certainly looked up for Sean once he completed boot camp. He was sent to the Marine Corps Air Ground Combat Center at Twentynine Palms, California, and assigned to an electronics school to specialize in small computers. It was right down his alley. He could not have asked for anything better. If 2001 had been a national year of tragedy, 2002 seemed to be Sean's year. His father enjoyed a similar position over thirty years earlier. Linn went from Parris Island to his chosen Marine specialty only to have things go terribly wrong. His son would follow his lead.

To his friends and family in Kentucky, Sean was the last person in the world to be accused of a crime. His Christian upbringing made it unreal. To the Marines he had come to know, including his recruiters, he was also the last person they would suspect could steal from his roommate. But it was what he was accused of stealing that made it all so incredible. Sean was accused of stealing a laptop computer. This was the same Sean Cassedy

79

who ran Computer Technologies, Incorporated. He used to customize computers for clients. He built computers. He owned no less than seven laptops. Computers to him were objects to be respected, not stolen.

His family background made it all the more unbelievable. It was a bloodline where honesty and personal reputation meant everything. His father's grandfather was one of the last schooner boat captains of the northeast. He was highly respected in his community. His dad's father was an athlete, a baseball player of the Babe Ruth era. His maternal great grandfather was a cattle rancher and part-time lawman. His mother's dad was a career Marine. After his military days were done, that same career Marine joined International Business Machines and the IBM team that developed the world's first standard computer language. Law, military, and computers. Sean came from a bloodline connected to all three. So, it was a great shock when the Cassedy household in Bagdad learned that Sean was accused of breaking the law in the Marines by stealing a computer from his own roommate.

The military justice system has an excellent reputation among civilian attorneys. Being accused of a crime in the military does not mean that Constitutional rights are left at the courtroom door. They are not. The rights of the military defendant and the civilian defendant are nearly identical, and this includes the right to remain silent. If anything, military members have expanded rights. For example, they can ask that a military lawyer be appointed to help them, they can hire a civilian attorney, and, in many cases, they can have both.

The main differences between the military system and the civilian system lie in the terminology used in each and the speed it takes to try a case. In the civilian world, a prosecutor is the district attorney or, in Sean's home state of Kentucky, the commonwealth's attorney. In the military, the prosecutor is called the trial counsel. The criminal defendant of the civilian system is called the accused in Sean's military world. A one-year delay between arraignment and trial is not uncommon in the civilian system. It is unheard of in the military justice system. That's because the military is all about the business of war. To be ready to fight should war break out, and to be able to continue the battle when war has already begun, military justice must be swift justice.

No less a legal figure than F. Lee Bailey, a former Marine fighter pilot and legal officer, has praised the military justice system. Bailey won fame for defending such high-profile clients as accused wife killer Sam Sheppard, the Boston strangler, and Captain Ernest Medina. Medina was accused of war crimes in Vietnam when civilians were murdered in My Lai hamlet. More recently, Bailey played a key role in the successful defense of O. J. Simpson. Bailey is on record saying that if he were accused of a crime and had a choice between the military justice system and the civilian criminal justice system, he would prefer being tried in the military system.

But to others, the military legal system can appear suspect. Part of the suspicion comes from a lack of familiarity. Part comes from the rapid pace of the system. When two U.S. soldiers died as a result of a grenade fragging incident on March 23, 2003, an American sergeant was arrested for the attack. The sergeant was taken back to his home unit in Fort Campbell, Kentucky, to await the results of the military investigation. A television reporter for one of the national cable networks reporting on the case ended her report by claiming that in the civilian criminal justice system, the accused is presumed innocent, but in the military, a defendant must prove his innocence. This is not true, but it shows how some think it's true.

The military has a number of different tools to enforce discipline in its ranks. The most basic way is by simple obedience to orders. The entire system of different military ranks is built on this principle, with lower-ranking troops always under strict orders to obey their higher-ranking superiors. It's a simple system and easy to follow. After this, the Code takes over. The Uniform Code of Military Justice sets out every crime imaginable, including crimes common to both the civilian and military communities, like theft, rape, and murder, and crimes unique to the military, like disrespect and absence without leave. Military commanders use something called nonjudicial punishment to deal with minor infractions, like failing to show up for duty on time or failing a military inspection. A GI accused of committing a minor offense is offered the choice of either accepting a commander's nonjudicial punishment or going to a court-martial. The different services refer to nonjudicial punishment in different ways. In the Army and Air Force, it is called Article 15 punishment, referring to Article 15 of the Uniform Code of Military Justice. The Navy and the Coast Guard call this captain's mast. The Marine Corps has a unique description for nonjudicial punishment, calling it office hours.

As military offenses go beyond the minor offense category, the military defendant faces one of the military's three types of courts-martial.

The least serious of the three is a summary court-martial. The potential punishment if convicted is rarely more than that which is found with nonjudicial punishment. Light jail sentences, however, are possible. The second type of court-martial is the special court-martial. It is roughly equivalent to civilian courts that deal with misdemeanors. Serious crimes like murder, aggravated assault, and major thefts draw the most serious kind of court-martial, the general court-martial. The sky is the limit as to potential punishment, including the death penalty for aggravated murder or for treasonous acts.

The Corps has a way of developing character. It has a way of pressing its young, of squeezing their minds in a vice, to find out what kind of mettle resides there. Sean Cassedy would find that out. His father found that out in almost an identical way. In early 1970, twenty-three-year-old Corporal Linn Cassedy was assigned to Skaggs Island Naval Security Base in Vallejo, California. He was assigned as a Marine guard. The Vietnam War was continuing with no end in sight. All Marines expected to go to Vietnam sometime during their enlistment. It was not a time to make waves.

Linn Cassedy was a man of great conviction even at his young age. His job at Skaggs Island troubled him greatly. He graduated fourth in his class at aviation supply school. He simply could not believe he had gone to a very specialized school only to be made a gate guard. He had enlisted with the understanding that he would be able to work in his chosen specialty field. This was a sore spot with him because he thought his recruiter had played fast and loose with his enlistment papers. When he signed his enlistment papers, he caught his recruiter marking "none" in the block that listed promised jobs. Linn told him to correct the papers. The recruiter crossed out the word *none* and inserted the job he promised Linn, aviation supply school. But his promise lasted less than a year. Linn went to the school that would qualify him for the job, but when he got to Skaggs Island, he was told he would be a guard, not an aviation supply specialist.

He decided to take matters into his own hands. No amount of complaining moved his superiors. No amount of persuasion did either. He showed them his enlistment papers, but he was still their guard. In February 1970, he wrote to Senator Clifford P. Case:

82

Dear Senator Case:

I am a Corporal in the United States Marine Corps, stationed at the Marine Barracks, San Francisco Bay Naval Shipyard. I have been in the Marines now at this writing one year eleven months. Before I signed up for a period of four years, the recruiter explained to me, and I have a contract to the effect, that I would go to aviation school and, I believed, work in that field.

Now, I did go to an aviation school at Memphis, Tennessee, to become an aviation supply man (MOS-3071) and finished fourth in the class. I had my choice of duty stations of which I chose USMCAS El Toro at Santa Ana, California. I was only at El Toro for eight months and only worked in my MOS for that short period of time before being transferred to the shipyard at Vallejo, Calif., to be put in the Marine guards.

Before I enlisted in the service, I was a college student, and after two years of college, I decided to take some time from school to study in Switzerland with Dr. Francis Schaeffer at L'Abri Fellowship Foundation, Huemoz, Switzerland. Upon my return, my draft board at Camden, N.J., notified me that I was reclassified, and I found out that I was probably due to be drafted. The Marine Corps got hold of my papers, and I was contacted by them. I do not especially agree with all our policies concerning Vietnam, but I did feel it was my duty as a citizen to serve my country. When I did sign up, I signed up for four years because I was led to believe what my contract promised me.

It was an amazing and brave letter for a Marine Corporal. It did not make him popular with his commanders at Skaggs Island. The senator sent him a short, noncommittal reply that emphasized the obvious: "The Marine Corps is well aware that the success of its recruiting program depends in large measure on the integrity of its recruiting procedures, and it has every desire to honor promises it has made." Translation: There was nothing the senator could do.

Linn's commander sent the senator his own assessment of the situation. In it, he only addressed Linn's secondary concern, the state of living conditions for Marines at Skaggs Island. He completely omitted the real thrust of Linn's complaint about a serious breach of his enlistment contract. The commander's letter stated that a Marine command report had graded barracks living conditions where Linn was assigned as "better than average." The report concluded that the squad bay where Corporal Cassedy slept had 2,584 square feet of living space for the twenty-six Marines residing there. This was in excess of the accepted standard of seventy-two square feet per Marine. Linn took no comfort in hearing that his living area measuring ten by ten feet was more than he deserved.

Linn's commander included in his letter to Senator Case something else. He attempted to smear Corporal Cassedy. He labeled Linn as a troublemaker when he mentioned to the senator that on March 13, 1970, Linn was placed on report for using obscene language to a superior noncommissioned officer, and this matter was referred to trial by summary court. This was a low blow. His commander tried to misdirect the inquiry away from Linn's complaint and turn Linn's own senator against Linn. The incident referenced in the letter came about in a very unusual way, and Linn's commander knew that. But he used it against Linn despite the fact that the case was still pending.

Linn was facing a summary court-martial because another Marine accused him of being disrespectful. The details would soon come out, but he still had to jump through a number of hoops just to defend himself against the accusation. A summary court-martial is the lowest level of court-martial. There is no jury in a summary court. Judges on the special and general courts must be JAGs with specialized training. But on a summary court, any commissioned officer can serve as judge. Though it's the lowest rung on the court-martial ladder, even a summary court can send a defendant to jail for up to thirty days. Linn's crime of using obscene language toward a superior noncommissioned officer grew out of a barracks incident. Another young Marine had tried to wake Linn. He was a recently returning Vietnam veteran. He was the lone survivor of a major firefight in Vietnam, and the entire episode with Linn was the result of a flashback. During a nightmare, he grabbed a large shell casing lying around in the barracks and was about to strike Linn with it when Linn woke up just in time to defend himself. The two exchanged heated words. The Vietnam survivor was a sergeant and so outranked Corporal Cassedy. He therefore pressed charges against Linn for displaying disrespect toward a noncommissioned officer.

As Linn prepared for trial, he asked to have a lawyer appointed to assist him. He received a sharp response from the legal office that was prosecuting him: "Neither the Uniform Code of Military Justice nor the Manual for Courts-Martial makes provision for appointed defense counsel in summary courts-martial." He found out about the loophole in the system. Defendants in special and general courts got a defense lawyer. They could even get two if they wanted. But in a summary court, Linn was out of luck. He would have to present his defense on his own. The same letter told Linn that he could consult with one of the judge advocates assigned to the legal office, but this was just another way of saying he could ask one of the prosecutors to help him with his case. Linn declined.

Linn prepared his own defense. While he did, his commander found a way to punish him before his court-martial ever took place. Despite how minor the charge was, his commanding officer placed him on restriction in lieu of arrest awaiting court-martial. He was confined to his barracks, with the exceptions of attending church and fulfilling medical appointments. Restriction to barracks was one of the punishments he could have received if he were convicted. His commander decided to impose it a little ahead of time.

Linn's case was as weak as a prosecution's case could get. But he still had to fight every inch of the way to keep his honor intact. He went on the attack from the beginning, testifying in great detail about how the argument started. He explained that the reason he got angry at the sergeant was because the sergeant nearly crushed the corporal's skull in with a shell casing. His testimony was just one part of his defense. He also placed his military character on the line. He submitted several letters attesting to his strong character and devout faith. A former teacher spoke of his having the "highest type of character and integrity." A lifelong friend from Linn's hometown spoke of him as an "ideal citizen." Every letter that he submitted to the military judge spoke of his honesty and of his Christian upbringing.

Linn fought for his pride and reputation during his trial. The summary court-martial took place on March 27, 1970. The trial did not last long, just six hours. The result was bittersweet. He was found not guilty. That should have ended the matter. He should have been able to go on with his enlistment. But within a week of his trial, he got orders for Danang, Vietnam. Like all of the Marines of his day, he expected to go, but because the orders arrived so quickly after his acquittal, Linn believed that he won the battle, but his commander won the war.

85

A little less than four months after his acquittal, the commanding officer of the Marine barracks presented Corporal Cassedy with a letter of appreciation to be placed in his permanent military record. It commended him for going above and beyond his normal duty and giving so freely of his time during Skaggs Island church services. "Your actions have provided an inspiration to not only the married personnel of the Station but also to the single personnel and the youth of our military community." This odd scenario of a court-martial followed by a letter of praise followed by combat would be repeated with Sean.

Marines are different. GIs from other services sometimes say that in the Marine Corps, a Marine really doesn't become a Marine until he has a couple of Article 15s under his belt. That's part of the lore of the Corps. Numbers add credence to the belief. The Corps is the smallest military service in terms of troop strength. The Army is the largest. Yet the Marine Corps out-punishes its sister services hands down. The Army had 858 summary courts in 2002, according to its annual report to Congress, and the Marine Corps had over a thousand.

Sean was next. He, too, would be charged with a crime by his commander. Like his father, Sean would have to fight for his honor. He would mount a defense very much like his dad's. He would take the witness stand and swear to God that he was innocent. To the Cassedys, this should have been enough. Swearing before God was a serious and profound act. It was not merely a courtroom detail. It was not going through the motions. Placing your hand on the Holy Bible in Sean's world connected him directly with his Maker. He could not lie under such circumstances. And he did not. Like his father did decades earlier, Sean would present witness after witness and letter after letter attesting to his good character. No one would be able to dent his testimony, and no one would be able to rebut the dozens of people who came forward to testify on his behalf. After all of his efforts, he would lose.

A few months after boot camp, Sean arrived at Twentynine Palms, California. Located in the Mojave Desert, the city of Twentynine Palms grew up around a natural oasis. After World War I, it was a place where GIs suffering from mustard gas poisoning would go in the hopes that the dry desert air would restore their health. Palm Springs is a little more than fifty miles south of Twentynine Palms. War with Iraq was eleven months away when Sean arrived. There was probably no other locale in the United States closer to the climate of Iraq than Twentynine Palms. Average temperatures, especially during March and April, are nearly identical.

Sean developed a small circle of friends while stationed at Twentynine Palms. Most of them were avid personal computer buffs. Sean was the unofficial computer expert, so the others always seemed to turn to him when a computer needed work. His time running his own company meant that he knew more than the others. He never turned anyone down. In April 2002, while he was attending the small computer specialist course, Sean developed a very serious case of tonsillitis requiring surgery. After the surgery, he was given two weeks of convalescent leave. He flew home to Bagdad, Kentucky, to spend that time with his family and friends. As part of his recuperation, he was prescribed a number of drugs. When investigators later searched his locker looking for the missing laptop computer, they saw this medicine. It would become part of the case against PFC Cassedy at trial. It would turn out to be one of a number of completely innocent things about Sean that would be turned against him.

The events that led to his court-martial began as he returned to base from convalescent leave. He got back just after midnight on Friday, April 26, 2002. He shared a room with two other Marines. It had been over thirty years since his dad had complained about the living conditions in the barracks at Vallejo, but Marines in 2002 still shared living quarters. One of his roommates had just purchased a new laptop computer. He showed it off to his friends including his bunkmate, Sean. Sean looked it over then went about the business of unpacking from his trip home and trying to get his mind back into being a Marine. He went to bed and awoke early the next morning. It was still April 26th. A routine barracks inspection was scheduled, so he spent some time cleaning his room. During a field day inspection, everything had to look perfect. Once his cleanup was finished, he went to his company office to officially sign in from leave. When he got there, he realized that he left his leave paperwork in his room, so he went back to retrieve it. He noticed the door was unlocked. He thought to himself that the inspectors must have left it open after the inspection.

At lunchtime, Sean asked his two roommates if they wanted to join him for chow. Both had other plans, so Sean went to lunch alone. Later that afternoon, he saw that his roommate was installing a latch on his desk so he could lock up his new laptop. He did lock it up and then went to work. But after he got to work, the roommate decided he wanted his laptop so he could watch a DVD while pulling duty. When he went to retrieve it from his desk, the laptop was gone.

The next series of events included no less than three separate searches of the three men's shared living quarters, with the third and final search resulting in the roommate's laptop being found in Sean's own locker. The first search was done by the three men. The three roommates took their living quarters apart looking for it. They searched the area thoroughly. They looked into each man's locker. No laptop. They unscrewed the air vents and found nothing. They went through each man's mattress. Nothing. When they could not find it, the military police were called in.

Military police called Sean in for questioning. It was the last hours of April 27th. Sean told the truth. He knew nothing about the missing computer. He was released during the early morning hours of Saturday, April 28th. When he returned to his room, Sean ran into the private who lost the laptop standing outside of their room. He said something to Sean that seemed a little odd. He told Sean that he had a mental condition and may have misplaced the laptop without knowing it. When he later testified at Sean's trial and was asked about this, he would tell the jury that he was only joking.

Sean spent much of that Saturday at a friend's house helping him with a computer problem. Sean's activities over the next couple of days seemed normal. Still recuperating from surgery, he was excused from the rigorous physical training. His morale was high. The two weeks he spent at home had buoyed his spirits. His training at Twentynine Palms in a specialty he loved was going well. He felt confident he would graduate near the top of his class. He led a spartan but good life in the desert. For entertainment, he had his X-Box. Life was good until something very unusual happened concerning the missing laptop. A third search of the men's room took place in a most unusual way. From that day forward, Sean's life as a United States Marine would change.

The military conducts barracks searches periodically to ensure that living quarters remain free of drugs and other contraband. These are known as health, morale, and welfare inspections, or, in the Marine Corps, as health and comfort inspections. They cannot be conducted as a cover to target someone suspected of a crime. The Fourth Amendment of the Constitution forbids unreasonable searches. Police cannot search based on rumors or mere suspicion. A search warrant cannot be issued unless the police have probable cause to believe a crime was in fact committed. In Sean's case, there was clearly no probable cause to justify a warrant. Two separate searches turned up nothing. The police had interviewed the two roommates who shared the living space with the Marine who lost his laptop. Nothing of any evidentiary value was discovered through this questioning. The time that had passed since the laptop was reported missing, a full four days, meant that even if probable cause existed earlier, the case was legally stale, and no civilian judge would have issued a search warrant. But Sean was not dealing with the civilian legal system. Somehow, contrary to the normal rules, a health and comfort inspection was ordered for Sean's barracks. During that inspection, Sean's roommate's laptop turned up mysteriously and conveniently inside Sean's locker.

Sean was again questioned, and again he told investigators that he had nothing to do with his roommate's computer. As he told them this, he could not have had any idea that by clinging to the truth he was committing another crime. Everything was becoming so unreal for Sean. He was in shock. The shock would continue as the pace of events picked up and the military justice system did what it does best. It moved swiftly, speeding him toward his own court-martial.

The Marine who lost the laptop later would take the witness stand during Sean's court-martial and testify that a friend of his promised to arrange for a health and comfort inspection. His friend was a Gunnery Sergeant, one of the most respected ranks in the Marine Corps. The legal import of this testimony was huge. It meant that a barracks inspection was used as a cover to target Sean when no probable cause existed to suspect him of a crime. Simply put, it meant that even if Sean was guilty, the evidence should have been suppressed and the case thrown out. But Sean was not guilty. He now had to prove that to a military justice system that seemed stacked against him with a questionable search as a starting point. Sean was beginning to think that things were upside down. He wasn't presumed innocent after all. He really did have to prove his innocence.

Outside the arena of war, there is probably nothing more unnerving to an active-duty GI than to be formally served with something labeled a DD Form 458. The name of the form reveals why. It is a charge sheet, the military equivalent of a grand jury indictment. The person charged with a crime in the military is called the accused. The accused is ordered to go to the commander's office or to the legal office so that a copy of the formal charges can be officially served on him. It is not a pleasant experience. Sean was now the accused. He had to report smartly to unfriendly territory so he could be officially called a thief. None of his friends could go with him to offer support. The class instructors from his computer course could not go. It was just Sean. After the official accusation was made, Sean Cassedy became a different kind of Marine. He wore suspicion on his face. The word spread, and other Marines at Twentynine Palms looked upon Sean very differently.

The charge sheet contains a capsule summary of the accused. It identifies him by name, by social security number, and by rank. It lists the member's specific unit, in Sean's case the Marine Corps Communication Electronics School, Marine Air Ground Task Force Training Command, Twentynine Palms. It contains the member's initial date of service [for Sean, 17 September 2001, the day he left Bagdad, Kentucky, for Parris Island] and duration of service [in Sean's case, four years]. It also lists his military pay. Sean made $1,239.30 a month according to the charge sheet. Gross pay. He made less than three hundred dollars a week to serve his country in peacetime and soon in the middle of a very hot war. Charge sheets list the pay so that military juries can compute fines and forfeitures should they find the accused guilty. But money or the lack of it meant nothing. Sean the accused was fighting for his honor and the right to stay in the Marine Corps. In less than a year, he would be facing Iraqi tanks, mortars, and bullets. He would be picking up dead bodies and would nearly die himself. He fought at Twentynine Palms for his right to fight in Iraq and do all of these things. Once he received the charge sheet, Sean knew that the battle was joined. A new type of Crucible had begun. Sean was humping just as he had in the boot camp exercise, but now he was humping toward trial, and it wasn't an exercise. It was real. He was fighting for the honor of his family name, the tradition behind that name, and he was fighting to defend his honor as a Marine.

The nightmare Sean woke to in late April 2002 only got worse. In addition to being charged with stealing, Sean was also charged with confessing. But that confession was like no confession anyone ever dreamed of. Sean confessed to being innocent! He denied ever taking his roommate's computer. Sean's commander charged him with making a false official statement by denying he stole the laptop. The charge sheet read: "In that Private First Class Sean S. Cassedy, U.S. Marine Corps, while on active duty, did at Marine Corps Air Ground Combat Center, Twentynine

Palms, California, on or about 1 May 2002, with intent to deceive, make to Investigator G., an official statement, to wit: 'I do not know how the laptop computer got in my wall locker,' 'I do not know how the laptop computer got in my backpack,' and 'I did not take PFC S.'s laptop computer,' or words to that effect, which statements were totally false and then known by the said Private First Class Cassedy to be so false." It is a peculiarity of the military justice system that a defendant's loud and clear claims of innocence can be converted into a crime.

There are generally two kinds of prosecutors in the military. By far, the first kind is made up of very honorable men and women. By far, these JAG officers seek justice. They charge only what can be proven by the evidence. There is a second kind. A very small minority of prosecutors seem to forget that theirs is a search for the truth and justice. Sometimes lacking experience and sometimes forgetting fairness, they press ahead just to get a conviction. Self-interest takes over. They seek to make a name for themselves. They are said to have blood on their teeth. Charging a young man with making a false statement because he makes a full denial of the crime is the cheapest shot that any prosecutor can take. Sean drew the second kind of prosecutor.

The Marine base at Twentynine Palms sits in the middle of the desert. Joshua trees abound. Mountains are visible in the distance. The military courtroom is located in a white building that almost fades into the surrounding desert. The courtroom where Sean was tried was small and very plain looking. An American flag stood in one corner and the Marine Corps flag stood opposite it in the other. On one end of the room, the judge's bench peered down over everything. To one side of the judge's bench, a small area was set up to seat the trial spectators. A mahogany guardrail separated the spectators from the participants. A dozen or so old office chairs were placed in the spectator's gallery. Only a few people watched Sean's trial. On the other side of the judge's bench was the jury box. It was so elevated that jurors actually looked down on the accused and the witnesses. Sean would get used to being looked down upon. Witnesses sat unprotected in a chair in the middle of the courtroom.

On Monday, September 23, 2002, the trial of Private First Class Sean Cassedy began. Linn Cassedy's trial lasted only a few hours. Sean's would last three days. There are many favorable comparisons between a civilian trial and a court-martial. But sometimes what seems like a good thing on the surface is not so good after closer examination. Both systems use the jury as a fact-finding body. But the military system uses a very elite jury. Military juries are composed of commissioned officers. Every juror has a college degree. The whole idea of a jury of peers is radically changed in the military. Most trials are trials of enlisted men and women, and most juries are juries of officers. So it is a rare thing for these defendants to ever get a jury of people just like them. Instead, they get a highly educated group of military officers who don't share common experiences with them.

Jurors do share something with the base legal office. Every juror has some contact with the very legal office that brings charges and provides the prosecutor. It is rare to see jurors laughing and joking with the defense team, but not so rare to see them smiling at prosecutors, especially when the prosecutors also prepare their wills and powers of attorney. This doesn't mean a prosecutor can't be fair, and this doesn't mean that jurors can't live up to their oath to be fair and impartial. But it's a fact of life that defendants like Sean must deal with. It isn't so much how jurors behave as how the defendant thinks they behave.

Civilian jury pools are created using very simple criteria. They are drawn from a list of local taxpayers, or they come from the registered voter list. In some jurisdictions, they are picked from the rolls of the licensed drivers. This opens up service on a jury to a wide cross-section of the population. But in the military, the base commander who authorizes the court-martial also personally selects the jury panel. Typically, a dozen or so names provided by the legal office in charge of prosecuting are given to the commander. The commander then initials the required number for a court-martial. Instead of a huge cross-section, a handful of officers who were handpicked by the person convening the court sit on the typical military jury.

In Sean's case, four junior-grade officers sat on his jury. They were four officers fairly new to the military and probably had hopes of making the military a career. In addition, the prosecution was not even required to persuade all of the four of Sean's guilt. The unanimous verdict is foreign to the military. In the military justice system, only two-thirds of the jurors is required to find an accused guilty. This meant that only three of the four captains needed to reach a verdict to find Sean guilty.

In the vast majority of cases, the military justice system means a fair trial and just results. This is in spite of the way the jurors are picked by the base commander and in spite of the emphasis on speed. But there are cases which lack evidence and which lack motive that reveal the military way of doing things is more like a bulldozer out to flatten a three-hundred-dollar-a-week Private First Class. Sean felt that way about his case. The bogus third search made no sense. It seemed more likely that someone wanted to find the laptop in his locker and took steps to ensure that result. The second charge of making a false statement, created from Sean's outright denial of guilt, seemed concocted. The military justice train kept coming at him, and Sean was powerless to stop it.

Sean's father flew to California to stand by his son. Linn watched every minute of every day of the trial. It was as if some cruel wizard, a black-hearted version of Sean's old Asheron's Call character, Mr. Dark Rogerz, had created a dark, distorted mirror for the Cassedy family. Linn Cassedy could look in it and see his son go through the same torment he went through thirty years earlier.

The heat outside was unbearable. It was typical Twentynine Palms weather, where summertime highs reached 115 degrees. Linn and his son entered the courtroom each of the three days from a room set aside for defense counsel. It was also a holding area for more serious defendants. So, each day they passed by the less fortunate, the poor souls already dressed in orange jumpsuits and already shackled. The military judge was a Lieutenant Colonel. Both the prosecutor and defense attorney were Captains in their late twenties. Linn took his seat in one of the office chairs of the gallery, and Sean sat with his appointed military lawyer directly in front of the military judge.

The only spectators Linn Cassedy noticed were officers. One of these was a gruff-looking Colonel in a camouflage uniform. Linn learned later that he was sitting next to the base commander who had convened this special court-martial against his son. This struck him as a move intended to keep the four captains on the jury in line. At least, that is what Linn thought. When the colonel who runs the base watches the captains who try his case, there is at least a perception that he is there to keep everybody straight. There is nothing in the military rules that forbids this, but to Linn it just didn't look right.

In a civilian trial, experienced attorneys take several hours and sometimes several days to select a jury. In the military system, it is condensed into a much shorter process, usually taking just a couple of hours. There is no real need to try to discover the criminal history of the panel, because there never is one. The result is that a criminal defendant like Sean gets precisely who the base commander gives him.

Sean's trial was neither exciting nor fair. The prosecutor used a cookie jar comparison in his opening statement. An opening statement is supposed to be a preview of the evidence, but since there was none in this case, the prosecutor instead fell back on a cheap and easy theory. It was a theory built on cookies. He compared Sean to a little boy caught stealing from a cookie jar. He claimed that Sean left a trail of cookie crumbs that led to the laptop. There was no such trail. What he really had was a case where Sean was at the wrong place at the wrong time. But more than the prosecutor's lack of evidence, comparing a United States Marine to a little boy was demeaning. Sean and his father grimaced at the thought.

The single image of a trail of cookies leading back to Sean's locker completely ignored the actual evidence in the case. First, there was no trail. There were two searches and an investigation, which turned up nothing. So there was no starting point for this imagined trail. Next, Sean was adamant and consistent in denying any guilt. Sean himself prevented a trail from springing out of thin air with his forceful denial. Third, the imagined trail led just as well to Sean's roommates. Even the owner of the laptop was a potential suspect, but the investigators never saw it. The owner of the laptop had told Sean the bizarre story about having a mental problem. This suggested that he might have planted the laptop in Sean's locker because of his problem. He might have needed attention, or maybe he felt so guilty after getting many people involved in his case that he had to show them he knew what he was talking about. According to Sean's testimony, he gave both of his roommates the combination to his own locker. Neither roommate would fully own up to this, but the prosecution theory never had any basis as far as the real evidence was concerned. It would have been a simple thing to fingerprint the laptop. But military investigators consciously chose not to look for fingerprints. There was no trail leading to Sean, but that's what the prosecutor told the jury as he opened his case.

Things only got worse. Not only did the prosecution focus the jury on such nonsense, but even Sean's Kentucky background was not immune from attack. Sean was portrayed as a young, impressionable man from the farm, as someone who led a sheltered life because he was home schooled. The attack on Sean was an attack on his very proud family roots, and neither

94

Sean nor his dad could do anything but sit there and hide the anger that was boiling inside them. The prosecutor simply did not understand who he was dealing with. Sean came from a large and close family that put a very high premium on Christian values. Instead, Sean was cast as the country bumpkin out of his element in the big time world of Marines. He was no longer defending just his own honor, but the honor of his home state, his county, his home town, and of the honor of his family's tract of land in Kentucky.

The prosecution's case quickly convinced Linn that his son was not going to get out of this. Sean's two roommates testified. Sean had given each one the combination to his wall locker. He considered this to be a relatively important piece of evidence to bring out through both witnesses. If he could show the jury that all three had access to the one locker, doubt would be cast on how the laptop got into his locker. But this crucial bit of evidence didn't come out the way Sean had hoped. One roommate stated that he did not remember Sean giving the combination to him. The other man said that Sean did give it to him, but he never knew what it was for.

Two military investigators testified against Sean. Both were allowed to tell the jury what no court should ever allow. One told the jury that Sean's body language suggested to him that Sean was lying. The second inspector was allowed to testify that he had a seventeen-year-old son, and that Sean spoke to him like his son did when he lied. Under normal rules, attempts like that to convert a police witness into a human lie detector would be grounds for reversing a conviction. But this damning evidence was allowed in Sean's case. One investigator went so far as to say that he found a watch in the same place the laptop was found, and he thought the watch was also stolen. Sean had owned the watch for some time. When he went to war in Iraq, he wore the same watch. Drugs were also found! But these were Sean's prescribed medications left over from his tonsil condition.

The trial continued, and father and son detected something throughout the entire presentation of the prosecution's case that all lawyers try to avoid. It was prejudice. It was the feeling that no matter what the truth was, there was only one side that was right in this case. It was the Marine side. It was the prosecution side. What they said, whether backed up by evidence or not, was what the four Captains were eating up. Just as everything looked stacked against him, Sean saw a glimmer of hope.

The hope came when the subject of the strange third barracks search came up. To show that this was a regularly scheduled inspection, the prosecution called the man who ordered the inspection. He was a Sergeant Major. He testified that this third inspection was part of a pre-scheduled unit inspection plan. Sean's defense counsel had only one question: Can you prove that? The sergeant major testified that he could because the inspection schedule was listed in a log book he kept. At this, the military judge ordered the witness to locate the log book and bring it to court after a recess. Sean began to see some daylight, especially if the log book could not be produced, or if it contained no such scheduled inspection of Sean's barracks. The Sergeant Major returned to court after lunch with the incredible news that he had lost the key to his own safe. The issue never came up again.

One of the turning points of the court-martial involved an event that hurt Sean's father deeply. Shortly after being accused of the theft, Sean spoke with his father on the phone from his barracks. A Marine standing near Sean overheard this conversation, but only a small part of it. Sean's father was offering his son the best advice he could. He told Sean that if he committed the crime, he needed to come clean and accept his punishment. On the other hand, he told his son that if he did not take the laptop, he should never give up. Linn asked him what kind of evidence they had against him. The bystander overheard this part of Sean's answer: "They don't have any evidence on me." To the prosecutor, this one sentence could be twisted into an admission that Sean was guilty, a statement that he would argue meant Sean was really guilty, but he was telling his father not to worry because they could not prove it.

Linn sat in the courtroom, a loyal father, watching it all unfold. The first two days, Monday, September 23, 2002, and Tuesday the 24th, were taken up with the prosecution's case. Toward the end of their evidence, they called the Gunnery Sergeant who overheard Sean tell his father that they didn't have any evidence on him. But the prosecution was not happy with just presenting the witness who overheard the statement. A simple little trial trick blew it all out of proportion. To exaggerate the importance of the testimony, the prosecution introduced phone records to confirm that a call had taken place when the witness said it did, between Sean in California and his dad in Bagdad, Kentucky, on the date and at the time the witness indicated. The idea was to show the jury that the government expended major resources to corroborate the testimony. So it had to be important.

The words overheard by the Gunnery Sergeant really were not relevant. In fact, they sounded more like a very early and adamant denial of guilt. But it didn't matter what Sean said. It only mattered what the prosecution said he said.

Linn was watching the undoing of his own flesh and blood. He had left his many duties at the farm and as head of his own company to watch these wheels of justice turn in the Mojave Desert. But what he was really watching was his son being dragged beneath those wheels. As he watched it all and tried to make sense of it, he heard something that he could not understand or believe: "Your Honor, the prosecution now calls Mr. Linn Cassedy to the stand."

This was a dagger. It was coated with poisonous venom and until now had been dipped in his son's blood. The prosecution was about to press it to Linn's heart. When he saw what they were trying to do, his emotions began to erupt. Linn had led a full life. He had studied science and the Bible, and believed strongly in both. He had served his country in Vietnam. Now he was being called to testify against his own son. He told Sean later, after the court-martial, that the easy road would have been for Sean to let a few misguided and misinformed Marines intimidate him. The easy thing for Sean to do after the humiliation of the court-martial would be to let them force him out. That's what Sean's DI had tried to do in boot camp. He had tried to force Sean to admit that he was destroyed. As tough as Linn Cassedy was and as tough as he encouraged Sean to remain, when he was called to testify against his own son, he was near the breaking point.

Linn took the witness stand and swore to his God to tell the truth. No amount of prosecution game-playing could move Linn from that truth. He told the court that there was absolutely no motive for Sean to steal and that most ridiculous of all was to think that his son could ever take another man's computer. He explained how Sean enjoyed a reputation as a locally famous teenager in Kentucky who had created his own computer company. He had no less than seven laptops in Bagdad and could have asked his family to send him one or all anytime he wanted one. Sean worked with clients who trusted him. A person's word was important, especially to the Cassedys of Whitestone Organic Farm and Bakery. Linn also testified about the way he raised Sean. He explained the method behind home schooling and the Christian values he tried to impart by teaching all of his children at home.

The defense of Sean Cassedy really began with the prosecutor's attempt to use his father against him. Linn spent his time on the witness stand speaking his mind and, he hoped, clearing his son's name. The charges against his son were bad enough. But when he saw how the prosecution's case was organized so that it looked as if Sean's own father was giving damning testimony against him, Linn lost something. He didn't lose his faith. That was unshakeable. He didn't lose his love of the Corps. But he lost faith in this small part of the Corps that was hell-bent on getting his son.

Once the prosecution rested, it was Sean's turn. The defense presented the one witness who could tell the jury in simple words how loyal Sean was to the cause. The defense called his senior drill instructor from Parris Island to testify on his behalf. Sean's drill instructor offered extremely strong testimony about Sean's character. It was unshakeable testimony, and no amount of cross-examination could move the drill instructor away from his high opinion of Sean. The real Sean Cassedy was a solid Marine and not a thief.

Sean walked in his father's footsteps of over thirty years before as he presented testimonials from people who knew him, all attesting to his honesty and trustworthiness. They came from people from different walks of life. The head of a real estate company from Shelbyville, Kentucky, wrote that his company had entrusted Sean with major responsibilities. He had given Sean the company credit card to make purchases. He spoke of the high trust his company placed in young Sean Cassedy. He also spoke of the high standing the Cassedy family enjoyed in the community. Finally, he praised the family's close relationship to God. A former probation officer from Louisville who had known Sean for over four years wrote the court, declaring, "I will never be convinced that Sean would do anything dishonest, or participate in any activity that would bring shame to himself, his family, and the Marine Corps." A toxicologist from tiny Eminence, Kentucky, filed an affidavit with the court stating that he had known Sean for seven years and was vouching for his impeccable reputation for truthfulness. A retired Army nurse wrote that she had worked with young adults for over ten years as a psychiatric nurse, and her five-year acquaintance with Sean led her to only one conclusion: Being a Marine meant too much to Sean to ever allow him to steal from someone else. There were several more, all filled with praise for Sean's work ethic, Christian morals, and honesty.

A defendant's decision to take the witness stand and testify under oath is one of the most important ones, if not the single most important one in the trial of a criminal case. It is the personal decision of each defendant. In Sean's mind, this had become a matter of honor. The shame began months earlier when he professed his innocence and watched his words form the basis for another crime. He had been frustrated from the start. The course of his trial only added to his sense of helplessness. He would not leave the courtroom until this jury heard from him.

Sean took the stand. He testified under oath and for a long time. It seemed like days. He turned every question the prosecutor asked into a springboard for Sean's side of events. He held nothing back. He tried desperately to show the jury that none of this made sense. He explained that as an owner of several computers, it simply made no sense for him to risk his Marine career and destroy his own family's proud Marine tradition by taking something he already owned many times over. He also told the jury that he had just spent two great weeks at home. His frame of mind on his return to base was great. So what would have motivated him to do something so bad? People just don't go from feeling great to feeling like stealing. What the prosecution was suggesting was akin to Sean's waking up one day and forgetting who he was, forgetting his Christian upbringing. The prosecution failed to shake him from his position no matter how difficult the cross-examination became. He did not take the laptop. He did not do it as a prank or for personal gain. Period.

A special court-martial can have extremely serious consequences. Even though the offenses were misdemeanors in the civilian world, Sean faced the possibility of being sent to jail for several months, not days. He also could be discharged from the Corps in dishonor. The jury had a weighty decision to make. Should it brand this young Marine for life because his roommate's laptop showed up in his wall locker? The trial gave the jury a lot to think about and a lot of testimony collected over three days to sift through. Linn and Sean left the courtroom after the case went to the jury, convinced they were in for a long wait. They were wrong. They were so wrong it wasn't funny. It took the four Captains fifteen minutes of deliberation to reach a verdict.

Every court-martial in every service has one moment in common. It is the very somber moment when the verdict is delivered in open court. The jury returns and hands the military judge the verdict form. The judge examines it and then hands it back to the jury foreperson. In the military, this is the senior-ranking person on the jury. After this, the judge orders the defendant and his counsel to rise and face the jury for the reading of the verdict. For Sean, all of the months of worry were now reduced to this moment.

"Private First Class Sean S. Cassedy. This court, after careful deliberation, voting by secret written ballot, does hereby find you guilty!" Then it was over. Life as Sean knew it was forever changed. In an instant, Sean's life as a Marine would be radically different. The jury found him guilty of taking the property. They found him guilty for professing his innocence. Sean resumed his seat. He and his dad sat in that desert courtroom shocked and stunned—in shock and awe. They knew it was coming. They both watched it unfold, and nothing seemed right. It didn't take a genius to see they never stood a chance. But it was not until the verdict was read that the reality hit the two men hard. But like so many things that happen in the United States Marine Corps, Marines understand that being tested during moments of exhaustion and weakness means mustering the courage and strength to go on.

Even at the absolute lowest point of morale, Sean had to go on because in the military the sentencing phase of a court-martial begins almost immediately. Sean had a choice, and it was a choice that no civilian defendant ever has. Sean could testify under oath, or he could make an unsworn statement to the jury. By opting for an unsworn statement, he could not be cross-examined on it by the prosecution. Military defense lawyers like the unsworn statement because their clients can avoid a barrage of harsh cross-examination questions. The unsworn statement is sometimes called the unsworn lie since a defendant can say just about anything.

Sean also had another choice. He could continue to maintain his innocence after the verdict, or he could throw himself on the mercy of the court, hoping to get a more lenient sentence. Taking the stand and then telling the jury you're innocent is risky. Saying you're innocent is telling the jury they were wrong. But that did not matter to Sean. There was no risk in his mind because he committed no crime. Without hesitation, Sean took the witness stand under oath, ready to answer any questions. He was not going to end his trial hiding behind unsworn testimony, and he was going to tell his jury something they didn't want to hear. He told them they were wrong. He said it as politely as he could. With all due respect to their status as jurors and officers, he told them they had made a terrible mistake. He told them they reduced a proud Marine from a proud Marine family to a pile of trash. He told them once, he told them twice, and he kept telling them. Sean would not be denied this last chance to defend his honor. Under cross-examination, each time the prosecutor tried to pin him down, Sean took the question apart, turning it into still another way to declare his innocence. He never stole anything. He had no reason to take a laptop. He left no room for doubt. The jury was wrong. The prosecutor was wrong. The commander was wrong. They had convicted an innocent man.

Sean and his father saw the military police outside the courtroom as court closed for the jury's deliberation on the sentence. They had shackles ready to take Sean to jail. The police just expected that Sean was about to become one of the orange jumpsuit crowd who hung out in the defense office. Sean and his father were both emotionally out of ammunition. They expected this deliberation to be over quickly, like the last one—fifteen minutes max—and they expected a very bad sentence to follow. They were bracing for a sentence that would send Sean to jail for several months. They also were preparing themselves for the worst part of the sentence, a bad conduct discharge from the Marine Corps. Sean had held up well through his three days in hell. It was roughly equivalent to the fifty-four hours he spent at boot camp struggling inside of the Crucible. That Parris Island trial now seemed like a million years ago, but it actually was less than a year in the past. For all of the humping and yelling and mind games he went through in the Crucible, there was no comparison with the torture chamber he was now in. At the end of the Crucible, there was a race to the parade ground to claim your full rights as a Marine. There was a Warriors Breakfast. At the end of the court-martial, only shame awaited him. He was about to take a step back, transforming himself back in time so that he would never reach that parade ground. If the jury sentenced him to a bad conduct discharge, he would lose all of his rights as a Marine. It would be as if boot camp never existed. It surprised father and son when no sentence was reached after the first hour of deliberation. In fact, the jury did not return for several hours.

Once again, Sean had to go through a few seconds in hell, standing at attention, waiting for the sentence to be read in open court. Sean took his million-year minute and thought of how horrible his life would be with a bad conduct discharge, with a BCD. He could not think of anything but the BCD. A BCD is known by military men and women in all branches of service as the Big Chicken Dinner. Sean had absolutely no appetite for the prospect of ending his Marine Corps career in this way. He never broke down once during any part of the trial. But if he was going to, it would be after the jury sentenced him to a lifetime of shame for something he did not do. The judge again issued an order to the two men sitting at the defense table: "The accused and counsel for the accused will rise for the reading of the sentence." The jury foreman read from the sentencing worksheet: "This jury, voting by secret written ballot, does hereby sentence you to be reduced to the lowest enlisted grade, to forfeit two-thirds of your pay for one month, and to a fine of $1,100."

Sean was confused when he did not hear any reference to either jail time or a discharge. Eventually, his confusion turned to satisfaction. He had evidently convinced them that he was not the bad boy the prosecutor said he was. His emotion at this relatively light sentence was not joy. He could not be happy after being found guilty. But he felt that he had achieved a small victory. He was satisfied that their sentence reflected this. They did not send him to jail, and they did not discharge him in disgrace. That should have been the end of this part of Sean's story. But there was one final twist to Sean's trial. After the sentence was announced, the prosecutor walked over to Sean and shook his hand. "I've never seen anyone take the stand after being found guilty to tell the jury they were wrong. That took balls."

What do you call it? What do you call it when a young man raised with strong Christian values is accused of a crime that belies those very values? What is it that describes a Marine whose entire teenage and young adult life has been steeped in computers? What do you call it when the prosecution attempts to associate him with a cache of prescription drugs to smear his name? What do you call it when a watch is found in his own locker and innuendos are made at trial that it is stolen, yet he owns that watch and wears it less than six months later into combat? What is it about a prosecution theory that belittles Sean's small town in Kentucky and Christian home-school upbringing? What do you call it when a young man denies the crime from the first moments of the investigation, tells his father he is innocent, takes the witness stand in his own case, and denies it again, and, when given an opportunity to beg for mercy during sentencing, he looks directly at the jury and tells them one more time he is not guilty of what they just found him guilty of? Sean calls it innocence. Linn calls it the same.

Within a week of his acquittal at a summary court-martial, Linn Cassedy had orders to Vietnam. After his court-martial, Linn received a letter of appreciation through the same command channels that sought to convict him. In Sean's case, he finished computer school, graduating near the top of his class. He also received a special commendation. It was more prestigious than his father's letter of appreciation. Sean received meritorious mast. This is a specialized award intended to promptly recognize an enlisted Marine's accomplishments that go beyond the call of normal duty. Sean's meritorious mast came less than a month after he was convicted for professing his innocence and for taking a computer he did not take. The award covered the period of July 2002 through October 2002. In other words, as he awaited trial and during the period of the trial itself, Sean did not let his own troubles affect his day-to-day job in the Corps. The award was for outstanding achievement in the superior performance of duty. The award recognized the real Sean Cassedy. The court-martial addressed a make-believe Sean, created by two investigators and a prosecutor to fit a trial theory.

In the aftermath of his trial, filled with shame and rendered penniless by the sentence, Sean began to let things slip. He drank more. He showed up late for work when he never did before. His ship was sinking, and he was barely treading water. His father, now back in Kentucky, could sense it. He knew that he was losing Sean. He could tell the Marine Corps was also losing Sean. Linn was also hit hard by his son's sentence since the family had to make up for Sean's loss of pay. There was only one place Sean could turn to for money, and that was his father. The sentence really had been a sentence on the entire Cassedy family, not just on Sean. But in the face of all of the hurt, Linn told his son something that seemed to take hold. He wanted his son to stop feeling sorry for himself and find a way to get on with his life. So, he spoke to Sean. It was simple talk from someone who had been there: *"You're letting them win. You have to be the better man. You know you didn't do it. Don't let them win."*

His father was not the only Marine who gave Sean this kind of advice. In Sean's unit, there was a quiet, battle-hardened Staff Sergeant. He represented the other Marine Corps. His Corps had no choices. He never thought of going to computer school. He could have cared less about trying to qualify for another MOS, or military occupational specialty. The Staff Sergeant belonged to one school and one specialty only—infantry. Marine infantry is a creed. It is a religion. It is a cult. The followers of Marine infantry don't need drugs to alter their minds. They need only a weapon. Marine infantry is the true grunt end of the Marine division. It is the sharp tip of the military spear. National security depends on Marine infantry. Infantry troops not actually in war are constantly preparing for war. Making rank is not important. The Corps gives them all of the basic necessities of life. In return, infantry grunts like the Staff Sergeant Sean knew paid back in sweat. They forever worked on physical conditioning, battle tactics, and weapons training.

The Staff Sergeant who came up to Sean was from this other Marine Corps. He was a grunt first, human second. The term *grunt* supposedly came from the Marine infantrymen of Vietnam. It was the sound made when they threw their full load of battle gear on their backs. Sean never noticed that this staff sergeant had been watching his slide, but he had been. He could tell Sean had lost his pride, his sense of being a Marine. He could see that he was fading out of the Corps, drifting away from it like ashes from a campfire. The grunt went up to Sean and said just two short sentences: "Cassedy, are you a bitch? You're proving to everyone out there that you're a bitch." Then he was gone. The words replayed in Sean's head over and over: *Cassedy, are you a bitch? You're proving to everyone out there that you're a bitch.* They seemed to knife through him. A Zen master could not have been any more effective. Sean took the words to heart. Coming from a grunt, they meant a lot. He stopped feeling sorry for himself. He let it go. He put the conviction and sentence behind him. He began to act like a Marine again.

Sean appealed his conviction to no avail. He followed his formal appeal with a plea to his congressman for justice. Sean got a polite but noncommittal response, just as his father had years before when he complained about a breach of his enlistment contract. Sean's father got orders to Danang. Sean got orders to Fort Lee, Virginia, and fabric repair school. The command section of the Corps was unforgiving. Sean's misdemeanor conviction meant the Corps would throw away the money it took to make him a computer specialist. Instead, they took a graduate of a highly technical specialty area and sentenced him to become a Marine Corps version of the seamstress.

The visions that brought him here were clouded now. His once extremely focused purpose—protecting his fellow Americans from terrorist attacks—was now obscured by the humiliation of the court-martial. In the face of his lowest point as a Marine and as a person, Sean did something the Marine Corps taught him to do. He kept going. He learned it at Parris Island. He learned it in the Crucible. It would not be easy. But the grunt was right. His father was right. Before he even turned twenty-one, Sean Cassedy understood that life was filled with obstacles. There was nothing in his upbringing that told him to take the easy way around. He was a Marine, the son of a Marine, and the grandson of a Marine. The jury didn't understand what that meant, but Sean did.

In early 1970 twenty-three year old Corporal Linn Cassedy was assigned to Skaggs Island Naval Security Base in Vallejo, California.

United States Marine Corps

This is to certify that

Private First Class Sean S Cassedy /4066

has completed the course prescribed by the
Commander of the Marine Corps for

Entry Level Small Computer Specialist Course

Given at

Marine Corps Communication-Electronics School
MCAGCC, Twentynine Palms, California

this 5 day of April , 20 02

_____
Commanding Officer

Sean's misdemeanor conviction meant the Corps would throw away the
money it took to make him a computer specialist.

Chapter 6

The Trip to the Edge of Hell

SUCH IS THE PATRIOT'S BOAST,
WHERE'ER WE ROAM,
HIS FIRST, BEST COUNTRY EVER IS AT HOME.
The Traveller by Oliver Goldsmith

Parris Island was merely a point of departure for the trip Sean would eventually make to Iraq. It was a reference point. Between the barking DIs of Marine boot camp and the desolate desert warscape of Iraq, Sean had to pass through a few more crucibles. Sean enlisted under the delayed enlistment program, reserving a slot in the Marine Corps in February 2001. But he did not depart for Parris Island until September 17th, actually entering boot camp on September 18th, or one week after 9/11. Boot camp lasted from September 18th through December 4th. After a well-deserved Christmastime leave at home in Kentucky, Sean headed to Marine Combat Training at Camp Lejeune, North Carolina, for twenty-two days of specialized weapons and combat training in the School of Infantry. This school is roughly divided into two groups: grunts, or those Marines wielding a weapon for a career, and all others. It was a grunt who turned Sean's attitude around after his court-martial.

Sean was part of the non-career grunt group at the School of Infantry. He was there to master the basic role of every Marine, the rifleman. But like so many other Marines, he had a life after grunt work. In Sean's case, he was going to be a small computer specialist, but the court-martial eventually destroyed that dream, and the Corps replaced it with another specialty, to be earned at Fort Lee's Fabric Repair School.

Grunts, on the other hand, took an expanded course at Camp Lejeune. Being a Marine rifleman was their specialty. When they finished the School of Infantry, they went to their bases and practiced their specialty until they were tapped for combat. In a hot war, they killed and destroyed better than any computer specialist or fabric repairman could ever dream of.

Sean spent much of his twenty-two days at Camp Lejeune in the field. He continued to hone his skills with the M-16, but it was a different rifle configuration than he used while in boot camp. This time, his M-16 had a grenade launcher attached. In boot camp, Sean became familiar with

107

machine guns; at Lejeune, he became an expert. Sean trained on the M2 fifty caliber machine gun, an eighty-four-pound piece of death. Nicknamed Ma Deuce, it can kill at ranges of up to four miles. Sean also mastered two sleeker machine guns, the M60 and the M249 SAW. After the First Gulf War against Iraq, the M60 was replaced by the M249 as the Marine Corps Squad Automatic Weapon, or SAW. Sean had to know how to fire both weapons since M60s were still being used. But his true expertise would lie with the Squad Automatic Weapon, the M249.

In addition to a very concentrated regimen of weapons training, Sean was immersed in combat tactics. According to the School of Infantry mission statement, students must master "infantry skills essential to operate in a combat environment." Raising the level of Marine survivability in combat was the goal. Saving Marine lives meant thorough training. It meant going beyond Parris Island. Sean also practiced critical land navigation skills. A map and compass became his constant companions, and he became proficient during day and night training.

After his School of Infantry training at Lejeune, Sean had become a lethally competent Marine. He was prepared to fight. But the transformation into a combat soldier was not complete. The Marine Corps does not stop hammering until time runs out. As war with Iraq became inevitable, Marine combat training only intensified, and Sean trained almost nonstop at Camp Pendleton prior to deploying. After he deployed to Kuwait, he humped nonstop for nearly a month in the desert. His unit and all of the coalition units deployed there used every minute they had to get ready for war.

His personal transformation had also gone through months of changes. Sean became a Marine as a teenager. He had literally left the chores of the family farm and the games he liked to play with Joshua and Stephen behind in Bagdad, and walked directly into the fierce and violent world of the United States Marine Corps. He never had time to enjoy a transition period. He didn't go to college, and he didn't leave home to take a holy journey to learn about his faith in the Swiss Alps as his father had. Sean jumped from his boyhood into the Corps as fast as September 11th changed the face of America. His Marine training almost overnight moved him away from the carefree teenager from Bagdad. His Marine life and its own unique experiences quickly matured him beyond his years. By twenty, he had experienced a court-martial. Like so many of the young military men and women of his day, the change happened so quickly he never had time to look back and realize that the other life was gone forever. Asheron's Call was no more. His country's call rapidly replaced the boyhood games. Virtual reality games were now combat maneuvers. For those who would have to die in the war that Sean eventually would survive, especially those as young as Sean, they missed so much as they moved from school days and teen problems to war and their deaths in the blink of an eye … all in the squeeze of a trigger.

Despite the advice from his father and from the grunt, and despite Sean's own re-dedication to the Corps, he still had to cope with his demotion and the loss of money from losing rank. He also had to face facts. He was a marked man, scarred by the special court-martial conviction. He also had to accept losing the computer specialty he wanted so badly. It was a lot of crow to swallow. But he did. Sean was sent to Fort Lee, Virginia, to become a needle-and-thread Marine. There is nothing, absolutely nothing, wrong with this specialty. Every Marine in every MOS provides a necessary piece of the entire Marine puzzle. It is simply the road that Sean traveled to get to this point that left him disillusioned and wondering if he could ever make up for what happened. *"Are you destroyed yet?"* To Sean Cassedy, it was embarrassing. It was degrading. And apparently that is exactly what his commander intended it to be. Yet, for all of the embarrassment that his Marine life had experienced up to this point, Fort Lee would also give Sean something he never counted on. There, he would search for the answer to one of the three big questions posed to him and his siblings during home schooling:

Where will you spend eternity?
What will be your life's work?
Who will be your life's partner?

Sean had a long history of love affairs. His first serious relationship was with a Chicago beauty named Jennifer. Coincidentally, she was the first girl he ever kissed. It happened one day while both were attending daycare. Sean planned to marry her when he grew up, but sadly the two drifted apart when his family moved from Illinois to California. In California, he dated a girl from his elementary school, but was discouraged when his older sister, Heather, and younger brother, Stephen, caught Sean kissing his girlfriend at the Cassedy house.

Things turned more serious when Sean was a teen living in Bagdad. He met Crystal at church. They dated for some time, but eventually they went their separate ways. Crystal was followed by Erin. By the time he was high school age, Sean's computer business interests took over. It wasn't long after running his computer company that Sean enlisted.

During his first few months in the Marine Corps, Sean was assigned recruiting duty. It was great duty and meant he could go home to Kentucky and show the flag and uniform for interested young men and women thinking about joining the Marines. During one of his recruiting stints, he met a young lady he came to like a great deal. She eventually enlisted in the Marine Corps. The two never really dated until they found themselves back in Kentucky, now both Marines and both of them assigned to recruiting duty. They worked closely together for the next several months. Despite how well they seemed to fit together, they never got into a serious relationship. That would change.

At the same time Sean was assigned to Twentynine Palms, his girlfriend was stationed not far away at another California Marine base. The distance between them was not so great that they couldn't see each other on a regular basis, at least every weekend. They did. They began to get serious, or so Sean thought. He tried to see her any time their two schedules allowed it. Sean started to think that this relationship was the one. She was the answer to that big third question his mom and dad asked him to ponder. Sean thought she was the one he wanted to spend the rest of his life with.

Sean and his girlfriend decided to throw a party for some friends at a room they had rented several miles from his base at Twentynine Palms. But at the party something was very wrong. Sean could tell almost immediately that his girl was acting strangely. Every time he got near her, she was extremely cold toward Sean. Then she dropped the bombshell. There was someone else at the party she was interested in. Making things even worse, that someone was one of Sean's best friends. Sean was seething with anger. He felt betrayed, and the only way he could handle it at a party he had planned and paid for was by drinking more. He drank so much he passed out at his own party. When he came to, the woman he thought was the one was tightly wrapped in the arms of his friend. Except for the three of them, the party was over. For Sean, the party was more than over.

Sean had woken to a nightmare. He was too drunk to deal with what he saw. Before he knew what hit him, his girlfriend left the party with her new friend. She took the room key and the car, and left. Sean was left literally outside looking in, locked out of his own room, miles from base.

All of his valuables were in the rented room. His shoes were also inside the room. Unable to break into the room without doing major damage to the property, Sean did the only thing a well-conditioned Marine could do under the circumstances. He ran the nine miles back to base. He ran barefoot through the Mojave Desert, slipping back on base undetected. He eventually made his way to his room where he passed out from total exhaustion.

Sean swore off women at this point. The woman who jilted him tried to call him several times over the next few weeks. Sean refused to speak with her and never let her back into his life in any way. Not as a lover. Not as a friend. Sean did not know it at the time, but his life was on a course that would lead him to the ultimate Crucible, where he would have to draw upon all of the lessons of life, including the survival lessons he learned as a Marine, and including the lessons of faith he had learned at home, just to survive the trip from Kuwait to Baghdad. Somewhere on the journey to Iraq, his life took a couple of wrong turns. After boot camp and after the School of Infantry, Sean lost his girl to another man. The court-martial dealt a serious blow to his pride. He also lost rank and relied more and more on financial help from home to get him through the tough no-pay periods. At the low-water mark of it all, he was sent to Fort Lee to become a glorified canvas patcher.

With the help of a caring father and a straight-talking grunt, Sean was able to convince himself to stop feeling sorry for himself. He began to rebuild his damaged psyche by first rebuilding his body through nearly constant physical training. He arrived at Fort Lee, Virginia, for fabric repair school on October 14, 2002. He was a magnificent physical specimen at six foot two inches, two hundred and twenty pounds with only six percent body fat. At least in terms of his physique, he was a poster boy for the Marine Corps. The bitterness from his unrequited love caused him to date-and-run. He went out with several women at Fort Lee, but never for more than a date or two. It was as if he wanted to attract them with his chiseled features and then dump them quickly out of revenge. But eventually he met someone who outflanked him.

Sean was in a mixed class at Fort Lee of both Marines and Army students. One day, he noticed one of the female Army students sleeping in the school break area. Marine that he was, Sean abruptly woke up the sleeper, and then chewed her out for being so lackadaisical even if it was a break room. Word soon spread about the incident involving the mean

Marine private. Virtually every Army woman in his class had it out for him. Sean did not count on committing the same crime he had chastised someone else for. But he did. He fell asleep in the same break area, and someone was standing by ready to pounce. He was startled out of his catnap by a five-foot-four-inch, blond, green-eyed tigress. She stomped her feet so everyone there would notice that she was waking up the big bad Marine. After waking him, she told him she did not appreciate how rude he had been with her friend. Sean had no defense at all. She had him. She even outranked the private. He had no choice but to sit there and take it. But even as he did, something inside him told him that he liked this little bundle of dynamite. It was an odd way for a man and a woman to start a relationship. But that day in the class break room, Private First Class Tiffany Fitzgerald of the United States Army Reserve woke up Private Sean S. Cassedy, USMC, and in the process, the revival of Sean began.

Sean paid little attention to her at first, but he felt some kind of chemistry working right away. The whole idea of dating a woman from another service was frowned upon in the Corps. Probably more important than that, Sean still had a big chip on his shoulder from his last relationship. Playing the field was much safer. Never committing meant no broken hearts. Despite the chemistry with Tiffany, he was adamant that there was no woman who could command his heart. None. No woman. Even if Tiffany's face kept popping into his head. None. Never. Even if he could not stop thinking of her. No woman on this earth. Well, maybe one.

His first real date with Tiffany nearly ended in disaster. Sean and Tiffany had entirely separate schedules at Fort Lee. It was difficult just finding a stretch of hours when both were not on the job. Tiffany made the first move. She had an entire evening free. It included an overnight liberty. She asked Sean if he wanted to spend a whole Saturday together. Even if he wasn't available for a long-term affair, he still thought it would be fun to be with the green-eyed tigress for a day. So he agreed. They were to meet at midday. They would wile away the afternoon hours together and then eat dinner. Sean went to the appointed rendezvous spot at the designated hour and waited. After several minutes, the thought of being stood up by Tiffany began to eat away at him. Twenty minutes passed. Then thirty minutes passed. The already-battered young Marine lost hope. He waited for an hour and gave up. He left.

In his room now, the hours passed. Five hours after the rendezvous time, the phone rang. It was Tiffany. She could not get out of her training session. The session had run long, and there was no way to reach him to warn him. She told him how sorry she was. Sean could tell it was no act. There was still time left on her pass, so she asked him to have dinner with her. They went to a steakhouse. The food did not matter. They found out that the two of them just loved to talk to each other. They almost wore out their welcome at the restaurant. Sean found out that his little tigress was not only beautiful outside but was also very intelligent, and she shared something with him. She had a deep, abiding belief in God. After dinner, Sean and Tiffany spent the rest of the evening getting to know more about each other. The process of answering question three was underway.

Sean and Tiffany met during the fall of 2002. It was when the United States was already inching toward war with Iraq. On October 4th the *Lexington Herald* printed an Op-Ed piece by a concerned local resident with the headline: "U.S. Attack Must Comply with International Law." The author argued for more of a reason to invade Iraq than "regime change," and worried about something called "reciprocity," where other, less principled actors would reciprocate if we implemented regime change, and openly targeted a sovereign country's leaders. Three weeks later the United Nations seemed to resolve the legal question. The Bush administration was able to wring out of the Security Council, Resolution 1441, a watered-down version of a final ultimatum to Iraq to disarm or else. The resolution passed on November 8, 2002. At about the same time, Sean was trying to get his mind off Tiffany. He was trying to avoid the unavoidable. He was headed for a showdown with his heart and with the warring world around him. Toward the end of his training, he and Tiffany saw more and more of each other. Despite this, Sean was convinced it would not last. The scars from his last serious romance were still fresh, and he did not want to repeat that failure with Tiffany. Lucky for him, he would be leaving Fort Lee and heading far, far away. He was certain that once he left Fort Lee, the miles between him and Tiffany would resolve this new relationship in favor of the single life.

He finished his training at Fort Lee on December 14, 2002, and went home for Christmas leave. After the holidays in Kentucky, he went to his permanent Marine duty assignment at Camp Pendleton, California. Once there, he and Tiffany continued to correspond. They talked by phone more and more. His feelings were mixed, wanting to avoid another bad scene, but also feeling something special deep inside. Tiffany was going through the same turmoil. She did not let out her feelings right away. But the feelings she had for Sean just got stronger. One day it happened, and they just poured out. During one of their calls, she told him. She said the magic words: "I love you, Sean." Sean had to muster up all of his Marine know-how and strength to figure out what to do. He did know what he felt, and he stopped trying to deny his feelings. He was in love with Tiffany. They had not spent a lot of time together, but the time they did spend was wonderful. Both were barely out of their teens, and both were absolutely certain that they had met the love of their life.

Sean's immediate problem was how to see the girl he loved. The two of them were nearly three thousand miles apart, and he was broke most of the time. The forfeitures and fine from his court-martial had left him virtually without pay for October, November, and December. He had been making ends meet with the money his parents sent him. Now it was the first of January, and he wanted to see Tiffany. Sean did what any red-blooded Marine madly in love would do in that situation. He bought a bus ticket on New Year's Eve and set out on one of the most uncomfortable trips of his life just to see Tiffany. It was a grueling eighteen-hour bus ride that he took across the country. But Sean really didn't mind the discomfort. Marines rarely do. It was no Crucible. It was no court-martial. And he knew a pot of gold was waiting for him on the other side. He knew it would all be worth it to see Tiffany and to hold her.

Before he arrived at his final destination, Sean did something special. There is one uniform that a Marine wears that makes onlookers take notice. It is the Marine dress blue uniform. For the first really important occasion of his life, Sean donned his dress blues. He also bought one long-stemmed rose to present when he arrived. He thought it was the most romantic thing that a broke Marine could do under the circumstances. Despite the painful bus trip it took to reach her, he tried to present to Tiffany the best, most sensitive Sean Cassedy he possibly could. He and Tiffany spent the next four days together. When this trip ended, Sean knew that he was very close to deciding who it was he wanted as his life's partner. Nothing short of war would stop him. Unfortunately, for Sean it did!

Sean had been hearing rumors for weeks, as far back as November 2002, that he would be heading overseas. But by the time he and Tiffany fell madly in love with each other, the war rumors began to circulate. Though they were just rumors, they also just made military sense. Marines deploy to the hot zone in case of war. First in and last out. By January 2003, it was clear to all that the United States was putting the pieces in place to go to war against Saddam Hussein. A CBS news report of January 24th spoke of a "massive Iraq deployment in the works" and mentioned a commitment by Great Britain to send 26,000 troops. The United States had 125,000 troops already in the pipeline.

The news report touted the Army's 4th Infantry Division as the "most lethal, modern, and deployable division." The 4th Infantry Division was supposed to deploy from Fort Hood, Texas, to Turkey so that they could attack Iraq from the north, establish a northern front, and secure the oil fields in that region. But politics got in the way. The Turkish government refused to let their territory be used for such an invasion. Some forty ships parked off the coast of Turkey loaded with 4th ID equipment, and weapons eventually had to be redirected. The Turkish rejection effectively bottled up the 4th Infantry Division for the critical first phase of the war. The tanks and Bradley fighting vehicles that made the 4th Infantry so lethal had to take the long way around, and the 4th Infantry would not be a lead element in the invasion.

It was the early stages of the massive deployment that found Sean Cassedy broke, in love, a convicted Marine, and about to be ordered into combat. Sean's orders came on January 16, 2003. They were the model of efficiency:

> *Effective 0730, 16 January 2003, you will stand detached from your present duties at Headquarters and Service Battalion. You are further directed to proceed and report to the Commanding Officer, FSSG HQ, 1st FSSG Camp Pendleton California, ISO Operation Enduring Freedom for a period of 179 days.*

Translation: Get ready to roll! Kuwait was on the horizon, and Iraq was just beyond that. He was being put into the rotation for war, "*ISO* Operation Enduring Freedom" meaning in support of the military mission to oust Saddam. Now things were getting totally real and unreal at the same time.

At Camp Pendleton, Marines were carefully being forged into billets, into specific war-time slots. Initially, Sean was picked to be a personal guard for one of the First Sergeants. A First Sergeant, or first shirt, is the primary link between the unit's commander and the enlisted troops under that commander. Providing personal security for the first shirt was clearly an honor. But this assignment quickly disappeared. Sean was next told he would be a guard for the commanding officer. That's when Sean took matters into his own hands, volunteering to go to combat survival training at Pendleton and serve as part of a security force team. He would forego his peacetime specialties of computer specialist and fabric repair specialist in favor of MOS 0311.

MOS 0311. The first two numbers (03) signify infantry. The second two indicate rifleman. When a Marine becomes a 0311, this means he becomes a scout, an assault troop, and an all-around combat troop. But to Sean, it meant more training. Now well beyond Parris Island and several months past the School of Infantry, he had to spend his time getting his body and mind ready for a shooting war. He had to push himself harder than he ever had with constant PT. He went on long runs and long marches. His humping now almost always included fifty pounds of gear. Because Sean was so well built and strong, he became a specialist within the 0311 MOS. He became a SAW gunner, assigned to handle one of the most powerful light machine guns in the world. It was after this training and still in the middle of the love affair of his life, that Sean began a journey that would change him forever.

Before he left for Kuwait, he spoke to two people who would help shape the way he approached his date with war. What do you say? What can you say? What does a father say to his son when he gets the news? When he learns that his son will go to war against a tyrant? When he realizes that his own flesh and blood will face the very real threat of a horrible death in the middle of a foreign land? Death in the desert. The chance that his son would be sending machine gun rounds into other human beings. That his own son would face death by some of the most ghastly weapons humankind ever devised? Sean might die from chemical or biological weapons. He might end his short life suffering unspeakable pain from nerve agents, blistering agents, or choking agents. Linn's son was part of this new age with such remarkable technology, and yet the crude weaponry of World War I was still out there. He could die from anthrax, the deadly biological agent that caused a nationwide panic in the fall of 2001. Death from anthrax is horrible. It is an agonizingly painful death preceded by skin lesions, and ultimately the victim's insides are eaten away. A lot of what Americans heard about the biological and chemical arsenal of Saddam was based upon educated guesses by the intelligence community. But there was also some well-established history to back up those claims. The world had substantiated Saddam's use of sarin and mustard gas to destroy Kurdish villages in 1987 and 1988.

Linn Cassedy had given Sean a pep talk in the aftermath of Sean's court-martial. He told him that no matter how bad things might seem, he was still a Marine, and no one could change that. Once a Marine, always a Marine! When the official word finally came down that Sean was headed overseas, father and son had a talk. Sean's father reminded him of two very critical pieces of family history. First, he told him that Sean's grandfather had gotten the call. He went off to war. He faced some of the bloodiest action war could ever produce. And he came home alive. Next, he himself had gotten the call. Linn went to war. For nearly a year, he faced the enemy in Vietnam. But he, too, came home alive. Linn reduced everything down to the bare basics. The conclusion was so obvious Sean didn't even have to think about it. Sean would be coming home alive, too. End of discussion!

It was the first week in February, and Sean was about to depart for Kuwait when he called the woman he loved. He told Tiffany that he would be flying out soon, heading to Kuwait and then to parts unknown, but she knew. Everyone knew. Everyone knew what Kuwait meant. The two lovers talked until Sean could not talk anymore, until time was up, and he had to get on the bus. There were a lot of Marines speaking to loved ones that day. There were buses and troops waiting outside of the barracks, men and women waiting near phones. They were the sons and daughters of moms and dads trying their best to say the final words to their families. They were husbands and wives telling their spouses on the other end how much they would miss them. They were moms and dads saying goodbye to little children. There must have been a lot of awkward pauses and horrible transitions as these tough Marines tried to end their conversations. They all understood the risk they faced and that a certain statistical percentage of them would not be coming back alive. They had to find a way to say "goodbye" and "I love you," and to do it all with the courage of a Marine, without tears, without a cracking voice, to say those tender words without revealing that once you were someone's little boy or girl, and you missed your mommy, especially now, and could use some old-fashioned hugs and kisses. Sean wasn't the only one.

Tiffany understood the gravity of the entire situation. She knew that she might never see Sean alive again. She did not want to think about it like that, but that was one of the stark realities of war, when warriors leave for war. She understood things better than most because she was a warrior, too. Sean wanted to end the call with the most important words he had ever said to Tiffany other than when he told her for the first time that he loved her. A few weeks earlier, he had made up his mind. After his cross-country ride to see her in early January, he realized that their love was something very special. She accepted him for what he was. Sean was amazed that she could do that, that she could love a completely broke and somewhat broken Marine whose future was about as uncertain as anyone's could get. Sean knew he wanted Tiffany, and he knew he wanted her for all time. He was torn because he was heading into the unknown, and he did not want to promise more than he could deliver. He ended his call to her by telling her that he would be coming back to her.

Sean felt confident he would return after speaking with his dad. If he worried at all, it was whether Tiffany would be there when he returned. Immediately after his call to Tiffany, Sean's unit assembled outside of the combat survival training building at Camp Pendleton. They had their full battle gear. Given his body weight of two hundred and twenty pounds, and his gear, which now included a twenty-pound SAW and a thousand rounds of ammo, Sean's total weight, called battle load, was tipping the scales at three hundred eighty-six pounds.

Sean reflected on the strange mix of emotions at the staging point. The world's best fighters were laughing, joking, and generally saying anything to burn off the nervous excitement over going to war. He thought to himself how odd it was to be heading off to kill people they did not know in a place none of them had ever visited, a thought that would return to him once he stepped foot in Iraq. Sean spent his moments at the staging point thinking it was time. It was time to put all of the training the Corps had given him to good use. He wanted to leave and go fight, but he also wanted to stay and find a way into Tiffany's heart. It was quite a place to be, the staging area. The really weird ones, Sean thought, were the Marines who dozed off. They apparently didn't have a care in the world. They had to be grunts.

Back in Kentucky, Sean's entire family was thinking about him. His older sister, Heather, probably was the most anxious. She became a war news addict. From the moment Sean left for Kuwait until he was injured, she developed a daily ritual of watching the war unfold on television. This included the time she spent at the office as a legal secretary. She tried to prepare the legal briefs for the attorneys she worked with, but she also had to get to a TV for her fix of the latest war news. As the war advanced, so did Heather's pregnancy. She was nearly eight months pregnant when Sean's parents got a frightening call saying their son was missing.

Sean's younger siblings had their own unique thoughts about Sean and his upcoming trip into Iraq. Eight-year-old Rebekah, dubbed the smartest of the bunch according to her father, thought that her big brother Sean was a little crazy. When it finally sunk in where he would be going and how dangerous it would be, brave Rebekah still claims she was only a little scared. Sean's thirteen-year-old sister, Sarah, thought Sean was a most unique brother. She wasn't worried about his safety. She was certain that he would be fine because she knew that he had put his trust in God. Eleven-year-old Hannah felt the same way. Joshua, fifteen, never gave the war a second thought. Sean was coming home. Seventeen-year-old Stephen was supremely confident and very practical. In his mind, Sean's deployment was just another job for a Marine. According to Stephen, there were so many things going for his older brother that he could not imagine anything bad would happen to him. Sean was one of the best-trained fighters in the world. He was also armed to the hilt. Not only that, but he was also surrounded by Marines who were just as well trained and just as well armed. Stephen thought Sean's safe return was a given. His brother was coming home, and he was coming back to Bagdad alive.

Sean's journey to the front began with a hundred-mile bus ride from Camp Pendleton to March Air Force Base in Riverside, California. The Marines of Sean's deployment arrived at the Air Force base at one in the morning, and then slept until seven thirty the next morning. After that, it was time to board the plane for the trip to Kuwait, a trip that took twenty-two hours. His first plane ride into the battle zone took off from the very base his father's last plane ride from Vietnam landed on over thirty years earlier. From March Air Force Base, the plane stopped in Frankfort, Germany, to refuel. Sean phoned home once more. He tried to call Tiffany but got the answering machine. He left a message, telling her he would see her in a few months.

Sean arrived in Kuwait City on Monday morning, February 11th. Immediately upon arriving, the troops were issued ammunition just in case they ran into an ambush on their way to their Kuwaiti camp. After sleeping off the long trip, Sean got down to business. It was time for more training. But this time, it all seemed very different. He was just miles from the war zone. Training now was as close to the moment of truth as it could get. This time it had to count. Parris Island seemed like a million miles and a million years away. Lejeune was far removed from the battlefield. Even the last-minute humping at Pendleton lacked true urgency because for all of the sweat, there was always a soft bed to fall into when training was over. In Kuwait, this final preparation had to get them through real battles waiting to be fought just around the corner. They had to be able to survive a hostile terrain, shifting weather conditions, a foreign army, bullets, mortars, artillery, and perhaps even dreaded weapons of mass destruction.

Sean arrived in Kuwait from the "world," as his father's generation referred to the United States. Sean's version of the world might be more accurately described as the accidental world. It was a place where people supposedly drove in straight lines. Theoretically, they kept their cars and trucks in their proper lanes and out of the lanes of oncoming traffic. But every day in the accidental world, someone drove crookedly, and people got hurt or were killed by the crooked drivers. The accidental world was a statistical world in which a statistical percentage of people died from gunshots, poison, and vehicle collisions. Yet no one felt the need to take special precautions or go through specialized training to live in the accidental world. Sean knew how to live in the accidental world. He drove as straight as he could, but he didn't really expect the people around him to do the same. He felt comfortable in that kind of world.

Kuwait was a transitional zone, separating Sean's accidental world from the violence of the intentional world he would be entering when Marines invaded Iraq. In some ways, it was like the accidental world. People drove straight, but accidents still happened. The first official coalition casualties of the war would take place in the transitional zone, when an American helicopter crashed, killing twelve British troops and four Americans. Between the nineteenth and twentieth of March 2003, very near to the moment President Bush announced the official beginning of the invasion, the chopper crashed ten miles south of Iraqi territory. To the families of the downed soldiers, it did not matter that war had not officially started. They just knew their loved ones would never be coming through the door of the family house again.

In other ways, Kuwait was like the intentional world. Snipers and infiltrators blew in with the desert wind. Things blew up, trucks were shot at, and soldiers died. Sometimes they weren't even soldiers, but they died anyway because someone intended for them to die. A couple of weeks before Sean arrived in Kuwait, two American civilian contractors were attacked near Camp Doha, Kuwait. One of the contractors was killed. The attacker used an AK-47 assault rifle. It was no accident.

Sean was about to jump off, out of the transitional zone, into one of the most austere parts of the intentional world. In Iraq, every bullet fired his way was intentionally trying to kill somebody. The statistics no longer mattered. The war zone of Iraq in March was an intentional world like no other. It was a zone of death filled with the most awful ways to die. To survive inside this world, a man had to block out all interference coming from that other world. Thinking too much about life back in the world was bad. Thinking too much about the girl you left behind was bad. Sean soon found it was impossible to stop thinking about Tiffany. Things could cloud your head in the intentional world. Marines simply could not afford any hesitation once the march to Baghdad began. The less interference that got through, the better it was.

Anti-war protesters live in their own world. Their world is generally part of the accidental world, but far from the intentional world of war. Their protests can have a profound effect on national leaders and the policy those leaders choose, as Vietnam proved. But there is a wide gulf between the men and women who exercise their free speech, and the men and women who fight to protect that speech. Protesters and warriors live in strikingly different worlds. Protesters do not survive on Meals Ready to Eat. They are not ordered to stretch a meal. They do not eat inside a tent soaked to the bone as a sandstorm howls outside. They have the luxury of taking time off from work to make placards and to travel to an assembly point. Some don't work at all. They don't need to. Protesters have more money and more free time than soldiers. But the most striking difference of all comes in the very right they are exercising, the right of free speech. Protesters are pressing this right to the limit and occasionally beyond, marching against the establishment and assembling sometimes where it is not lawful. Soldiers swear an oath of allegiance that shrinks their right to speak. Free speech for the GI is actually a restricted right. The limit imposed on American soldiers is good order and discipline. If their expression threatens the good order and discipline of the service, then it is forbidden. They have no choice. There is a clear disconnect between the avid and sincere protester, and the loyal and hamstrung military member. The protester thinks she's there to stop a

Marine from firing at the enemy, while the Marine is certain he's firing his weapon to protect the right of the protester to protest.

Sean knew this as well as anybody. He sincerely believed he was fighting to protect the freedoms of other Americans and of Iraqis, too. Inside the intentional world, troops don't care if the protesters are right. They only care about surviving … the next day … the next hour. During a firefight, they care about making it through the next minute. They have to pull the trigger of a powerful weapon like the M-16 rifle. Sean had to be ready to fire his awesome machine gun. What well-intending protesters back in the world have to say cannot come between the order and the fingers that have to squeeze the triggers to comply with the order. Sean had little room for freedom of action, freedom of speech, or for personal choice inside the zone of death. Those were foreign concepts to him and potentially deadly distractions.

Even at his young age, Sean was not overcome by the idea of dying. He did not dwell on it. He did not spend his waking time thinking about it, even in Kuwait as the invasion order was about to be issued. One of Sean's Marine brothers asked him point blank if he was afraid to die. Sean could tell his friend was scared. It was a very basic question and maybe the most important thing a person could ask given the circumstances. Sean thought about it and surprised himself at how little fear he had. He felt an inner peace inside and trusted that feeling. His peace came largely from the fact that he was raised as a Christian trusting in God. He had issues with his mom and dad, like all sons and daughters do. He especially had difficulty being the boot camp son to a drill instructor dad. Yet even at his age, Sean had matured into a faithful Christian believer whose faith gave him tremendous strength. To his anxious Marine buddy, Sean gave a very honest and practical answer. He told him that when it was his own time to die, Sean Cassedy's time, or when it was his friend's time to die, all of the worrying in the world could not stop it. Sean gave his friend some brotherly advice. Instead of worrying about the chance he might die, he should concentrate on keeping his weapon clean and ready to use. Through his fifteen days in Iraq, securing refueling sites and guarding airstrips, Sean lived his life according to the gospel of SAW. Through desert heat and cold, through sandstorms that stopped the coalition forces in their tracks, and through frequent mortar attacks, Sean always made sure his weapon was ready and able to fire. It never failed him once.

It was during Sean's holding pattern in Kuwait that the British news media became intrigued with Sean's hometown. Bagdad? Baghdad? Do you mean to say there are American troops who come from towns in the United States named like the capital of Iraq? This sideshow led to the Cassedy family's own little international incident. It happened when the nation of France took on a single American woman. She was the daughter of a career Marine. She was a baker. She was the wife of a former Marine. She was the mother of seven. She was the mother of Marine Private Sean Cassedy. Carol Smith Cassedy was pitted against one of the original great powers of the western world, against one of the world's nuclear powers. It was not a fair fight. France never had a chance.

During Sean's journey into the Iraqi warscape, he would endure a blinding, howling sandstorm in Iraq toward the end of March. But just one month earlier, Kentucky experienced one of its worst storms in history, an ice storm that blanketed much of central Kentucky and all of Bagdad. Two reporters from the British Broadcasting Corporation picked this precise time to do a story about Bagdad, the American version. On the fifteenth of February, four days after Sean arrived in Kuwait, BBC reporter Oliver Conway landed in New York City to cover the anti-war demonstrations. Conway and a second BBC reporter, Linda Duffin, left New York after spending just one day there and flew into the ice palace that central Kentucky had become. Virtually every tree in Shelby County glistened with a thick coating of ice from the massive storm. Thousands of Kentuckians lost power, some for over a week.

Conway and Duffin were there to discover Sean's hometown and other towns in America sharing the name with Iraq's capital. The result would be a BBC news article of February 28th under Linda Duffin's byline with the headline TRAVELS IN BAGDAD, USA. In that article Bagdad, Kentucky, was prominently featured. The article captured the town's patriotism but made the place look a little like the old Wild West: "This is the sort of place where strangers are asked who they're kin to, and nobody blinks if a Vietnam veteran shops at the general store with a gun strapped to his thigh." While it was an attention-gathering line, it seemed to miss the real essence of Bagdad, a beautiful and quiet farming community built around God and the Bagdad Roller Mills. Other than the B & N store and Keystop station, there was nothing like a general store. As for people going to shop with a gun strapped on, there really is only one known to do that. The article went on to describe two other places with a similar name, Baghdad, Arizona, and Baghdad, California. But it was not this article that led to the international incident. It was when these BBC reporters found out that a Marine from Bagdad, Kentucky, was headed to fight against the dictator of Baghdad, Iraq, that the Battle of the Chief Baker of Whitestone Organic Farm and Bakery began.

The BBC news crew was ferried around Bagdad for interviews and town research by Sean's parents. When they learned that the Cassedys had a son in Kuwait who was about to go into Iraq with the rest of the coalition forces, they did two live satellite interviews with Carol. One of these aired on the BBC radio program *Radio Five Live*, with Mr. Matthew Bannister, the BBC's night presenter on loyalty and fashion. The second interview was carried on *BBC World News*. Carol was asked to give her opinion of the French. She gave a short but telling assessment that sent shockwaves across the Atlantic, and which eventually led to a modern hybrid of *Saving Private Ryan*. But in this case, the U.S. military was not trying to save the remaining son from combat; the French were trying to save face. Incoming Cassedy mortar shell number one: Carol told the interviewer that, historically, the French have been obstructionists and, as far as Iraq goes, they still are. In just one line using one loaded word, she implied a vast outline of history. She had opened old wounds from France's obstructionist past. And she opened fresh ones caused because the United States and France stood on opposite sides on how to handle Saddam Hussein.

The old wounds involved France and its position from bygone days over the best way to handle terrorism and terrorist acts. The Marines are well known for their famous hymn describing their exploits that extend from the halls of Montezuma to the shores of Tripoli. Marines, with the help of a large band of mercenaries, won a major battle at Tripoli. Pirates were the terrorists of their day. They were regarded as enemies of the human race and subject to any nation's armed forces. In 1805, U.S. Marines were dispatched to defeat them all the way to the Libyan coast. Nearly two hundred years later, terrorists sponsored by the Libyan government targeted innocent men and women at a West Berlin nightclub in 1986. Two years later, terrorists blew up Pan Am Flight 103 over Lockerbie, Scotland, and they too were linked to the government of Libya. The 1986 Berlin disco bombing killed an American soldier and an American civilian. Over two hundred people were injured, including sixty-three GIs. The Lockerbie explosion killed two hundred and seventy innocent human beings of many nationalities.

The nightclub attack took place on April 5, 1986. U.S. intelligence sources traced the attack to Libya. Some countries doubted the validity of the intelligence, but President Reagan acted on it to protect Americans abroad from similar attacks. Ten days after the bombing, he launched Operation El Dorado Canyon. The operation was a secret bombing raid against military targets in Libya that supported terrorism. The five pre-selected targets were located near the very heart of the Tripoli of Marine song and lore. Four of the five targets were directly linked to terrorism, and a fifth target, a Libyan airfield, was bombed to prevent enemy fighters from attacking U.S. bombers. The raid was launched from Britain. There was only one major obstacle and that involved the distance to the target. It was so great that overflight of France was considered essential for the safe return of the bombers. France refused.

In the instant that it took for Carol to speak her words, the ghost of another dictator was revived and the memory of another Anglo-American response came back. It was a classic case of French déjà vu. The United States and Great Britain joined forces to combat terrorism, while France took its own independent course. In 2003, the same year Sean took part in the invasion of Iraq, the Libyan government neared an agreement to pay compensation to the victims of the nightclub bombing, the victims of Pan Am 103, and even to the victims of another terrorist attack against a French airliner that exploded over the Sahara Desert in 1989. In December 2003, Libya's president made a surprise announcement, renouncing all of its programs to develop weapons of mass destruction and inviting the United States to send inspectors into Libya to watch the dismantling of those programs. In June, 2004 a German court denied the appeals of four people convicted of the nightclub bombing. Their sentences ranged from twelve to fourteen years.

But Carol did not stop with calling the French past and present obstructionists. Incoming shell number two came when she described the French as the "dilettantes of Europe." A dilettante is not necessarily a bad thing. It can mean someone who loves art or someone who dabbles in something. But in the context of this interview, the meaning was clear. Carol had called the French amateurs when it came to world politics and the use of the country's military. The BBC interviewer told Carol that as soon her comments aired, the phone banks in the studio lit up. It would be a great irony for this family that their Marine son would be contacted on the battlefield by a French news crew, and Sean would be given a satellite phone to call home in the middle of combat.

As war with Iraq was about to begin, Sean fired off e-mails to his family and friends. The pace of this conflict was too fast to depend on snail mail. The intensity of his last minute training did not allow leisurely evenings of letter writing. The time he spent in Kuwait had to be devoted to getting ready to fight. Through all of the frantic last days he spent in the transitional zone, he never stopped thinking about the woman he wanted to spend the rest of his life with. It might not have been a good idea to dwell on somebody back in the world, but Sean could never stop thinking about Tiffany.

He was startled out of his catnap by a five-foot four inch blond, green-eyed tigress.

Sean might die from chemical or biological weapons.

The BBC news crew was ferried around Bagdad for interviews and town
research by Sean's parents.

Photo of the ice storm at the farm by Sarah Cassedy.
...Kentucky experienced one of its worst storms in history...

Chapter 7

E-mails of Love, Life, and the Possibility of Never Coming Home Alive

—*"Greetings from Bagdad, Kentucky"*

"WE'RE GOING TO DO SOMETHING. I KNOW I'M NOT GOING TO GET OUT OF THIS."
HE RECITES THE LORD'S PRAYER, THEN: "ARE YOU READY, GUYS? LET'S ROLL."
United Flight 93 Passenger Todd Beamer's phone call to the ground on September 11, 2001.

So many things changed for Americans after the tragedy of September 11th that it is nearly impossible to identify them all. But one special and very specific thing changed. It was the way a loved one acted toward a loved one. The way sons and daughters acted toward their parents. The way brothers looked upon sisters. The way those once-distant relatives came back into view. Everyone hugged each other just a little bit more often and just a little harder. Doomed terrorist victim Todd Beamer was just one of the many who died that fateful day trying to reach out to loved ones before the end came. Fallen hero Beamer was able to communicate with the outside world from his doomed plane just long enough to pass on his last wishes. Most of the nearly three thousand innocent people who were murdered by a heartless band of terrorists on September 11th died without any chance to make peace with their Maker and without any time to pass on a final "I love you" to their loved ones. The last phone calls of those who knew their fate like Todd Beamer shook the nation's psyche. These were calls made out of utter desperation. Some of those who died in the World Trade Center collapse attempted to make these desperate calls only to reach answering machines. But at least they got a message out before they perished.

The legacy of Osama bin Laden is that he violated the basic rules of human decency, rules upon which all of the world's faiths are built. Mounting a cowardly sneak attack against innocent men, women, and children broke the cardinal rule of protecting those who are helpless, unarmed, and unsuspecting. The attack was an insult to any religion including Islam, Christianity, and the Jewish faith. The Koran forbids murder and condemns indiscriminate killing. The 9/11 terrorists were part of a larger group that never tried to achieve their goals through the political process or through civil disobedience. The legacy of bin Laden lies in the method of targeting those who never saw it coming, those who had no fight with him and his followers, those who were not in the military, and those who were the true innocents of our times. When he did this on such a massive scale, he made the country that he targeted feel pain, fear, and tremendous anger also on a massive scale. In that way, he helped marshal the forces of good, and he helped unify an entire nation against his murderous plots.

After the simultaneous attacks, Americans assumed a new urgency about life. A sea change took place, and the old television public service announcement "Have you hugged your kids today?" expanded into a stark and realistic everyday concern: Have you hugged your family today? Have you told your mother and father that you love them? Have you called your aunt recently? Have you visited that relative in the nursing home? It was a Pearl Harbor wake-up call only much, much more frightening because the enemy was not in uniform and because he did not even pretend to strike at military objectives. He struck at the heart of America. The attack of 2001 gave Americans a new nervousness. It translated into a very real fear that the train, boat, or plane trip they were taking next might be a final ride. *I love you, Mom*—the once unspoken and understood sentiment began to be said aloud more and more and with feeling.

It was against the backdrop of this 9/11 state of mind that Sean Cassedy prepared for war and deployed to his new staging ground in Kuwait. Throughout his days in combat, until his mysterious fog-of-war incident of early April, Sean found ways to say what all Americans were getting better at: I love you, Mom. I love you, Dad. I love you, big sis. I love you, little sisters. I love you, my Asheron's Call teammates, Stephen and Joshua. And maybe most urgent of all of his I love you's: *I love you, Tiffany Fitzgerald.*

During the first week of 2003, the press reported that the buildup of U.S. forces in Kuwait was steadily increasing. It was at this time that Sean was going through intense training at Camp Pendleton. Troops were already deploying ahead of him. As the United States and its primary coalition partner, Great Britain, prepared for war, the United Nations International Atomic Energy Commission issued a final ultimatum in early January concerning weapons of mass destruction. But it was not to Saddam Hussein, and it had nothing to do with Iraq at all. It was an ultimatum addressed to the government of North Korea, giving it one last chance to abandon its nuclear program. That program was no longer secret. Unlike the Iraqi weapons of mass destruction, no inspectors were needed for verification. It was an admitted fact by one of the world's most dangerous regimes, a regime that chose to starve its own people to promote its desire to remain isolated from other worldly influences. North Korea formally withdrew from the Nuclear Nonproliferation Treaty on January 10, 2003. The war with Iraq would take place, and in its immediate aftermath, no weapons of mass destruction would be found. The diplomacy with North Korea would continue and so would the North Korean nuclear weapons program. In one instance, mere suspicion led to war. In the other, certain knowledge led to talks.

Sean's life was about as logical. He joined the Marines out of sincere patriotic fervor, a fervor greatly fueled by the terrorist attacks. Then he was court-martialed. After graduating near the top of his computer school, he was shipped off to fabric repair school as punishment. He fell madly in love with someone he could not be with. The cycle of his life, with its wonderful highs and miserable lows, continued as he worked and trained at Camp Pendleton. Patriotism once again consumed him as his country was on a timetable for war. Sean had returned to the reason he was proud to serve in the Marines, a reason that became crystal clear as he headed off to boot camp one week after 9/11.

He was getting conflicting reports about the job he was expected to do in the upcoming war. First, he heard he was not going at all. That changed almost instantly. On January 9th, he sent an e-mail from Camp Pendleton to his dad in Bagdad:

Dad,
Well, I reported back to my shop this morning, and they told me that I wasn't going to be deployed. When I got to the office, all pissed off that I wasn't going to be working within my MOS [military occupational specialty], *the admin chief told me that I was going to be attached to the security detail that is going to Kuwait. So, that means that I will be working with a lot of weapons over there. Kinda sounds like fun. But I have to go get my anthrax shots right now.*
Later,
Sean (I'll try to call tonight)

As Sean was trying to determine his exact role in the war, a Marine Corps reserve tank unit from Fort Knox, Kentucky, was shipping out to the

Persian Gulf. The same unit had deployed during the First Gulf War against Saddam and helped liberate Kuwait ten years earlier. The commanding general of the tank unit told his Marines, "You are on the verge of something big."

On January 10th, Sean wrote again to Bagdad, this time knowing a little bit more: *Hey Dad and family, I have some good news and some bad news.* The bad news was not so bad. He was being transferred to his company's headquarters unit: *I will be on a guard detail for the headquarters in Kuwait. I start combat survival training next Thursday. CST* [combat survival training] *is kind of like MCT* [Marine combat training], *except I get to shoot more weapons and train with pistols. I also get to learn riot control and all kinds of fun stuff.* Sean explained what that fun stuff might include: *I might even be able to blow stuff up!*

The pace of his Marine life had picked up. He had returned from leave in Bagdad and was thrown immediately into a nonstop training schedule. This was probably a good thing after the court-martial. He finished this e-mail with: *There hasn't been any time for me to even unpack my belongings, that's how busy they have kept me here. Yesterday, I had twenty hours of duty. I had been up for forty hours before I went to sleep. To say the least, I was very tired. Yesterday, I got my first anthrax shot. I have to get my second one on the 23rd, a day before my birthday. I got two other shots yesterday as well, not sure what they were, but I have to go back to get two more shots.* He would turn twenty-one years old on January 24, 2003. He had been through a lot, but nothing like the next four months would bring. He would reach the legal drinking age in Kentucky two months before he went to war.

Two days after this e-mail, a Knight Ridder newspaper ran the headline: "Poll—U.S. Should Wait on Iraq War." The article referred to a poll that showed that a majority of Americans would support war with Iraq only if the United Nations got behind it and only if a multinational force carried it out. Only a third of those polled would support war without both of these conditions being met. On January 16th, an editorial published in the *Detroit Free Press* warned the Bush administration not to go it alone. The newspaper cited the same Knight Ridder poll. Knight Ridder, the editorial noted, owned the *Detroit Free Press*.

Sean sent a very short e-mail home on January 16th telling his family not to worry about a recent illness. At first, he thought his tonsils had become infected. He assured them that his tonsils were fine. The doctor told him he had inflamed tonsils from a combination of not drinking enough fluids and stress. His family could stop worrying. If only Sean could do the same.

On January 20th, a statement attributed to Osama bin Laden encouraged all Muslims to end their own bickering and unite against the forces that were readying an attack against the Islamic world. Other news reports the same day spoke of how "bundled and buoyant, legions of protesters marched on their nation's frigid capital." Closer to Sean's own home, over one hundred Kentucky protesters staged a peace rally outside the Blue Grass Army Depot near Richmond, Kentucky. Since 1944, the depot had become a storage center for the nation's chemical weapons. At the time of this protest, the site held approximately two percent of the nation's original chemical weapons stockpile.

Sean arrived in Kuwait on February 11th, beginning his most frenzied phase of preparing for war. His e-mails reflected the hectic pace. They also assumed a more serious tone, reflecting the fear of the known that was on everyone's mind. Combat was about to begin. On March 5th, he wrote to his family in Bagdad:

Sean here. I hope this e-mail finds all of you in good health and spirit. I don't have much time, so I am going to make it short. I am doing well. I am a grunt over here. I have a SAW [squad automatic weapon]. I wish I could send you some pictures of what I do; it's cool. We are all preparing for war right now. No one knows when it's going to happen though. I sent Tiffany an e-mail as well. Can you call her on my cell [phone] and see if she got it? And if she didn't, give her this e-mail address as I will be able to check it every once in a while. I haven't gotten any letters from you yet; I have gotten five from Tiffany. Tell her I love her and miss her, please. It is very hard to be this far apart from the people that you love without any communication. OK. I have to go, but I love you all. Please pray.

Sean created an e-mail address that allowed his family to reach him without violating the security rules of not giving out his specific location. The address he created was: somewhereinkuwait.com. E-mail for Sean was what snail mail was for GIs of previous wars. For any military person stationed far from home, mail has always been a vital link. For those stationed overseas, mail becomes even more important. But for soldiers on the brink of war or, as in Linn Cassedy's case, for those in the middle of war, the postal link to the world is the last thin thread of communication that connects them to their loved ones. For Sean, it was the e-mail link, and every message he sent and every one he received verified in its own way one very important fact. It was the fact that he was still alive, able to send and receive.

The e-mails he got from home were his lifelines as he moved toward the edge and got ready to jump into the intentional world where some would not come back alive, where others would not come back whole, and where everyone would be changed forever by what they did and by what they saw. Everyone would become a General Sherman to some degree. Everyone would feel and smell the hellish part of war. The only links between Sean Cassedy and what his father and Vietnam veterans like him called the world were electronic letters sent and received on a computer screen.

Tell her I love her. The five words to Tiffany caused a slight problem for his Marine-tough father. Linn was embarrassed. But this was his son asking, so the loving father called Tiffany and said the words his son told him to say: "And, Tiffany, he told me to be sure to tell you that he loved you." Remaining completely true to his word, he added, "And he misses you."

It was so very, very hard for Sean and the tens of thousands of Seans preparing for war to be so far from the people they loved. *I have to go, but I love you all.* Sean's home schooling, his family bonds, and the sense of urgency that war brings all came together as he signed off: *please pray.* If death to a young man of twenty-one looked like a far-off eternity under normal circumstances, it looked right next door for the same young man training in Kuwait, waiting to go.

Sean's family answered his e-mail of March 5th the same day. Love in the cyberspace world could be answered with lightning speed. The subject line of their reply message read: "Greetings from Bagdad, Kentucky!" They told Sean that one of the worst ice storms in Kentucky history had struck, and three-quarters of an inch of ice coated trees, while three to five inches of solid ice covered the ground. Sean also learned about the BBC reporters and about his mother's worldwide interview about the French. Linn told Sean how he and Carol had taken the BBC crew to town where they interviewed people at the Roller Mills, the post office, and the B & N Market. Sean's dad said he was in close touch with a military support group. Linn and Carol had helped this support group set up an e-mail network.

Stephen included a short note: *We have used all the wood in the barn except for a half a pallet; lots of cutting ahead.* He offered his own version

136

of the rifleman's creed: *May God guide your aim and steady your hand.* Joshua said he had nothing to say because Stephen took the words right out his mouth. Eight-year-old Rebekah told Sean how much she missed him. She also said she was reading McGuffey reader number 2 in her home-school program. McGuffey readers were originally designed to provide the children of America's pioneer days an education in reading, science, the Bible, and many other subjects. They have been around for over one hundred and fifty years. They were begun by the Reverend William Holmes McGuffey at the urging of a Cincinnati publisher. The principles they teach are some of the same ones taught by the Corps, such as punctuality, goodness, honesty, and truthfulness. In its original formulation, the second book Rebekah was reading not only addressed reading and spelling, but also biology, astronomy, history, table manners, and one's attitude toward God.

Hannah added a short, sweet message about how everyone missed Sean and wanted to see him soon. Thirteen-year-old Sarah gave her big Marine brother a little picture of what life was really like back on the farm: *Hi Sean. Today Buffy peed on Hannah when she was playing with her Barbies outside.* She was referring to Buffy the cat.

Sean was told to expect a large package of goodies via regular mail, a package put together by his sister, Heather, and her many friends in the law office where she worked. Linn added that his own package was headed to Kuwait with one of Sean's favorites—gingersnaps!

Linn closed on a serious note: *There are many people praying specifically for you and for the approximately 300,000 troops, President Bush, and General Tommy Franks, that they are under the power of the Holy Spirit in their decisions.*

The e-mails flew back and forth. After the exchange of messages on the 5th, Sean sent one to Tiffany the next day: *I want to tell you that I miss you and I love you.* He followed this with another one to his family in Bagdad, again imploring his dad: ... *if you're able to get a hold of Tiff, let her know I love her and miss her.* Combat neared, and the most basic expressions of love came out over and over again. He told his family in Bagdad that he had not received any packages from them, but that it was probably because the post office was understaffed and a lot of mail had backed up. A one-month delay was not unusual. He also apologized for not phoning, but that was only because the troops were not allowed to use the phones.

His father responded to Sean's frantic plea for help in contacting Tiffany, again on the same day Sean sent his e-mail: *We continue to call Tiffany, and when we talk with her, we tell her your message.* The "we" he referred to was really just Linn. He asked Sean for Tiffany's e-mail address, hoping to cut down on the need to act as Sean's designated love messenger. Linn passed on some farm news from Whitestone Organic Farm and Bakery: *Our dog Tippy got sprayed by a skunk today, and I got some residual. Everyone stayed away from me. Things just don't change on the farm. Six deer continue to hassle us, and we will probably put one of them in the freezer soon.* He also told Sean that his sister Sarah was attending a reverse dinner in the high-rent district. The children would begin their meal with dessert and work backwards to the main course. Sean's mother was sending a homemade pizza to that dinner from the low-rent district. Linn ended with his signature Marine ending—*Semper Fi*—as well as an expression of faith: *We continue to pray for you specifically and the powers that be.*

Those powers were at that very moment trying to work around the Turkish problem. On March 7th, the *New York Times* reported that the military leaders had presented President Bush with options for attacking Iraq without launching the main attack from Turkey, meaning without launching the main assault using the awesome might of the Army's 4th Infantry Division. Sean reported that the desert weather was always windy, sandy, sunny, and warm. During the awful sandstorms he would encounter ahead, he could only wish this was true. At the very end of his message, Sean mentioned that he was heading to class. It was a class on ROE. He was going to learn who he could shoot and when.

ROE stands for rules of engagement. When battle plans are drawn up, the military drafts the precise rules that each troop must follow as combat unfolds. Every troop knows the ROE for a given battle zone by heart. The rules are usually reduced to a handful of *do's and don'ts*, sometimes even printed on cards. Rules of engagement serve many goals. They should give each Marine heading into danger enough freedom of action to defend against all threats. They should also be flexible enough to account for virtually any kind of threat. The rules must also limit the firepower, so that when coalition forces go around killing the enemy, they take care not to hurt innocent civilians caught in the crossfire. This last objective is something terrorists reverse. Terrorists have no rules. If anything, they seek to harm as many innocent people as possible.

Linn's experience with ROEs in Vietnam had been a lesson in how not to create rules of engagement. Firing at the enemy depended on whether command allowed it. If it wasn't allowed, then time passed as command considered the request. Enemy truck depots located away from roads could not be attacked, but enemy trucks bearing down on American forces could be. Quotas were placed on ammunition. It got so ridiculous that Linn Cassedy, serving in his grunt role on the ground, had to ask for permission to fire rounds at some of the dog-sized rats in his own security compound.

U.S. forces fighting in Vietnam could not possibly reduce the rules of applying lethal force to a few simple *do's and don'ts.* The rules differed depending on the location, the target, and the weapon selected to take out the target. Vietnam was about a president micromanaging what the generals could do. U.S. aircraft could target Vietcong anti-aircraft artillery sites, but not the means of local food production. When the Vietcong located their anti-aircraft gun batteries on farm dykes in the middle of rice paddies, the entire ROE process was thrown into confusion.

Sean went off to his ROE class. There would not be issues like anti-aircraft located in rice paddies. There would, however, be guns in the mosques and weapons caches in hospitals and schools. There would be fake surrenders in which the Iraqis would try to lure Americans into the kill zone with white flags. Fortunately for Sean and the Marines he fought with, command and control of this war had been passed down to the military commanders in the field. There would be no managing the details of the battle from the White House. Sean would be given the freedom to use his firepower to take territory, take out the enemy, and to win.

His ROE e-mail had one short postscript: *Love my SAW.* Sean headed into war as one of the light machine gunners at the rear of his squad. His job comforted him. The Marine rifle creed was no longer an abstract training requirement. It had merged with Sean's way of thinking. He not only respected his new weapon, he also knew it might just be the thing that got him out of Iraq alive.

Sean's family continued to send him messages throughout his stay in Kuwait. They sensed that he was approaching the point of no return. They would not think about a bad ending to this war. But they could not escape that possibility. War was in sight, and their son and brother was far, far away. Sean's father wrote:

Hi Sean,
We sent Heather your e-mail address, and you should hear from her. We sent an e-mail to Tiffany and will call her aunt again. Last night, we left a message, and we also left a message on your cell phone. We will keep trying. We will e-mail Nana [Sean's grandmother in Minnesota] *today. How about this? Heard on Paul Harvey that an Iraqi reporter questioned Secretary of State Colin Powell: "Is it true only 13% of Americans can identify Iraq on a map?" Colin Powell's answer: "That might be true, but you should know that all United States Marines know where Iraq is." End of discussion! Heather will be getting an ultrasound next Tuesday, March 11th. We should know if the baby is a boy or girl. Joshua is making cinnamon raisin rolls right now. It's cloudy and cold in the 40s. Supposed to be sunny soon. Keep us informed. More later. Keep us informed. Cassedy over.*

This was followed by one from Heather:

I put a picture of you, Brian [Heather's husband], *and me in there. Well, a lot has been going on at home. The weather has been crazy. We had an ice storm two weeks ago that knocked out the power in Lexington and here in Frankfort. We didn't go to work one day. Then it has been snowing, too. But, finally spring is finally getting here. Today it is 55 degrees, and Saturday* [next day] *will be 67. The Louisville Cardinals were second in the nation, but they have lost some games and are eleventh. Hopefully, they will do well in the Conference USA. Next Tuesday, I go to the doctor for another ultrasound. We are supposed to find out what the baby is. Hopefully, the baby will be positioned just right so they can tell. My stomach is sticking out now. I am six months along. I wish you were home so you could see me. I will send you a picture of me. The baby is due June 6, 2003. Everyone is thinking about you and hopes you are doing well. Take care of yourself. I have your picture on my desk and have a yellow ribbon up for you! I am very proud of you and thank you for serving this country. Be careful and come home safely and in one piece! We love you! The baby says hello, too!!! We miss you!!!*
The exclamation points in her e-mail told the story. She was worried about her brother and could not hide it. As war was about to begin, and with the

distance between Heather and her brother being so vast, it was all becoming so deadly serious. Heather was overpowered by a feeling of helplessness. Once an unindicted co-conspirator who watched her little brother spray-paint the neighbor's house, now Heather was reduced to relying on media reports to see if her brother survived or not. It was a horrible feeling.

The day after Heather's e-mail, Sean's father wrote to him that United States Army Reserve Private First Class Tiffany Fitzgerald was about to deploy with her unit, but he did not know where she was going. Linn dutifully continued his role as relay man between the two lovers: *She told me to tell you she misses you and loves you.*

When Tiffany finally got some time to herself, she began to reply to Sean's e-mails. On March 10th, she e-mailed him: *I miss you terribly, and I can't wait to see you again.* She told him that her reserve unit was being deployed to Pennsylvania. She said she would later be sent to Fort Dix, New Jersey. She closed with a lover's cry: *I love you! Don't forget about me, okay? Love always, Tiffany.* Sean sent a quick reply, but it took much longer than normal because the military authorities had cut off access to computers and e-mailing for a few days. As to Tiffany's fear that he might forget about her, he told her: *But have no worries though, I will never forget you. Never. And that is a promise. I love you so much and miss you. It is storming outside right now.* And it was storming inside his heart. He told her how to reach him in Kuwait just in case her unit was sent there, too, closing with, *I love you; no matter what goes on, I will always love you.*

As these messages went back and forth between Sean and his family, and between Sean and Tiffany, the media was filled with war analysis. On March 8th, the *Los Angeles Times* reported the Iraqi government was boasting that the war would be anything but a swift U.S. victory. The French government, holding a veto over any further U.N. Security Council resolutions, announced that it would oppose a U.S.-British effort to impose a March 17th deadline for Saddam to disarm. On March 9th, the *New York Times* reported that the United States was considering a number of options for dealing with the North Korean nuclear program, from diplomacy to tactical nuclear strikes! At the same time, the Mideast peace plan proposed by the president, dubbed the roadmap to peace, receded farther and farther into the background as war with Iraq took center stage.

Also on March 9th, a private from Kentucky—not Sean—got lost for three hours, fighting his way back to his own tent in Camp New Jersey,

Kuwait, through fifty-mile-an-hour winds during a sandstorm. On that Sunday, an editorial writer for the *Lexington-Herald Leader* published a column labeling the president a madman: "The madness of King George II has the United States in one helluva Middle East mess. Thanks to his obsession with Saddam Hussein's carcass in a body bag, this nation is in a lose-lose situation." Two weeks later, during the early stages of heavy combat, the editor of the same newspaper issued a modest clarification. She wrote that the role of the editorial page was to persuade and inform, and in this case to convince the readers that marching headlong into a war "without world support was perilous." But she assured everyone that "our paper's thoughts and hopes are with the servicemen and women in Iraq."

The world was sharply divided over the war. France and Russia opposed the invasion. Spain joined the United States and Britain in their plan to conquer Iraq. The Islamic world itself was divided. Some countries even had split personalities. Qatar, a tiny Persian Gulf emirate—once part of the Ottoman Empire and once a British protectorate—provided the United States its main military headquarters for the war. United States Central Command headquarters was transferred from its home base in Tampa, Florida, to Doha, Qatar, during the war and General Tommy Franks would oversee the execution of the war plan in Iraq. But also located in Doha, Qatar, was one of the most vocal media critics of the war, the Al-Jazeera Arab news channel.

The national press was also divided. The *New York Times* and the *Los Angeles Times* remained highly critical of the plan to invade. To conservatives, both the *Los Angeles Times* and the *New York Times* were naysayers, bent on reporting what went wrong with the coalition's invasion. To others, they were the country's fourth estate necessary to keep the organs of government honest through careful public scrutiny. Conservative media outlets focused on the patriotism shown by young men and women sent into harm's way, and on the need to oust a dictator who was hiding weapons of mass destruction. The pros and cons about this coming war seemed to be everywhere every day and said in every way.

A new cadre of reporters emerged during the publicly declared war against Iraq. These were the embedded journalists, adding a unique and risky way of covering the war. They were attached to the military units they covered and reported on the war at ground level, as tanks and armored personnel vehicles rolled thunderously northward from Kuwait. This new journalistic machine would be tested under combat conditions. A handful would not survive the combat. Over seventy embedded journalists covered just Marine units, including the 1st Marine Division and the 2nd Marine Expeditionary Brigade. Embedded reporting was not a novel idea. Reporters during Linn's time covered the war in Vietnam, traveling with U.S. military units. But they lacked the technology that accompanied reporters in Iraq. During the assault on Baghdad, real-time war video footage could be sent via video phones as cruise missiles exploded or as battles raged on in Iraqi cities.

None of the noise over disagreements affected the Cassedy family in Kentucky. They were not paying attention to the split in opinions. Theirs was about just one position, one opinion, and one voice. Sean must only get a constant message of hope from them. They loved him. They stood steadfastly behind him. As his father had reminded him, no matter what, no matter how tough the war would become, he was coming back alive!

Tiffany followed her March 10th message with another one the very next day, telling Sean that she got three letters from him. She also told him that she was lonely, sad, and feeling very, very lost. She told him, *I love you more than anything; my prayers are with you always.*

When Sean finally got the care package of goodies from Heather's office, he wrote to her that he passed out the cookies and other items to the other members of his platoon. He also revealed a little bit of the anxiety he was feeling: *I hope that this war doesn't get out of hand, as it will be a long time before I come home.* He had no way of knowing it then, but his words were deeply prophetic. The war would take on a whole new look after Baghdad fell. The fresh troop pipeline would dry up. Guard and reserve forces would have to assume a radically different wartime role. But what Sean could not possibly have foreseen when he wrote these words was that his beloved Tiffany would one day be sent to Iraq. Sean broke some really big news to Heather. He and Tiffany were getting married.

Heather's next e-mail was filled with both enthusiasm and worry. She was excited over the news of Sean's plans to get married. But she had her own big news. The ultrasound confirmed that she was going to have a baby girl. She tried her best to let her younger brother know how important this new life was as Sean was about to head into peril. She told Sean about Brooke Elizabeth, her yet-to-be-born daughter: *We saw her little parts, and she was moving all around. She was glad to see us! Her eyes and mouth were moving.* She followed this news with words of prayer for Sean, something that was becoming a constant from the Cassedy family: *I know that the war is going to be starting soon. You are in our prayers every night. I wish you did not have to be over there a long time, but I am proud of you! We all miss you! And of course love you, too!* The sense of urgency was increasing.

By March 12th, Sean had learned a few sobering facts about his role in the war. For one thing, his unit would be going into Iraq in the first wave of troops. Though he could not reveal precisely where he was headed, he let his family know in no uncertain terms that he would be at the forefront of this war. He told them that he expected to be in Iraq soon "so please pray for me." His platoon would join other units, units specializing in mortars, .50 caliber machine guns, and MK-19 automatic grenade launchers. They were to launch a lightning assault that would place them ahead of the full-time grunts. Sean would be part of a forward element charged with securing a toehold so that Marine infantry could follow right behind and start the leapfrogging maneuvers north toward Baghdad. Sean told them this proudly but with a hint of fear: *We shall be the first ones in a certain area. But I know God is on my side and that all shall be well.* He also informed his family that e-mails would cease "once we cross over." Stephen reacted to this last bit of news with a blunt "that sucks." He also told Sean that he must be pretty darned good to be heading into Iraq first. Sean couldn't help but respond with just how good they were: *My platoon is trained to the teeth. We are good. I can completely break down a SAW* [squad automatic weapon, or, light machine gun] *in 58 seconds and rebuild it. I have been trained on just about every weapon the Marine Corps has including the big ones. We are supposed to move out in a few days. That is about all I can tell you.* He finished with: *I got Dad's and Heather's e-mail. It's cool she is having a baby girl and that we will all be uncles and aunts and grandparents.*

Linn wrote to his son on March 12th another "greetings from Bagdad, Kentucky" e-mail. It was an unusually long one. Everyone was bracing for the start of the war. Linn wanted to give Sean some special words he could take into battle with him. He began very simply and ended with words he thought would inspire:

Hey Sean,

> *Everything here is fine. Weather continues to be cold, and we have to build fires every day using a lot of wood. We disked the fields as it finally dried out, and then today it rained!*
>
> *I guess you got my last e-mail about Tiffany. I talked with her on the phone, and she was at the PX* [Army Post Exchange] *purchasing items for deployment. I read the e-mails from you, and she said to tell you the same. She was not sure where she was going when I talked to her.*
>
> *Once again, we were contacted by Sky News, London to do a TV interview from Bagdad, Kentucky, regarding the viewpoint of heartland America about the war efforts. They were aware that you were in Kuwait and will be mentioning this during the interview. Unbelievable, the interest the British have in Bagdad, Kentucky. They need support for Prime Minister Tony Blair and to rally the people in England behind Bush and Blair.*
>
> *Many people are praying specifically for you and now for your platoon. Your mother and I are running the military support group e-mail list at church, and all sons, daughters, husbands, etc., in the military are prayed for.*
>
> *Remember the story of Jehosaphat in II Chronicles 20: Thus says the Lord to you: "Do not be afraid nor dismayed because of this great multitude, for the battle is not yours, but God's."*

Jehosaphat, according to the Book of Matthew, was born from the stock of Abraham, the Biblical figure respected by Jews, Christians, and Moslems alike. He was eighteen generations removed from Abraham. As the King of Judah, he faced a great enemy and was vastly outnumbered. Linn filled his message with hope straight from the Bible. He was desperately trying to bring his family's faith in God to bear upon one of his seven children, the one he felt was in the greatest need because he faced the greatest danger. What a wide swing of emotions Sean's parents were experiencing with their two oldest children. Heather was just a couple of months from her due date, and Sean was about to risk his life in war. Linn reinforced the story of Jehosaphat with a long and eloquent passage on the power of prayer from one of the Christian Church fathers from the early years of Christianity:

> *The potency of prayer hath subdued the strength of fire. It has bridled the rage of lions, hushed the anarchy to rest, extinguished wars, appeased the elements, expelled demons, burst the chains of death, expanded the gates of*

heaven, assuaged diseases, repelled frauds, rescued cities from destruction, stayed the sun in its course, and arrested the progress of the thunderbolt. Prayer is an all-efficient panoply, a treasure undiminished, a mine which is never exhausted, a sky unobscured by clouds, a heaven unruffled by the storm. It is the root, the fountain, the mother of a thousand blessings.

It was a remarkable message that Linn Cassedy delivered to a son located nearly seven thousand miles away. Linn's power of prayer passage had come from Bishop John Chrysostom, a revered Christian clergyman who lived in the fourth century. He was the son of a high-ranking officer in the Syrian army and was born in Antioch of Syria. Chrysostom became the archbishop of Constantinople and was renowned for his sermons on the Holy Scriptures. An American Marine was being steeled for combat against an Iraqi army using the Christian teachings of a Syrian.

Linn's long e-mail concluded with short bursts from the children. Rebekah got right to the point, telling Sean that she missed him. Hannah told him that she was about to enter sixth grade in her home-school curriculum. Sarah, the family horse-riding expert, broke some really important news: *I am now riding a white pony named Sparky, and he is really fast. Tuesday* [the day before] *Rebekah and I fed all the horses candy.* Linn ended the message with: *Cassedy over but not out.*

While these messages of love helped Sean's family cope with the difficulty of the situation, e-mails could not heal the blind spot. For virtually every family with a son or daughter in Kuwait, there was this huge news blackout as far as what their loved ones were actually doing in the sands of Kuwait. What they were doing was building upon all of the combat training they ever had. Grunts had to get stronger. Non-grunts were being trained in areas they had not spent much time learning. Sean had a crash course in EPWs, or enemy prisoners of war. Considering the very high probability that they would take a large number of Iraqis prisoner, this was a vital area to master. American forces are among the best trained in the world on how to comply with the Geneva Convention on the treatment of prisoners of war. The rules require above all else humane treatment. Prisoners must be given necessary medical care and enough food to maintain good health. Sean learned how to build prisoner detention facilities from available materials. He also took his turn at role playing. It was a far cry from the life-giving mage he liked to portray in Asheron's Call. As war was about to begin, Sean pretended that he was an Iraqi prisoner so that he could feel what it would be like on the other side. By going through these exercises, American forces became more sensitized to how their defeated enemy would feel once under American control. Long after the march to Baghdad had ended, allegations would surface that U.S. Army personnel had abused Iraqi prisoners. At the end of April 2004, the deputy chief of coalition operations admitted that, if the charges were true, they violated "every tenet we teach in the Army about dignity and respect."

But Sean also had to be prepared for the nightmare scenario of becoming a POW himself? It was an unthinkable idea, especially to a Marine. It was a painful, frightening thought given the nature of the enemy and given the murderous character of their leader. Sean and every GI who headed into this war took with them a simple little formula to help guide them through enemy prison camps. It is less than twenty lines long. It is the Code of Conduct. The Code is taught in every boot camp of every service. It begins with the military reason for being: "I am an American, fighting in the forces which guard my country and our way of life." The second line is a very sobering promise that every service member makes before ever going to battle: "I am prepared to give my life in their defense." Despite the awesome and lethal group of Marines he was a part of, Sean and all Marines understood this line and the naked truth it held. American POWs are required to "resist by all means available" their captivity including making "every effort to escape and to aid others to escape." But the Code is flexible enough to provide an escape clause when brutal torture means that resistance will clearly lead to death. Though American prisoners are supposed to reveal no more than their name, rank, service number, and date of birth, the Code tells them that giving out any further information will depend on each prisoner's individual will to resist. Different soldiers have different abilities to resist, different breaking points. Sean knew the Code forwards and backwards. But he never dreamed he would have to use it.

In the days leading up to invasion, Sean also learned a series of simple but critical combat codes. These were essential in surviving the war. One code signaled that you were out of ammunition. Another one told his assistant SAW gunner he had a hot barrel, and they needed to break down his SAW and install the extra barrel. A third code meant his gun had malfunctioned, and he wasn't able to fire it at all. They were simple, barked-out codes that kept Sean and his squad fighting.

Sean's squad had twelve men and two women. They would be moving north aboard a seven-ton, canvas-covered truck. The squad had to be configured for maximum firepower and maximum safety. Each Marine in Sean's squad had a specific combat role. Sean and his squad practiced combat relays. The NCOIC, or noncommissioned officer-in-charge, gave an order, and fourteen Marines had to react instantly according to the situation. Sometimes the order meant they were to jump out of the truck and take up defensive positions. When Sean's legs were crushed between two trucks and mass confusion prevailed, his squad formed a 360-degree defensive position around him. Sometimes they rehearsed being on patrol outside of the truck. But everyone knew exactly where to go, where to point their weapons, and what to do according to a pre-planned set of orders.

Sean also practiced his role as part of a Marine fire team. Four Marines constituted a fire team. Every fire team was pretty standard. The fire team leader ran the show. After the team leader came a SAW gunner, an assistant gunner, and a point man. In Sean's squad, Sean was the primary rear SAW gunner. In or out of the vehicle, each fire team knew how to deploy, react, fire, and coordinate with one another.

At boot camp, Marines learned how to defeat the enemy in hand-to-hand combat using the skills developed during the Marine Corps Martial Arts Program, or MCMAP. This was the relatively new Marine Corps program that emphasized martial arts. In the sands of Kuwait, the Marines trained doggedly, striving to go beyond the basics. Sean's Combat Service Support Battalion-10 mastered the advanced techniques as quickly as they received them. A platoon of military police challenged Sean's platoon. MPs have the reputation of knowing martial arts skills better than anyone else, with the possible exception of elite Marine combat units like Force Reconnaissance. So this was supposed to be a walk in the park for the MPs. It was not. Sean's squad soundly defeated the MPs in nearly every match.

Linn was able to send one more e-mail before the war began. On March 13th, he sent Sean a message entitled "You are famous in Bagdad, Kentucky." He told Sean of the *Sky News* interview beamed from London, England, and of an upcoming live interview of the family by the BBC. This was Sean's last e-mail from his father. But it wasn't his last e-mail before the invasion. He got one more from a very special person. It came from his grandmother, Nana Erkenbrack of Minnesota. On March 16th, she wrote:

Dear Sean:

We received your letter, and we were very glad to hear from you. I also spoke with your parents this evening, and they also received a letter postmarked the 28th of February. We are delighted that Heather is going to have a little girl in June. We want to go back to see them all at that time. I sent a package off to you last Thursday, March 13th. I sent it priority, and how far it can go that way is unknown to me, but I think you'll like what I sent. I mailed Girl Scout cookies, gummy bears, jelly beans, Snicker bars, shampoo with conditioner, soap, toothpaste, a St. Christopher medal blessed by our parish priest, and a hunting magazine. I hope it arrives in good condition, and you enjoy it all.

Our prayers are with you, and you ask your guardian angel for special protection. I surround you with a protective shield. Lots of love and prayers, and tell the troops that we are all praying for them.

Lots of love,

Nana

Maybe all loving grandparents by virtue of being grandparents are transformed into protective mages like Nana. Maybe the love of grandparents for their grandchildren is so uniquely special that they sincerely believe they can erect a protective force field around a grandchild facing danger. That's what Sean's Nana told him. Nana is Carol's mother. She knows what it means when a loved one has to go to war. She was married to Carol's Marine father.

The press headlines appearing between the middle of March and the start of the invasion on March 20th ran the gamut of support, criticism, and outright disdain for the upcoming war. On March 15th, a Democrat from Virginia relinquished his U.S. House of Representatives leadership post after suggesting that Jews were pushing the country toward war with Iraq. On the 16th, an Associated Press story carried this headline: "Protesters in D.C., Worldwide Cling to Hope of Stopping War." Also on Sunday the 16th, Vice President Richard Cheney appeared on NBC's *Meet the Press* and stated the U.S. goals should war begin: dismantle the regime of Saddam Hussein; eliminate all of Iraq's weapons of mass destruction; preserve the territorial integrity of all nations in that region; and create a broad, representative form of government for the people of Iraq. He would learn after the fall of Baghdad that virtually none of these goals would be easily achieved. The remnants of the regime would form an insurgency movement that would target the occupying powers and prove as difficult to defeat, if not more so, than regular Iraqi troops. The weapons he said should be eliminated could not be located. The integrity of the nations of the region still depended on the stability of post-war Iraq. Terrorism would become a daily problem in Iraq. The ousted Taliban would strive to regain a foothold in Afghanistan. There was a threat of outright religious civil war in Iraq between Sunni Moslems and Shi'ite Moslems. Creating a representative government after Saddam was removed would prove to be a tremendous challenge.

On March 17th, Saddam Hussein issued a defiant statement that he would fight this war any place in the world where there was sky, land, or water. In December, some nine months later, on Friday the 13th, Saddam would be found hiding in a hole with little water, no sky, and not enough land for even one man to launch an attack. His war had come down to an eight-foot-by-thirty-inch-wide and thirty-inch-high crypt. He was discovered near the village of Ad Dwar, eight miles southeast of his family stronghold in Tikrit, and just three miles south of the village of Al-Ouja where he was born. Unlike the prisoners of his regime, the captured dictator would receive a representative of the International Committee of the Red Cross to ensure his health and safety.

Also on March 17th, Walter Pincus of the *Washington Post* suggested that there existed little specific information as to the quantity of weapons of mass destruction in Iraq or their precise location inside the country. *Business Week* saw the country's economic and foreign policies "on a collision course." Slashing revenues through massive tax cuts led to massive deficits, while the war led to massive spending. Something had to give.

Various wire services previewed singer John Cougar Mellencamp's anti-war song titled "To Washington." It included lyrics like: *What is the thought process, to take a human life? What would be the reason to think that this is right?* It was a far cry from one of the most popular anti-war songs of Linn's Vietnam era, "I-Feel-Like-I'm-Fixin'-To-Die Rag" by Country Joe and the Fish. "Rag" is sometimes referred to simply as the "Vietnam Song" and is much more strident than Mellencamp's song, using a rousing ragtime beat with this refrain:

One, two, three, what are we fighting for?
Don't ask me, I don't give a damn,
Next stop is Vietnam!

The lyrics are also lethally blunt:
And you can be the first ones in your block,
To have your boy come home in a box.

Protesters opposing the invasion of Iraq, whether in editorials, in large crowds at various places around the globe, or through song, all had a right to express themselves. One soldier on his way to the war zone was asked about the protests and about protesters in particular. He said that he wore the uniform for them. He said that he was out there to protect their right to speak.

A Knight Ridder headline on March 18th coincided with Sean's journal entry that he was packing up to cross over into Iraq: "Troops, Marines in Kuwait Ready to Execute." An Associated Press article described the French as upset over the apparent end to diplomacy. On March 19th, one day before D-day for Operation Iraqi Freedom, an article appeared by Drew Brown, the military affairs reporter for Knight Ridder. Brown described the real focus of the combat troops: "If you ask an infantry troop what he's fighting for, it usually has nothing to do with grand ideas about protecting loved ones back home. When battle comes, an infantry troop fights for the man to his left and his right." Thought processes narrow on the battlefield. Orders have to be executed. Survival depends upon it.

After all of the talk and all of the planning, the time had finally arrived. Senate Minority Leader Tom Daschle declared that the president failed "so miserably at diplomacy that we're now forced to war." The American troops in Kuwait probably never stopped to think if their president failed at diplomacy. All they knew was that their country sent them there, and now they had to fight for their lives. Sean's e-mail pipeline had ended. Now it was time to fight.

Chapter 8

Inside the Circle of Death

AND WHEN HE GOES TO HEAVEN
TO SAINT PETER HE WILL TELL:
ANOTHER MARINE REPORTING, SIR;
I'VE SERVED MY TIME IN HELL!
Epitaph on the grave of PFC Cameron, USMC, Guadalcanal

March and April in Bagdad, Kentucky, are months of severe weather changes. Spring planting means tornado season for the farmers around Bagdad. Winter generally refuses to leave Kentucky completely in March, and early April can signal weather of extreme violence. In 1974, nearly 150 tornadoes ripped through the south causing massive devastation. Kentucky was not spared as a swath of destruction cut through the state, along Interstate 64 from Louisville, past Bagdad, and into the state capital of Frankfort.

Drastic weather changes during these same two months are also present in Iraq. Despite mild average temperatures in the mid to upper seventies, a windstorm can combine with sand and rain to create a cold steel knife of weather that cuts right through the most well-protected American GI. Average statistics simply don't tell the true story. The average rainfall for Iraq in March and April is less than one inch per month, but when a blowing rain occurs during your fire watch, the averages don't mean a thing. The weather for Sean was an almost daily dose of desert heat and cold. Once the sun was up, the sweating began. By ten o'clock, Sean was stripping off as many of his outer garments as the rules allowed. Once the sun dipped below the horizon, the chilliness of the desert evening took over. If a sandstorm kicked up, the comfort level suffered even more. If the sandstorm continued during the overnight, worse still. And if rain accompanied the sandstorm at night, worst of all. Sean and his fellow Marines rode this weather merry-go-round in the desert.

War is hell—no matter what kind of war, whether it was the war fought in the Pacific during WWII, or war in Vietnam, or any war. Now it was Sean's turn to test this principle in the middle of Operation Iraqi Freedom. During war with Saddam, war really was hell. War in the desert was very much like hell. It was filled with fire and poor souls condemned to its hot sands, wanting to be anyplace but there.

War can be dressed up so that it seems less threatening. Panoramic camera shots from afar can even make it look pretty, even artistic. Filmmakers perform plastic surgery on the stark ugliness of war in this way all the time. Films can portray a battle in Vietnam with stunningly beautiful color combinations. They can take the D-day invasion of Normandy and set the deadly landings to majestic symphony music. The almost suicidal assault on Guadalcanal can be transformed through film magic into something moving and beautiful. Battles can be choreographed to portray the dance of death unfolding like a beautiful ballet. Mini-packs of red dye are triggered electronically so that they explode in sequence, revealing the bullet tracks on a dying soldier's body. Movies about war become movies with pop music, and combat soldiers are portrayed by Hollywood actors. They are movies with themes. They have majesty and panoramic depth. They are in a word totally and completely *unreal*!

Many movies have tried to depict the war in Vietnam. In such films as *The Green Berets, The Deer Hunter, Apocalypse Now, Platoon, Full Metal Jacket,* and *We Were Soldiers*, war is shown with varying degrees of realism. During Linn Cassedy's Vietnam era, one director tried to document the Vietnam War in a very unusual way. The war hadn't ended, yet in 1974 Peter Davis created the Oscar-winning documentary, *Hearts and Minds*. He tried to answer three questions: *Why did we go there? What did we do there? What did this doing do to America in return?* Sean's parents taught him that life could be understood, with all of its explosiveness, by searching and answering basic but crucial questions along the way. *Hearts and Minds* received great critical acclaim, but it was also attacked as a propaganda piece that showed America in a bad light, while doing very little to analyze atrocities by the North Vietnamese. The film's method of editing was called into question.

In Sean's day, over a year after Baghdad fell, one director tried to document how the president of the United States responded to 9/11 in the wrong way. *Fahrenheit 9/11* received great critical acclaim, winning the top award at the 2004 Cannes Film Festival, but it was also attacked as a propaganda piece, quick to show America in the worst light, while minimizing the brutality of Saddam Hussein. The film's method of editing was also called into question. But whether they were based in fact, fiction or fantasy, no war movie really dealt with what Sean had to deal with on a daily basis, and sometimes on a moment-to-moment basis. His drama in the combat zone was always real, always dangerous, and filled with sights, sounds, and smells that only a hot war has.

Private Sean Cassedy was not part of any such scenery or music or acting. When he hit the ground running in Kuwait and later crossed over into Iraq, everything he did and everything he thought revolved around just one reality theme—living through this thing. It was not about what was pretty or artistic. It was about surviving to go home again. It was all about making it back to Tiffany. She had been willing to accept a penniless Marine so readily. Sean had to survive. He had to live. He would return and ask her to marry him.

War here was his personal hell, and he had to be ready for the worst. That meant keeping his own arsenal of weapons ready to use. This included his grenades and mortars. It also included his utility knife, something that would eventually save his life. Even his bare hands and the hand-to-hand combat techniques he learned at Parris Island were part of his lethal array of weapons. He did what the Marine Corps taught him to do. This was about following orders. It was about constantly cleaning his weapons. It was about his SAW: *I will keep my rifle clean and ready, even as I am clean and ready.* It was about keeping his eyes on the prize and being an effective killing machine so he would not be killed. Sean was a perpetual-motion machine, always moving, acting, and thinking as part of the team—a team dedicated to a mission—and never, ever could he become complacent, lazy, slow, or overcome by fatigue or worry. That was for the non-Marines. That was for dead men.

He was not Sean anymore. The senior DI had it right all along. "Sir, this recruit did not mean to kick sand on the Senior Drill Instructor's corfams." Not "I did not mean it." There was no "I" anymore. Not in the transitional zone, and definitely not in the intentional world. If he could enjoy his own person, his own individuality after boot camp, he certainly could no longer. Here, everybody was part of the team. As the team rolled into Iraq on the President's orders, individuality rolled out. Iraq was war. It was not Parris Island. In boot camp, the worst thing that could happen was to wash out. But here, with the slightest screw up you could take a bullet from a stranger and go lights out in the desert. It was lights out far, far from home. It was death in an instant. Just a few complacent moments that it takes for an enemy bullet to travel, strike you in the heart, and change the resting face to one resting forever. Sean fought all urges to rest and let his guard down. Living was his full-time job, and he did that by staying part of the team.

"War is hell." The famous words of William Tecumseh Sherman were not said in isolation. They were not uttered as an eye-catching one-liner like the BBC used when it described Bagdad as a place where a Vietnam veteran could carry a gun into the general store without raising an eyebrow. There was more to the quote. Sherman's fame, or infamy, came from his scorched-earth policy of destroying everything in his Union army's path, including most of Atlanta. But Sherman's famous march through the South began in 1864. It was not for another fifteen years that he uttered the famous three words. He spoke of war after living with its nightmares for years: "I am tired and sick of war. Its glory is all moonshine. It is only those who have neither fired a shot nor heard the shrieks and groans of the wounded who cry aloud for blood, more vengeance, more desolation. *War is hell.*" His words answered the dreamy, untested soldier who thought the battlefield would be a romantic place. They answered television analysts who reduced war with Iraq to troop movements and long-distance air strikes, but who forgot the grunt pain of fighting close in with the enemy, bleeding, sweating, and sucking in the dust of a firefight. Sherman was a great teacher because he came around and was taught himself by the death and destruction his forces caused. He was answering those who saw war as something glorious, like some moviemakers of today. He told them to stuff it. He told them, if you haven't been there, shut the [expletive deleted] up! Sean was now headed for Sherman's hell.

In some ways, the war the public sees is defined by how it is reported. Sean's father, Linn, went to war in Vietnam. That war began as a war of liberation. Our boys were heading over to save the south from the spread of Communism. National pride was strong. But the war took an ugly turn. Liberation wasn't working. The job was much tougher than expected. The President wanted victories that didn't lose support with Vietnamese civilians. The number of casualties kept growing. Inside of the situation, during the 1960s, the greatest military minds and the most powerful man in the world couldn't figure out what they were doing wrong. U.S. troops were told to win without making a mess. It was not their native battleground. The enemy was invisible and ruthless. Military plans that seemed so clear in Washington were not carried out that way in Vietnam. Things became blurry, except for the one thing reporters could report with absolute clarity:

Our GIs were dying in great numbers. This was no longer a small stone thrown in a farm pond where one young man's death was felt by one town. The ripples of hometowns all across the country were being stirred up every week by the death toll broadcast on the major television news shows. The reporters began to spread the word. It was a bad war. That explains a lot of what happened to Linn when he returned from Vietnam and the homecoming that was not there for him.

On the other hand, Sean's war unfolded in the papers and on television in a rush of patriotic fervor that seemed to carry everyone along, down a torrent of battles and maps and videophone coverage. The invasion of Iraq looked so surgically sterile at times. The shock-and-awe war used such incredibly accurate weapons. The mosaic of war strategy kept lethal firepower precisely focused on the targets. The goal of Operation Iraqi Freedom seemed simple and easy to define. Defeat Saddam's army and oust Saddam. What could be clearer? The reason for war was clear: Saddam himself was evil incarnate. Therefore, when the case was made that he was hiding weapons of mass destruction, it was so much easier to believe this would be a just cause. Just wars are good. They are popular. They do not depend on something as tenuous as a domino theory that sent over half a million U.S. troops into combat in Vietnam. It would only be in the aftermath of a perceived quick victory that the just cause of Sean's war would be compared to the tenuous cause of Linn's war. It would only be when deaths from roadside bombers occurred almost daily that the clarity of purpose would be called into question. It would only be when the elusive weapons of mass destruction became impossible to find so that even administration officials began to admit they might never had existed, that this war also would begin to lose popular support.

Sean's war was characterized by combat where the true bloodiness of battle could sometimes be lost by the distance of high-tech weaponry. His war was also different because those reporting it were so close to their subjects. Many targets were taken out without grunts on the ground. Cruise missiles, Predator drones, and other air-power assets could make it look cleaner and more humane than it was. Like the Hollywood directors, the military directors of war in Iraq could pull the camera back and show war from afar. A cruise missile launched from a ship in the Persian Gulf and followed by video camera over Baghdad, finally slipping through a window was just a clean shot. Shock-and-awe bombing attacks that used stealth bombers over Baghdad, hitting strategic targets, military headquarters, could be summarized as precision bombing. The images of that bombing shown at press briefings at the United Nations and all over the world made it all look so humane. Yet, everyone involved in that missile on the launching end or those bombs on the dropping end, and everyone on the receiving end of both the missiles and the bombs, they all had families who wanted to know if the missile shooter and bomb dropper, and the missile and bomb targets were okay.

The war at ground level, at Sean's level, involved a war within a war. It was a battle fought by men and women in uniform wrestling with vulnerability, with fallibility, and with mortality itself. This war of emotions and the struggle to overcome fear in the face of death became the human-interest angle of embedded reporters. They traveled with the men and women fighting the war. They ate and slept with them. They loaned satellite phones to combat troops so they could phone home. They ate the same MREs as the troops. They slept inside the same greasy, smelly armored vehicles. Their proximity to the fighting and to the fighters made this kind of journalism unique, and to some it was also suspect.

Every single troop went through this emotional war as the ground war got underway. Probably all troops who ever headed into combat fought this war, the war of wondering who out there loved them. If they were lucky, an embedded journalist helped them reach out with a satellite phone. If they weren't so lucky, they looked into their helmets at fast-wrinkling pictures of the family or loved one back home in the world. Sean was no different. He fought this war within a war every day, from the moment he landed in Kuwait until his injuries took him out of combat. He would return over and over again to Tiffany's picture, and when he was evacuated from the battle zone, with two crushed and bleeding legs and a bullet hole no one could explain, he clutched Tiffany's dog tags.

It is an amazing thing, the American fighting machine. Somehow it all comes together. Men and women, once boys and girls, once young adults enjoying themselves, turn into warriors. The Corps hammers them into human bundles of lethal energy through training that never seems to end. They train at Parris Island. They train again at their Marine bases. When war approaches, they train again, more intensely and tailored for the task at hand. They fine-tune their fighting skills, practicing urban warfare or how to fight in the worst conditions dressed in a chemical warfare suit.

While the media spotlight is on the big picture, daily headlines, and how generals move pieces around on the battlefield, somewhere through all of this macro-war is the individual. The grunt. The ground troop who gets lost in a sandstorm going to the bathroom. The convoy's lead driver who makes a wrong turn. The average GI hunkering down in a very dangerous war, just trying to follow orders, eat an MRE, clean sand-clogged equipment, and just keep going. In one way, it is a beautiful thing to watch. A war machine marching forward. In another way, it is the craziest animal imaginable, filled with these tiny individual creatures—the troops—who laugh, shout, cuss, excrete, and, through it all, maintain their eyes on the prize.

But even Marines about to attack find ways of relieving the pressure. While Sean and the others trained around the clock in Kuwait, they used Marine ingenuity to play harmless pranks on each other. Sean built MRE bombs. These consisted of pouring the dry powder from an MRE into a water bottle and combining it with a heater pack, a small package of instant chemical heat. The combination resulted in a messy but harmless explosion that drenched some poor Marine on the other end. Sean also built a special hybrid of the MRE bomb known as the MRE artillery shell. He dug a hole in the desert and form-fitted a plastic bottle in the hole. Then he added the MRE powder and heater pack. He liked to use green powder for nighttime blasts, topping it off with a chemical light, a light source created like the heater pack when the chemicals inside mix together. The pressure from being packed tightly inside the hole would force the entire mess skyward, like a crude-solid fuel rocket, and the green MRE powder combined with the chemical light substance sent an eerie glow across the night sky of Kuwait.

Living on meals ready to eat was nothing unusual for Marines. They began MRE training in boot camp and continued it every time they encountered field conditions. Once Sean left the transitional zone, he knew there would be little or no creature comforts. Drawing MREs that suited his taste was one small comfort. He really liked the hamburger, chicken and noodles, and bean burrito MREs the best. But the Mexican rice and beef stew varieties made him gag. As Sean's unit trained, they occasionally ran into packs of wild dogs in the desert. Sean's squad found a pup from one of the mongrel packs and made it their mascot. They named him Duke E. Nukie. Duke stayed with the squad until they invaded Iraq. After that, little Duke was on his own. Duke was the recipient of the MREs Sean couldn't stomach. Duke E. Nukie wasn't a picky eater.

Sean was about to jump off into the intentional world. He was also about to take a leap back into the ancient world. Coming from one of the world's younger nations, they were headed into an ancient land where history itself was first recorded. Two hundred and twenty-seven years of U.S. history was just a pinch of sand in Iraq's hourglass. Sean was about to take a military journey through the legendary cradle of civilization. Iraq had evolved from the ancient kingdom of Mesopotamia, the land between two rivers. American forces would use the Mesopotamia strategy to reach Baghdad. One large contingent of American troops led by the U.S. Army would travel roughly parallel to the Euphrates River to the west. The other main force, led by Marine forces, including Sean's CSSB-10 unit, would follow the Tigris River on the east, eventually attacking Baghdad from the southeast.

As he fought his way north, Sean would sweep past the city of Ur of the Chaldees, reported birthplace of Abraham. It was the Abraham factor that brought American soldiers to this land. Abraham is the Biblical figure revered by Jews as the seed from which their religion grew. He is greatly admired by Christians and held in high regard according to the holy book of the Islamic faith. The march to Baghdad invoked all three religions in varying degrees. Saddam's weapons threatened Iraq's neighbors, but they also threatened Israel. An army from a largely Christian nation was about to invade a largely Islamic one.

Sean had to cross the land known as the Fertile Crescent, the large expanse of land lying between the Tigris and Euphrates. His Marine convoy would pass ancient Babylon, once the center of Babylonia. Babylon is a name that means the gate of God. The ancient Babylonians destroyed Jerusalem, the capital of the Kingdom of Judah. Babylonians built magnificent towers called ziggurats. The story of the Tower of Babel originated here. It was the story of man's attempt to reach heaven through a gigantic tower. To thwart this show of human arrogance, God made it impossible for the tower builders to communicate with each other, turning their common tongue into many languages in an instant. Now British and American troops armed with the world's most advanced weapons were racing through this ancient land, and Sean was along for the ride of his life.

He was headed into a time warp, armed to the teeth with this twenty-first-century gear, passing through the literal sands of time, over two thousand years of sand, on his way to liberate the Iraqi people. His convoy would race through miles and miles of endless brown, of little towns with low, sandstone structures. Tanks and trucks filled with the most sophisticated weapons would pass roaming tribes atop camels moving their sheep and goats. This was a land once home to ancient Sumerians. People of centuries past obeyed the law known as the Code of Hammurabi, a code intended to establish the rules of the righteous. It was a harsh code, and death was a common punishment. Now the coalition was seeking to liberate the Iraqi people from the harsh code of Saddam Hussein.

Sean learned a very important lesson from his father: record as much of your life as you can in any way that you can. Linn Cassedy had tried to do this while he was in Vietnam, but had only succeeded in preserving his memories there through a few photographs. Sean, on the other hand, snapped pictures throughout his unit's march through Iraq. He also kept a small war journal in which he was able to jot down a few observations in between the action. He began the journal with these three underlined words: *Operation Enduring Freedom*. His first entry was short, but it marked the critical start of his journey through Iraq with the rest of his platoon. It revealed that sometimes military men and women sent to fight have to follow orders without ever knowing where they are going or what lies ahead once they move: *March 17. We didn't know why, but on this day, we prepared our gear and trucks for departure.* Sean was in the dark during much of his time in Iraq. He only got the details he needed for the mission he was assigned. What other units were doing he did not need to know. It was like a massive game of Piñata. He knew what his stick was for and how to use it. But what went on outside, beyond his blindfold, and what he would find inside the enemy positions he pounded with his stick, he would have to wait for those answers.

The same day that Sean began his journal, a speech that took less than fifteen minutes changed world history. The president of the United States dropped all pretense of waiting for the United Nations to approve his plan to invade Iraq. He delivered an ultimatum over the airwaves directly to his enemy: "Saddam Hussein and his sons must leave Iraq within forty-eight hours. Their refusal to do so will result in military conflict at a time of our choosing." This was a radical departure from the normal language of diplomacy. Telling another country's leader to, in effect, get out of Dodge or else had not been done like this before. It also signaled that the invasion was close at hand. This was an invasion justified in large part by the suspicion that

Iraq was hiding a stockpile of weapons of mass destruction. The President's ultimatum changed the rules. It admitted publicly for the first time that the world's greatest military power could do something once thought unheard of. When George Bush's father geared up for war, an Air Force general was fired for suggesting out loud that the coalition forces of Gulf War I might be going after Saddam himself. As this war was about to start, the leader of the United States of America told the world that his country and a few allies would initiate regime change in another nation, even when that nation was not in the same hemisphere, even when that nation was not tied directly to the war on terror. This was not like the war waged in Afghanistan, against a Taliban regime that gave comfort and refuge to Al Qaeda terrorists. This was not the same as invading Panama when a dictator threatened American citizens just down the block. This was different. It was a change in U.S. foreign policy that shocked many countries, especially America's traditional foes.

As Sean's platoon was packing to leave Kuwait, it was two trucks short of what it needed to transport all of the gear necessary to go to war. Private Sean Cassedy and his Sergeant stepped in to remedy the problem. The two of them walked into the motor pool in Kuwait like they owned the place. They quickly picked out a truck, jumped in, turned on the ignition, and didn't look back. A couple of Marines challenged them, and they bluffed their way through, talking about some vague set of orders officially requisitioning the truck. Whatever they said, they got their much-needed truck. Then they returned later to get the second one. They picked out a large seven-ton truck that would be their squad's home for all of the war that Sean would see.

It was the second truck that nearly sunk them. Because it was so large, it had a hydraulic system and ignition system totally unfamiliar to Sean and the Sergeant. They had no idea how to start it. So, they went back to the motor pool person who signed it out to them and got detailed instructions. By the time they figured out how to start it, the sun had set and it was getting dark. This presented a new challenge since they didn't know how to turn the headlights on. Afraid that if they went back in a second time for instructions, someone would figure out what they were up to, they put their Marine ingenuity to the test. They drove away wearing their night-vision goggles! A few puzzled Marines watched this bizarre sight of two Marines driving a seven-ton truck down a dark road with its headlights out, looking like two creatures from another planet. But they got the two trucks their unit needed, and that's all that mattered.

Sean would learn to love the seven-ton truck. It looked like a large dump truck with the dump bed removed so that only the flat bed remained. Three-foot rails lined the sides of the bed, and a canvas tarp bowed from side to side creating a Conestoga wagon in the desert. It was not exactly the log home Sean was used to in Bagdad, but it was his home away from home. He was part of a different family now. Back in the world were his parents and six siblings, just a little more than half a squad. His Marine family was twice the size and a thousand times more deadly!.

His journal entry for the 18th was terse: *Bombing campaign started. We slept all night on a seven-ton ... Freezing cold that night.* Also on March 18th, Saddam's elder son, Udai, decided to turn the tables on President Bush. He gave Bush an ultimatum, urging him to relinquish power. Four months later, thirty-nine-year-old Udai would be dead, killed with his younger brother, Qusay, by powerful TOW missiles fired into their compound in the northern Iraqi city of Mosul. Photos of their dead bodies would be promptly released to the media. Because of damage done to their faces by the missiles, the photos would prove to be unconvincing to Iraqis who feared the two brothers. To remedy this, media would be invited to visit a building containing the bodies to confirm their identity. The bodies would be touched up so no one could mistake who they were.

By March 19th, Sean's platoon was on the move: *Drove to the staging area. Changed into MOPP suit. Moved to RP 2. Bombing still going. Night time we could see the light from the bombing against the clouds. Provided security for RP 2.* Throughout his unit's push north toward Baghdad, Sean would refer to RPs. These were the re-supply points his security force was sent to guard. While the RP numbers generally went higher the further north the Marines went, there was no real logic to the numbering system.

Changed into MOPP suit. These words reveal the great discomfort the coalition forces had to endure because of the uncertainty as to whether Saddam would use chemical or biological weapons against the coalition forces. The fear of being killed with a gas attack must have been constant and overwhelming during the opening hours of the invasion. To meet the uncertainty, Sean's platoon and all of the forces moving into Iraq had to don the very cumbersome MOPP suit, or Mission Oriented Protective Posture suit. The threat would never materialize, but until the operation was well underway and the confidence level that no such attack was substantially increased, MOPP suits were the uniform of the day. Later, the state of readiness was relaxed so that just the gas mask had to be within reach at all times.

At 0100 hours Greenwich Mean Time on March 20th, the Bush ultimatum expired. Shortly after that, the war officially began. Acting on intelligence from the CIA, a coordinated air attack struck a Baghdad target thought to contain Iraqi leaders, including Saddam Hussein. It was a decapitation strike, aimed at beheading the Iraqi leadership. Two F-117A stealth bombers were diverted from their normal missions for this attack, unleashing bunker-buster bombs. Tomahawk cruise missiles were launched from ships in the Red Sea and Persian Gulf and fell on the exact same location as the bombs. Other pinpoint air strikes took out targets in Baghdad as the Second Gulf War began in earnest. American news coverage began reporting the impending coalition campaign using the phrase *shock and awe*. The first hours of the war seemed less than shocking, and it became clear that this new description for the air campaign had less to do with noise and numbers and more to do with lethal precision.

The picture of the war presented in the papers and the images on TV rarely matched what was going on individually with the troops. The news accounts spoke of the battles in the major cities, the collective number of killed and wounded, and the thousands of Iraqi prisoners of war. War was what the analysts said it was. Retired generals took to the air with daily assessments of the war. But that was the macro-look, or big picture assessment, of the conflict. Down on the ground was Sean and a hundred thousand vignettes of personal struggle and discomfort. They were the micro-war of blood, sweat, and tears sucking up the desert sand; firing guns, mortars, and grenades; and being fired upon in return.

At Camp Pendleton, Sean had been part of the Combat Survival Training School. Once he deployed, he became attached to Combat Service Support Battalion-10. The pecking order of Marine units leading to Sean's unit began with the 1st Force Service Support Group, a large organization dedicated to providing combat support services to the men and women of the First Marine Expeditionary Force, or IMEF. When IMEF deployed for combat in Iraq, 1st FSSG broke into various support elements tailored to match up with different units of the deployed combat elements. Once war broke out, the main ground-combat element of IMEF became the 1st Marine

Division. Sean's unit, Combat Services Support Battalion-10, was assigned to directly support the 1st Marine Division.

Support units normally provide vital non-combat services, but Sean's was assigned the job of force protection, meaning it was armed to the teeth to help units of the 1st Marine Division leapfrog north. Other CSSB troops had jobs as commonplace as mailmen and water purifiers. Others were the military police in charge of enemy prisoners of war. But no matter what their assigned role in the combat arena, every Marine was a part of the overall firepower directed at the enemy. In Sean's case, he was part of a security force that helped the 1st Marine Division fight its way to Baghdad.

The firepower of CSSB-10 was tremendous. Sean's fourteen-person squad alone proved that. No less than five members of Sean's truck squad wielded SAWs. This light machine gun combines the accuracy of a rifle with the rapid fire of a machine gun. Ammunition can move through it a couple of different ways. Rounds can be fed with a belt or loaded individually. It also has a magazine well that is designed to accept an M-16 magazine cartridge. A SAW could be fired in a number of ways. A SAW gunner could use it just like an M-16 service rifle. It could also be mounted on a bipod or tripod in a semi-permanent position. The SAW fires between seven hundred and fifty and a thousand rounds per minute. In Sean's squad, two Marines carried SAWs up front, charged with front area security, and three Marines wielded SAWs in the back of the truck. Sean was a rear SAW gunner.

Sean's assistant gunner, or A-gunner, was armed with the dependable M-16. But the A-gunner's primary duty was to keep Sean firing at the target. An A-gunner carries an extra SAW barrel for the SAW gunner. During long firefights, when the SAW is fired nonstop for a long time, the barrel gets hot and has to be replaced. The A-gunner also carried additional ammo, including a 200-round drum that attaches to the SAW, as well as cleaning and lubricating material for Sean's SAW. In addition to these five machine guns, seven other Marines had their own M-16s and a large assortment of deadly weapons. Grenades and bazookas were loaded under the seats of the seven-ton truck. Sean's brother, Stephen, thought it was a no-brainer that Sean would return home alive. He could not imagine anything else given Sean's training and weapons and the Marines all around him. But even Stephen had no idea just how well armed his older brother was as he traveled the roads of Iraq.

The convoy of military vehicles that Sean traveled with moved along the highway to Baghdad as fast as it could. This meant as fast as the enemy threat allowed. On average, the long snake of a convoy traveled at twenty or twenty-five miles an hour. Everything in front of them was suspect, including the ordinary civilian-looking people of the Iraqi villages they swept past. In addition to threats posed by the people along the way, the speed of the convoy was slowed by the possibility of landmines in the roads. There was no way of knowing what fleeing Iraqi soldiers left in their path.

The array of vehicles in the convoy was a mix of old and new. It resembled an old-fashioned Kentucky car auction where everything must go. The main difference was that Sean's mishmash of clunkers and high-tech vehicles were all painted with the same desert camouflage outer coat. The convoy included a collection of military vehicles from the seven-ton trucks like Sean's to Humvees to the megaton lumbering logistics vehicle system monstrosities. It was not pretty, just a dirty caravan of camouflage-painted, Marine, covered wagons, rattling down a very dangerous highway.

When the convoy moved depended on the mission. Whether it was daytime or night had little to do with it. American forces are trained to move and fight at any time in any weather. So the view of war for Sean was sometimes through night-vision goggles and sometimes through sunglasses. CSSB-10 stayed near the front of the long convoy because of its mission and its firepower. As threats materialized, Sean and his squad would alight in fire teams to neutralize those threats.

By March 19th, Sean had been at war for two days no matter what the press reported and no matter what the official deadline set by the President. None of his platoon had slept more than five hours in those two days. They were constantly on the move. As they reached a designated checkpoint, or RP, they set up an outer perimeter defensive line. They dug fighting holes that were surrounded by endless desert. They protected one another by dividing the platoon of forty in half. Half of them slept while the other half pulled fire watch. Sean volunteered for the first fire-watch shift. During his shift, he saw the coalition aircraft fly overhead. He could see them drop their bombs just a few miles in front of their defensive line. The reality of the situation struck him hard as the planes were unloading little bundles of hell on the enemy. As he took it all in from his fire-watch position, it finally sunk in. While he was watching the eerie glow of the explosions transform the clouds and nighttime into something surreal, he thought to himself, "I am in combat."

According to the Chairman of the Joint Chiefs of Staff, the ground war officially began on March 20th when the 1st Marine Expeditionary Force crossed into Iraq from its staging base in Kuwait. Marines were first in again. Sean was one of the first of the coalition forces to set foot in Iraq. The Marines were quickly followed by the United States Army 3rd Infantry Division, a division consisting of approximately 20,000 troops and 300 tanks, rolling through southern Iraq at break-neck speed. By 10 PM of March 20th, Bagdad, Kentucky, time, or 6 AM on the 21st, Baghdad, Iraq, time, the ground assault had begun in a massive way. Sean was now most definitely in combat. The Marine Corps rifleman's creed became his mantra. *My rifle is my best friend. It is my life.* He depended upon it—his upgraded SAW version—for his very survival inside the intentional world. Throughout his fifteen days in Iraq, his weapon never jammed. He knew his life depended upon it, so he cleaned it four or five times every day. He knew combat awaited him. He saw it almost immediately. He could see the glare of explosions. According to his journal, he could hear it as well: *March 20. Still at RP 2 providing security. Bombing still going. We could hear division in front of us fighting.*

Within one full day of the ground war, elements of the Army's 3rd Infantry Division punched through Iraqi defenses covering nearly a hundred miles. General Tommy Franks, United States commander for all coalition operations in Iraq, described the war as "unlike any other in history." He described the general strategy as a mosaic war plan, referring to the many options open to him and the coalition planners in terms of weapon systems and troop packages. U.S. Marines joined battle with British Marines around the Iraqi port city of Umm Qasr. Oil fields, oil and gas terminals, and a whole array of strategic targets were seized in the first days of the war. American Special Operation Forces as well as troops from other coalition allies took part. Sean's war journal recorded the results of this mosaic of lethality: *March 21. Moved to RP 7. Crossed the Lod into the oil fields. The landscape looked like something out of hell. Supposed to regroup with the rest of our platoon here. Saw a lot of death and destruction caused by us. Once we got to RP 7, we all slept the whole night. Division provided security.*

A thousand cruise missiles and another thousand coalition air strikes lit up targets all over Iraq. The Lod Sean mentioned stood for "line of departure," the border between Kuwait and Iraq roughly defined by tank trenches running along the entire length of the border. The leapfrogging technique had begun. Marines from the 1st Marine Division took charge of providing Sean's platoon security. Elements of 1st Marine Division and Combat Service Support Battalion-10 would now take turns beating each other to the front, to a key frontline position, so the movement was always forward. One bunch of Marines would grab the forward ground and hold it, while another to the rear would follow, sometimes rest, and then jump ahead. In this way, the entire military beast was always moving north toward Baghdad.

Twenty-one-year-old Sean Cassedy of Bagdad, Kentucky, ex-computer specialist and current fabric repairman, was now providing full-time force protection for his fellow Marines in the most violent part of the world. His farm days were long gone. His entire life history, from Chicago to Bagdad, was in the distant past. Now he wielded a SAW for a living, and a truck was his home. His actions were controlled by standing orders and an enemy bent on killing him. As he headed into combat, the *Chicago Daily Herald* reported that anti-war protests were taking place in downtown Chicago, near Sean's birthplace of Arlington Heights. The protests coincided with the first two days of the invasion, March 20th and 21st. One Arlington Heights protester characterized his conduct as the actions of a true patriot. Sean never heard this patriot or even realized that the war he was fighting in was being opposed by so many patriots. He was too busy doing what he was told to do and just trying to survive.

The general ground strategy had the Army tracking in a northwesterly direction roughly parallel to the Euphrates River. The Marine Corps pushed northeast in two great waves of fighters, both following the Tigris River. Sean's convoy headed initially toward An Nasiriyah. Less than two days into the war, Sean's platoon was part of the Marine combat force that secured the oil fields at al-Ramallah. This was one of the early strategic targets of coalition war planners. At the oil fields, he saw a tank trench that ran for miles, and barbed wire was placed all along the trench. His journal description barely scratched the surface. The barbed wire, the long trenches, and the burned-out buildings formed another picture. General Franks had spoken of the mosaic of war. What Sean saw at the oil fields was a mosaic of hell. Oil fires burned all around him. A great battle had obviously taken place just before his unit arrived. The road was filled with holes, and defeated Iraqi tanks were still smoking like great carcasses in the desert.

Sean's platoon overtook 1st Marine Division on the morning of the 21st, and as it did, Sean caught a glimpse of a platoon of defeated Iraqi troops being marched past by their American captors. He thought that they looked like hell. But the battlefield was ever changing. No sooner had he surveyed men soundly defeated in their own land than something almost ridiculous wandered before him. As he stood in a field of death, an Iraqi shepherd calmly tended his sheep amid the fires, the destruction, and the burning oil wells.

The smells of this invasion varied. The obvious one was the smell of the open desert with its sharp, dry, sauna-like blast to the nostrils. But Sean found that there was a contrast between the unique desert odor and the smells created by the living. Moving in and out of small villages, he could readily detect smells of cooking, of animals, of vehicles, and of human and animal excrement, all smells that added color and texture to the desert air. But of all of the smells he experienced, with the single awful exception of the smell of the dead, the smell of burning oil was the most powerful. It was strong and pungent, and overrode all other odors. It seemed to be everywhere, and after his unit helped secure the oil fields, it was a smell that stayed with him long afterwards.

By March 22nd, the fighting was becoming fierce. Heavy combat was reported at Umm Qasr, a key port city a few miles north of the Kuwaiti border and located on a bay emptying into the Persian Gulf. Intense fighting was also reported near An Nasiriyah, a provincial capital on the Euphrates where the ruins of the ancient city of Ur are located. For Sean, it was slow going and uneventful: *March 22. Moved out in the afternoon. Spent all day on the truck. Nightfall came, and we got separated from our convoy. That night we moved 8 miles in 9 hours.* The British 3 Commando Brigade fought to take control of Umm Qasr. The U.S. Army 3rd Infantry Division was halfway to Baghdad, or 150 miles from its starting point at the Kuwaiti border. Like Sean's Marine units, the Army was leapfrogging its way north, with one brigade punching forward, then stopping, while the next brigade moved ahead during the stop.

The 1st Marine Division had taken control of the oil fields outside of Al Basrah. The battlefield was filled with tanks and artillery. Other Marine units entered An Nasiriyah, and urban warfare training was severely tested as the Marines encountered stiff resistance inside the city. Enemy dead, wounded, and captured were mounting in all areas of combat. Approximately three hundred Iraqis were taken prisoner near the Talil airfield, members of a surrendering Iraqi 11th Infantry Division. At the end of the fighting on the 22nd, over one thousand Iraqi troops had surrendered.

Also on the 22nd, a major coalition accident resulted in one of the highest casualty figures for the still-unfolding war. Two British Navy helicopters collided in the Persian Gulf killing six British crewmembers and an American. A bizarre tragedy the same day occurred when an American Army troop allegedly tossed grenades into the command tents of 1st Brigade Combat Team, at Camp Pennsylvania, Kuwait. Two Americans died, and fourteen others were wounded. Two more Marines died in southern Iraq in the general vicinity of the southern Iraqi oil fields where Sean was. Sean had left out of his journal the details of why it was so slow going. The reason his outfit could only cover eight miles in nine hours was because he was surrounded by pitched battles. His platoon took advantage of the situation and spent the night of March 22nd getting several hours of sleep while these battles raged all around them.

Sleep in war is a special kind of sleep. Sleep in an oil-leaking, greased-stained, smelly seven-ton truck, where a dozen bunkmates are crammed next you, is a desperate act. It can only occur if the body and mind are so worn out with the filthy, hourly grind of war that fear itself can stay awake no longer. All of the basic functions of a human body are drastically changed in combat. Going to the bathroom in enemy territory during a sandstorm becomes risky. Eating a meal takes on an entirely different meaning. It's taking in enough sustenance, primarily through MREs, so that a body can remain strong enough and alert enough to pull the trigger fast enough. Sean had prepared for the conditions they encountered in Iraq. But even he was constantly surprised at how unreal those conditions seemed under the strain of fighting. Parris Island, that horrific nightmare they all once feared, was now his best friend. The dreaded Crucible all of a sudden made perfect sense.

On the fourth full day of war, Sean was deep inside the battle zone. Major fighting was taking place all over Iraq. Despite taking the upper hand from the start, coalition forces continued to experience resistance in Umm Qasr. Baath Party militia engaged elements of the Army's 3rd Infantry

Division near An Najaf. The mosaic strategy resulted in a friendly fire incident as a U.S. anti-missile Patriot battery locked on to a British tornado aircraft returning from a mission. Both crewmembers were killed.

The Patriot in this war had evolved from an anti-aircraft missile to an anti-missile missile, purportedly able to knock down incoming enemy missiles like Iraqi scuds. The Patriot's track record in the First Gulf War came under close media scrutiny, and the number of successful interceptions initially claimed by the Department of Defense in that war was sharply refuted by later analysis. The new generation of Patriots continued to stir controversy. One other friendly fire incident would occur during the Second Gulf War when a Patriot missile knocked down a U.S. Navy F/A-18C Hornet fighter on its way back to the carrier *USS Kitty Hawk*. On March 23rd, a U.S. fighter mistakenly struck a Patriot battery with no reported casualties. The mosaic strategy sometimes led to the unavoidable intersection of high-tech offense and high-tech defense. Sean would soon have his own brush with a friendly fire incident. March 24th was also a bad day for unfriendly fire. A U.S. helicopter went down, and the two-man crew showed up on Iraqi TV. Then the weather in Iraq began to go bad.

The fourth day of war also signaled a new military tactic by the Iraqi forces. Until this day and this year, the rules of war clearly outlawed certain practices that no combatant force would ever use. Tricks in wartime are not prohibited. Building a tent city using inflatable, full-size, fake aircraft and tanks was a ruse used by the U.S.-led coalition in the first war against Saddam Hussein. But war, despite its goal of utterly destroying the enemy, holds certain things inviolable. Fighting forces are required to direct their firepower at military targets, and away from non-combatants. Places with special cultural and historical significance are supposed to be avoided as targets. Iraq is filled with history and is therefore filled with places that the law of war tries to save from the ravages of combat.

One of the most time-honored rules in the history of warfare is the rule against firing on surrendering soldiers. If the enemy raises a white flag or puts down weapons and raises hands in surrender, firing upon that enemy is an ironclad violation of the rules of war. The flipside of this rule is that troops can never use a recognized signal of surrender to lure unsuspecting soldiers into a death trap. On the fourth day of the Second Gulf War, coalition forces approached a group of Iraqis displaying a white flag of surrender.

The Iraqis opened fire. The breach in custom killed nine Marines. This war was ugly, and this kind of treachery proved that in the worst way.

Sean recorded his platoon's close call with Iraqi plans to ambush them: *March 23. Got to RP 5 during the night. We had incoming mortar fire landing all around us. We had a company-size* [four platoons of approximately sixty troops each make up a company] *Iraqi army about 200 meters from our position that had been re-supplied the day before pick up and run away when they saw our trucks. They left their weapons and everything they owned in their holes. Intel reported that they had maps with grid cords of our position in their mortar positions. Thank God they didn't fire on us.*

On this date, Sean's platoon was tasked with providing security for a FARP site. This kind of assignment was critical for this kind of war. A FARP site is a Forward Arming and Refueling Point. It's like a gas station for helicopters built quickly and stocked with everything a chopper might need for arming and maintenance, including missiles and even extra rotor blades. It's sometimes called an aviation oasis. A network of FARP sites stretched from just north of the Kuwaiti border to just outside of Baghdad. By stocking these and protecting them, the firepower of coalition helicopters was multiplied many times over.

On March 24th, Sean's unit was sent to RP 7. Given the sights and sounds of the last twenty-four hours, they were all on edge. As they arrived at RP 7, they could make out the silhouettes of enemy troops cast against the light of the oil fires in the distance. The squad dug in. Sean shared a fighting hole with his assistant gunner, a tough female Marine. Sean had to relieve himself and told his A-gunner he would be back shortly. As he returned, the A-gunner mistook him for an intruder. She came at him with her foxhole shovel, the E tool, short for entrenching tool. Caught completely by surprise, Sean raised his SAW to defend himself. Had he pulled the trigger, his assistant gunner would have been shredded to pieces. It was a bizarre silhouette in the Iraqi desert, a man and a woman facing each other with vastly different weapons. One had a machine gun, and the other had a trenching shovel raised in return. When the danger of the moment passed, they stood frozen and silent until one of them laughed, and then both of them laughed. It was the nervous kind of laughter that comes from a close call. His journal captured the incident: *March 24. Provided security for the RP. Division re-supplied and punched further up last night. While digging our fighting hole, I had to use the bathroom. I told my A-gunner where I was going. Upon returning, my A-gunner was surprised by me and jumped up screaming at me with an E tool in her hands. I brought my SAW up to fire as I was very startled by being screamed at. I almost pulled the trigger. Thank God I didn't. I cussed her out for being so jumpy. But all of us were. It got really quiet, and we both started to laugh about it. EOD blew up all the weapons.*

By EOD, Sean was referring to the explosive ordnance disposal unit. Marines from EOD were experts in blowing things up and in deactivating bombs left behind by the enemy.

Day five also saw continued coalition air attacks against selected targets. Iraqi Republican Guard units in and around Baghdad received the shock-and-awe treatment from above. Waves of aircraft also struck the northern Iraqi city of Mosul, preparing it for a large force of Kurdish fighters assisted by U.S. Special Operations troops. Perhaps the most frightening news of the day was the discovery by U.S. Marines of 3,000 chemical weapons protective suits in An Nasiriyah. A day or so later, the Royal Irish regiment came upon another 100 such suits in an Iraqi command post. The threat that Saddam's forces would use a forbidden weapon still persisted.

Sean was so busy with his wartime duties on the 25th that he only had time to make a one-line notation in his journal: *March 25. On the move again. We stopped at RP 15. Provided security there for the night.* The coalition assault on the port city of Umm Qasr was succeeding. The attack on Karbala was progressing, but the outcome was far from clear. As war raged at many sites in Iraq, an article appearing in the *Washington Post* suggested that Saddam's army could give American forces a very tough time. The 10,000-man Medina Division appeared especially ready to fight the invaders. With the combined firepower of the Army's 3rd Infantry Division and the 101st Airborne, Karbala would be captured in short order.

On March 26th, a powerful new Iraqi force moved in that stopped Sean, the Marines, and the Army from their northward push toward Baghdad. It was probably the most potent weapon in the Iraqi arsenal. It was Mother Nature and the weather that she brought. Sean explained how it happened: *March 26. Sandstorm moved in during the night. Around midnight we were relieved by the MPs [military police]. Couldn't see my hand in front of my face. I was tasked to make sure everyone got back to the truck safely. It took almost an hour to get all…in my squad to our truck. Slept outside the seven-ton.*

Charged with the headcount, Private Cassedy went out into the storm to gather up the troops. This normally was not a difficult job except that conditions got so poor that Sean could not see anything. Just maintaining his balance was a challenge. Even his night-vision goggles proved useless in the sandstorm. All of the technical wizardry in the universe could not stop the sand from filling up every crevice of the goggles. It took Sean nearly three hours to locate everyone in his squad. At one point, the private was challenged by a corporal who wanted to pull rank. He told Sean it wasn't right to be told to get back in the truck by a mere private. Sean told the corporal he didn't think it was right for a private to have to do a corporal's job. The corporal said no more. Sean would later compare notes with his father. The incident with the corporal in the middle of a war zone in 2003 was eerily similar to something that happened to Linn Cassedy in Vietnam over thirty years earlier. Sean's squad huddled together in the truck, trying to do the impossible and snag a few hours of sleep in the middle of a sandstorm that blew like a hurricane.

On the first full day of this awesome sandstorm, day turned to night as the storm blocked out the sun. It was the seventh day of the offensive. After an ambitious start to the invasion, the storm threatened the advance. But even as coalition forces were slowed, coalition attacks persisted throughout Iraq. The mosaic strategy continued to work. In some cases, the weather worked to the advantage of the advancing coalition forces, masking certain ground maneuvers. In addition, U.S. and British air strikes maintained the pressure on Republican Guard units dug in around Baghdad. Columns of Republican Guard vehicles made the deadly mistake of going south, toward the advancing coalition forces. The head of coalition air operations reported that over 1,400 sorties were flown. Coalition air power cut the Republican Guard units to ribbons. Similarly, Iraqi forces in Al Basrah attempted to escape from their British pursuers under cover of night, but over a dozen Iraqi tanks were demolished by the British forces.

U.S. ground forces were reportedly within fifty miles of the Iraqi capital. Secretary of Defense Donald Rumsfeld warned of the possibility that Iraqi forces may use chemical weapons as coalition forces closed in on Baghdad. In executing its own version of a left hook up the Euphrates, the Army's 3rd Infantry Division engaged in fierce fighting around An

Najaf, about 110 miles south of Baghdad. Leading the circling and flanking maneuvers for 3rd ID was the 7th Cavalry Regiment. This was the modern-day successor of George Armstrong Custer's regiment that was once stationed in Elizabethtown, Kentucky, to stop the Nightriders, even sending a small force to Sean's home of Bagdad. It was the 7th Cavalry that gave the Army its worst defeat by Native Americans in the country's history, when approximately 250 men including Custer were wiped out at Little Bighorn in 1876. News reports put Iraqi casualties during the first seventy-two hours of the battle at An Najaf at 1,000.

The fighting continued to rage unabated in some parts of the battlefield, but the sandstorm kept Sean's convoy from advancing. Sean took advantage of the halt and the storm to invent a new war game. He and a friend tied a poncho to their boots and let the wind drag them along. It wasn't exactly reliving his days in Southern California, skateboarding and windsurfing, but under the circumstances, it was a welcome diversion from the relentless and deadly advance. During those California days of his youth, he lived next door to a family from Iran. He used to skateboard, doing long jumps over ramps he constructed himself. Now he was in southern Iraq, neighbor to Iran, doing his unique version of windsurfing. There weren't many diversions like this on the road to Baghdad. Everyone was too busy just surviving. Sean did don his Walkman from time to time, especially when he was just sitting aboard the seven-ton motoring along the road to Baghdad. He did not listen to tunes of his day or music of his age group. Sean preferred classical music. He liked its calming effect. For every hour of his trek north, his unit was on high alert. So, he tried to dampen the effect of the noises of war by putting on his headset and listening to the soothing sounds of classical symphony music. To him, this kind of music calmed his violent soul.

The storm worsened as the wind and the sand were joined by rain. The hot desert climate that everyone feared turned instead into a bone-chilling nightmare. The storm blew in and cast a huge curtain over the shock-and-awe and mosaic strategy. More than that, it made the life of a grunt absolutely miserable. The war had only begun. Friendly fire and military accidents had marred the start. Then Nature herself seemed to check the advance of the world's finest fighters. Despite the many embedded reporters, the news coming from the front was limited. Sean recorded his personal misery during the peak of the bad weather in a March 27th journal entry: *March 27. Bad, bad sandstorm. Hard to breathe. We were supposed to move. Sandstorm prevented that. Grounded for the night. It started to rain. I was soaking wet and cold. I was wet from keeping down the cover of our seven-ton. No one else was doing it, so I did. I didn't sleep that much that night. I was up providing security for our truck most of the night.*

Before the bad weather subsided, Sean decided to try his hand at erecting a two-person tent. Back home, his family enjoyed a snug log house, and millions of Americans were safe and cozy in thermostatically controlled houses. All Sean Cassedy wanted was a brief break, a temporary shelter from a storm in the middle of a war. He thought that he could get that if he took advantage of one of the military's high-tech tents. It took a lot of work to deploy it in the high winds, but Sean and a fellow Marine successfully erected their tent during one of Iraq's worst sandstorms. The two of them crawled inside to savor the luxury of being fully protected from the storm. A third Marine could not resist crashing the party and joining the other two. All three fell sound asleep, and for a few hours, the war and the chilling effects of the wind went away. When they woke up four hours later, they were sweating, the tent was so effective in blocking out the cold.

Even at that, sand still found its way inside. One of the three tentmates was an African American, but three white-faced Marines emerged from the nap, all with faces caked with desert sand. Sean had to literally break off the caked sand around his eyes in order to open them. All three men broke out laughing after they realized their cozy little tent had turned them all into Pillsbury doughboys. They took the tent down just as the rain began to pour down. The Marines of Sean's squad now retreated to the seven-ton truck to stay dry and warm until they got the word to move. Sean was already soaked through, so he stayed outside and pulled security for the truck.

In fact, the weather began to break on the 27th itself. The Army's 3rd Infantry Division had split in two, with part of it halting at An Najaf to finish the job it had started in capturing the city. The other part drove to Karbala, a city much revered by Moslems. It was only sixty miles southwest of Baghdad. By now, Al Basrah was surrounded by British forces, and the nearby strategic oil complex was completely secured by coalition forces.

President Bush issued his ultimatum on March 17th, and war officially began on March 20th. But Sean's journey into the intentional world started a day earlier on March 19th when he loaded up the trucks and crossed into Iraqi territory. After a full week of war, twenty-eight U.S. service members had been killed. Of these, twenty-two died in combat, four died in combat-related accidents, and the remaining two died at the hands of a grenade incident in which a U.S. Army sergeant reportedly rolled three or four hand grenades into a tent in Kuwait. In the middle of it all was a twenty-one-year-old from Bagdad, Kentucky.

By March 28th, the official ninth day of the war, Sean knew he was in the fight of his young life. The news from the front, if there was a front, was largely fragmented. Embedded journalists were careful not to disclose precisely where they were. Under the rules, journalists had to consult with commanders before releasing any information that could be deemed to contain sensitive military data. Descriptions of a completed military operation were carefully restricted to avoid letting the enemy piece together the tactics and strategy of coalition forces. Off-the-record interviews with combatants were strictly forbidden. Journalists were not allowed to reveal current locations or identify any future targets. So the public at large saw the war in a much more restricted way than did Sean. They got only the limited information fed to them by embedded journalists, information that had already been filtered by the rules. They also got whatever news the military sources gave out during daily press briefings.

Sean saw the war as it happened all around him. He did not know the overall strategy, but he knew what he saw, felt, and smelled all around his convoy. He was riding inside the belly of the beast on a seven-ton truck. He could smell the stench of death as he passed dead bodies, and sometimes as he policed up dead bodies. He could hear the moans of the wounded. The only blinders he wore were to that other world beyond. The blackout for him and for all of the coalition forces was a blackout of news from the world. He could not talk to his family. He could not communicate with his beloved Tiffany. The only view for him was the war, and it was an awesome view at that.

There were battles happening all over Iraq that the American public heard very little about. There were great tank and artillery confrontations reminiscent of land battles fought in bygone days. Tank battles occurred in and around Al Basrah, and later near Saddam International Airport. Paratroopers, like their World War II counterparts, surprised the enemy at key airfields. U.S. Special Forces joined Kurdish fighters in northern Iraq. Navy SEALS and British Royal Marines operated in the waters off the Iraqi coast, in the Persian Gulf, around the Faw Peninsula, to secure critical port, oil and gas terminals. The front was Iraq, and something was happening everywhere. U.S. M1 Abram tanks were cutting Iraqi forces to pieces. Apache helicopters were delivering ordnance in the form of 30-millimeter rounds, up to seventy-six rockets, and sixteen Hellfire missiles. Unmanned aerial vehicles called Predator drones were flying 20,000 feet above selected targets and delivering up to 3,000 pounds of ordnance in smart bombs or missiles. The mosaic of battle was a massive array of firepower, and despite the tunnel vision embedded journalism was forced to adopt, the battleground was a quilted patchwork of lethality.

Sean's journal began to reflect how deeply he had sunk into the bowels of war. Everything that did not contribute to his survival was rendered useless. He was fighting to win and to live. Sometimes it was just to live. At other times it was to win. The line between victory and survival never seemed very clear. He was reminded at every turn that something deadly could land on him. It was a surreal landscape that he was visiting now, filled with exploding and spent ordnance, and filled with former men who were now very real corpses. The war was hitting him hard from all directions, but still he had the presence of mind to record his thoughts: *March 28. Moved to what was going to be RP 24. Punched ahead of Division. Mortar and artillery fire all around us. We punched out from our truck about 30 meters for security. Sgt. H. and I punched out about 300 meters from our truck to recon the area. We had mortar fire shot at us. Landed about 80 meters away. We got covered in dust. Our division behind us fired back. Bodies all over the place. We got back to the truck after the incoming fire stopped. We jumped out to provide security. 2 dead Iraqis right next to our truck. Bloated and blown up from the shelling from our troops. We punched out about 100 meters from the road. Bodies all over the place. The area we moved to had been an area in which the Iraqi army tried to ambush our convoy. They were dug in and heavily armed. RPGs [Rocket Propelled Grenades], mortars, RPKs [rifles], and all kinds of ammo were lying around. My hole that I was in was dug by the dead man lying ten feet behind us. Sgt. H. and I were tasked to find all the holes and report all the ordnance and dead bodies. EOD didn't tell us that they were blowing up a bunch of stuff. Sgt. H. and I were walking when an explosion just in front of us went off. We hit the deck with fragments and burning stuff flying all around us. We couldn't see because of all the dust. Sgt. M. and some of our troops were 200 meters behind us when they saw the explosion. They thought we were killed. That night, we were told we had to provide 100 percent security. Longest and coldest night of my life. A firefight broke out about 100 meters on the other side of the road from us. I was expecting contact any minute. Incoming mortar fire all around us all night. Intel told us in front of us was a minefield. I was with Sgt. H's team of mortars when we shot back. Intel reported that we killed over 50 Iraqi army guys. In our sister platoon, one of their guys got hit by some of the incoming frag. He got hit in the chest. He was airlifted out.*

Sean was making notes in his journal as fast as the war would permit. He was writing like a man about to die. He wanted his loved ones to know as much as possible about his final moments. As Sean's platoon was taking incoming mortar, Iraqi civilians were being shot at by Iraqi irregular soldiers as the civilians tried to escape the battle raging in Al Basrah. In Baghdad, over fifty Iraqi civilians were killed by an explosion in a marketplace, which Iraqi officials claimed came from U.S. bombing. As this war continued all over Iraq, the United Nations Security Council passed a resolution to authorize humanitarian assistance to Iraq.

On March 28, 2003, Sean and his sergeant jumped out of their truck to pull reconnaissance duty in front of the platoon. Incoming mortar fire increased, and shells hit all around them. Coalition artillery answered. Sean answered too, but his rifle spray of the landscape, shooting in the general direction of where he thought the mortars came from, was really out of frustration. He just needed to do something in return. It was ineffective, but it made him feel better. The two men got back into the truck, and all Marines inside took up a defensive posture with weapons trained on anything that moved on the outside. Suddenly, three Iraqis popped up like targets in a carnival shooting gallery. One of them pointed his RPG launcher at Sean's convoy. Two Humvees were in front of Sean's truck, and someone from one of the Humvees opened up with a .50 caliber machine gun, cutting the Iraqi soldier to pieces. The blast sent the grenade he tried to launch flying harmlessly straight up in the air. The same machine gun took out the other two Iraqis. Private Cassedy and his sergeant jumped out of the truck again, now tasked with clearing holes and locating unexploded ordnance. They came upon a suspected ambush site, but 1st Marine Division discovered the site too and covered the position with artillery shells. Sean saw only the end result. He only saw the dead bodies.

While still on foot clearing the way for his own platoon, Sean was surprised by a flash, and then he felt fragments fly past. He and his sergeant hit the ground. At first, Sean thought one of them had stepped on a landmine. For a few moments, he even thought he was hit. He must have been. Pieces of metal had zipped past his head. The explosion was just a few feet away. But despite the lights and noise, neither of them was hit. They found out that their own EOD unit had set off an explosion to destroy a cache of Iraqi ammunition in a nearby tank trench.

The night of the 28th, Sean's platoon pulled an all-nighter. There was simply too much going on to take a chance on sleeping and not waking up. Incoming mortar fire continued the whole night long. A firefight broke out on the opposite side of the road Sean was guarding, about one hundred yards from Sean. He expected contact with the enemy at any moment. The contact never came. In the middle of the night, Sean left his own encampment and went to assist his sister platoon. This was a mortar platoon, and Sean was helping them fire back at the Iraqis who were shelling Sean's position. During this watch, Sean saw a fellow Marine take a mortar fragment in the chest. It was a sickening sight to see the wound. It came at a very bad time. Sean had been up for two days straight. There was no safe haven out here. Like so many of his fellow troops, Sean's nerves were shot. He had to admit that. He didn't have time to stop and wonder why at the time. But he had been through a lifetime in a little over a week. This was for real. Fighting his way to Baghdad was tough, and things only seemed to be getting worse. Amazingly, his best friend during these awful two days was the desert cold. It kept him awake and alert.

This was clearly a different kind of war. When tanks faced tanks, it looked like a conventional conflict. But when surrendering troops lured their enemy into a kill zone with white flags, the normal rules no longer applied. There was nothing normal about it. There had been a rule against the use of indiscriminate weapons since mustard gas used in World War I killed anything in its path, and the wind itself determined that path. Weapons of mass destruction had been outlawed for decades, too. The massive destruction of the atomic bombs dropped on Japan only solidified the world's stand to enforce the ban. But in Iraq, Sean faced the very real possibility of dying from badly guided scuds, from mustard gas, from anthrax, or from any other chemical or biological agent that Saddam chose to unleash.

It was a different war in terms of lethality, too. Shock and awe signified cruise missiles going through the windows of buildings and taking out very specific targets. In a sense, it was a second generation computer war. The First Gulf War was generation one. Shock and awe in that war translated into taking out the power grids with saturation air strikes, using lots and lots of dumb bombs. It was loud, ugly, and far less precise. In the second generation, Gulf War II, technology had vastly improved. Predator drones, F-117 stealth bombers, B-2 bombers, Patriot anti-missile missile batteries, and cruise missiles employed smart technology to maximize the chances of taking out precise military targets and to minimize collateral damage, a military euphemism for civilian casualties.

But it was also a different kind of war because it was a war against terrorism as well as a war involving terrorist tactics. Prior to invading Iraq, there were allegations that Saddam provided a safe haven for Al Qaeda terrorists. In June, 2004, a staff report from the bipartisan commission investigating 9/11 concluded that there was "no credible evidence" of collaboration between Saddam Hussein's government and Osama bin Laden's Al Qaeda terror network in planning the infamous attacks on the United States. This did not mean that there wasn't any such coordination, just that this commission found none. The conclusion made the Bush administration's relatively vague claim seem a little vaguer. But what was well established was Saddam's checkbook. He had a checkbook for martyr families. He provided rewards for the surviving family members of suicide bombers who successfully attacked Israeli targets. Sadly, these targets were often buses filled with innocent men, women, and children. Sean found himself a post-9/11 warrior in the middle of a war that was far from conventional. It was about as crazy as the war his father fought in three decades earlier. Maybe the lesson he was learning was that all war is insane. War is not just hell; it is crazy.

On March 29th, the insanity got worse. On the tenth day of the invasion, the suicide bomber also became part of the mosaic of war in Iraq. As an Iraqi taxicab passed through the U.S. checkpoint at An Najaf, a bomb inside the cab was detonated. Four American troops were killed. Tariq Aziz, Iraq's deputy prime minister, defended the tactic in an interview with ABC News: "This is not a new policy; the people which is being threatened by an invasion has the right to fight by all means to defend itself. This is one of the means to defend Iraq against the invaders. So it is welcome; yes, it is welcome." This Iraqi policy overlooked an age-old custom that opposing forces wear a recognizable uniform or emblem, identifying themselves as organized fighting forces. It also overlooked the requirement that troops carry their arms openly. But this war obviously was different. Also on March 29th, an Iraqi missile successfully damaged a shopping mall in Kuwait City.

There was also an irony in how the world's most powerful superpower seemed to follow the rules of war, its enemy did not, and yet it was the rules violator whose forces were literally demolished. Sean's journal entry of the 29th documented the everyday bizarreness of war in Iraq: *March 29. Hajji man and his kid with a mule came up to our positions begging for food. Provided security. Mortar and artillery fire continues. Division moved back in front of us. Picked up all the bodies and buried them in a mass grave. We were replaced by the Marines that came in on the convoy today. We got a full night's sleep. We were told today that yesterday a major and a gunnery sergeant got run over by a tank.* A hajji man means one who has made the pilgrimage to Mecca. It also means an old man. It can also be a very derogatory way of referring to Iraqis or any of the people of that region. Sean used it to identify the old Iraqi man seeking help. The old man he saw had walked through a minefield to come up to Sean's position to ask for food. He not only survived the minefield, he also survived the Marines he had approached, all of whom had trained their weapons on him, thinking he might be another Iraqi suicide bomber.

Sean saw many Iraqis who greeted the Americans with loud cheers of support on his journey north. He saw them in many of the small villages his convoy passed through or passed by. Marines and local Iraqis bartered with each other. Cigarettes were in extremely short supply for the Americans, so the Iraqi villagers helped alleviate the shortage. The invasion was not fighting and killing all of the time. Sean saw other things, humane things that happened, even in a war zone. The Marines traveled with a supply of humanitarian MREs. These were meals ready to eat just like the ones Sean lived on and sometimes gagged on, but a little larger and containing food that met the indigenous population's diet. One humanitarian MRE contained enough food for a whole day's sustenance. Sean and his fellow Marines would take turns handing them out.

Sean was part of the body detail. During one major body detail, he collected at least forty Iraqi bodies for burial. It was just another job for a Marine. But added to all of his other jobs, it was one that was pushing him to the very edge. It was like the time in boot camp when the slug in front of him couldn't climb the wall and Sean snapped. But the emotional drain on him on this battlefield was a hundred times worse than he experienced at

Parris Island. He was nearing the end of his rope emotionally and physically. The corpse detail was his last chore before going to sleep. It was a lousy way to lie down to rest, having just carried dead soldiers to their graves. At the time he finished the detail, he hadn't slept in nearly three days. He caught a nap here and there, but no solid sleep at all. He thought about the dead souls he was picking up. Handling the actual bodies forced him to think hard about life and death, and what he had done. These were men his men killed. They were men like him who were sons to a mother and father, or brothers to brothers and sisters. It wasn't that Sean had a lot of time to dissect his thoughts as he handled the dead. It was just that the only kind of thinking he could do during this task was to wonder to himself about the lives of the men he clutched so closely to his own body. He reduced everything to one absolute truth. It was either them or him. It was so much better to gather them up than to be gathered up. After struggling with these morbid thoughts, he finally let it go and sunk into a really deep but temporary sleep.

Sunday, March 30th, was a normal day of rest in Bagdad, Kentucky. Some miles south of Baghdad, Iraq, Sean was entering the eleventh day of the war. A man in a pickup truck drove into a group of U.S. troops in Kuwait, injuring fifteen. The push to Baghdad gathered momentum as the forward elements of the Army's 3rd Infantry Division reached Hilla, southeast of Karbala. The war's outcome, as far as defeating the Iraqi army, was starting to become evident. The reports from the embedded reporters had given the world public bits and pieces of the puzzle, but by the 30th, the impending coalition victory seemed certain. Coalition forces had gained control of the strategic approaches to Baghdad, at An Nasiriyah, An Najaf, As Samawah, and Karbala. The only real uncertainty was how fast coalition forces would defeat the Iraqi Medina Division dug in south of Baghdad, the Al Nida Division to the east, and the Baghdad Division somewhere even farther to the east. Statements from the Iraqi military indicated that thousands of Arab volunteers would launch suicide attacks against coalition forces. The Palestinian group, Islamic Jihad, reportedly sent several recruits for the suicide army.

The noise of the worldwide anti-war protest movement reached a crescendo during the days of March 29th and March 30th. An estimated 100,000 people in Germany protested. Tens of thousands more joined the anti-war chants in New York City, one of the main targets of the 9/11 terrorists. Police had to use tear gas to control protesters in Kuala Lumpur, Malaysia.

Another 10,000 protesters gathered in Egypt. The international anti-war movement included 3,000 in Amman, Jordan; 6,000 in Moscow; and 15,000 in Athens, Greece. Eight thousand protesters met in Pennsylvania, the state where Flight 93 went down on 9/11. More protests were heard in Dublin, Ireland; Chile; Venezuela; and South Korea. Even America's principal coalition partner, Great Britain, saw protests in seventeen of its cities.

Sean was oblivious to the protesters. During his entire time in Iraq, only one sound from the outside world got through to him, and it didn't last long. One of his buddies found a radio as they were clearing an area of enemy threats. He clicked it on, and Sean enjoyed a few minutes of American pop music. That was it. That and one amazing satellite phone call from his fighting hole. Good, bad, or indifferent, he was only concerned with doing his job and, in doing so, surviving the war. His brief journal entry of the 30th shows how full his hands were just taking care of business: *March 30. Moved across the road to provide a stronger force over there. Intel told us that the Iraqis had surrounded us on that side. AAVs* [Amphibious Assault Vehicles] *with 50 mike mike* [fifty caliber machine guns] *punched out about 1,000 meters in front and on the side of us. We had many contacts. 13 Iraqis spotted and taken out. I didn't sleep much tonight.* By this date, forty-three U.S. troops had been listed as killed or missing in action, and over one hundred were listed as wounded. Sean would join two of these three categories soon. One year from the start of the invasion would find the American death toll at nearly 570. Fourteen months after the invasion the death toll would approach 800.

News was being reported with lightning speed. News of coalition gains and coalition problems. A debate would later rage over media sources that appeared to put a negative slant on their war reports. Certain print media was associated with the liberal Left and accused of only reporting the problems encountered by the coalition forces. Certain instant-expert war analysts, especially those from the previous presidential administration, suggested that coalition forces ran the risk of getting bogged down. They offered so-called expert opinions on why Secretary of Defense Rumsfeld had committed too few ground troops and how this would threaten the goal of a swift victory in Baghdad. Since Baghdad was the goal, and since the war being reported was centered on that goal, virtually no one spoke of the endgame. No experts really predicted what would happen after Baghdad fell.

The speed of the reporting and the rapidly changing situation in the war left little room for reflection and for national grieving. In this war against Saddam, families were being touched every single day. They were the families of loved ones blown up, shot, and maimed for life. They were the families of those killed by friendly fire. They were the families of those GIs who fell into statistical columns, but to these families, these troops were not statistics. They had names. They had dreams. They used to come home on military leave and hug little nephews and nieces. But the coverage of the war did not stop for them. The speed of reporting the war had to match the speed of the coalition march to Baghdad.

Sean's platoon depended upon solid intelligence to keep them out of harm's way. The hajji man who walked right up to them and begged for food walked through what the Intel section had identified as a minefield. The ability to know where the enemy was and what he was up to saved many lives during this war. On the 30th, Sean heard a very disturbing Intel report. They were surrounded. An Iraqi armored division had outflanked the Marines on the side of the highway where Sean's platoon was. To get unsurrounded, the Marines simply moved back across the road, away from encirclement.

The last day of March was a Monday. The weekend had been filled with protests around the world and bombing throughout Iraq. Defense sources said that 3,000 bombs had been dropped on the 29th and 30th combined. Coalition ground forces were now just forty-five to fifty miles from the Iraqi capital. Sean and his Marines were roughly forty or fifty miles south of this. As he continued on the march to Baghdad, 2,300 fresh Marines were being off-loaded at Camp Patriot, Kuwait. Battles raged near the cities of Hindiyah and Hilla, south of Baghdad. Army troops fought in Hindiyah, street by street. The 101st Airborne encircled An Najaf and began a full assault. The 82nd Airborne Division picked apart the Iraqi artillery system defending As Samawah. With all of the ground, air, and sea actions occurring throughout Iraq, Private Sean S. Cassedy had a most unexpected visitor to his foxhole and a highly improbable lifeline home. His mother's assault on France would now be answered: *March 31. Still in the holes, providing security for the FARP site behind us. Sniper attacks on us today. 2 people got hit on our line of defense. The fighting hole next to us got hit by some frag and rounds last night. A reporter stopped by my hole and did an interview. I got to use his satellite phone and talk to Mom. I wish I was able to talk to my baby* [Tiffany]. *We are supposed to move north tomorrow.* Sean was going through every imaginable emotion. The fighting had become continuous. The images that passed before his eyes were sometimes comical, sometimes pathetic, but mainly gruesome and grotesque. One moment he was dodging mortar shells, and the next he was picking up dead bodies. People all around him were killing and being killed. But on the 31st of March 2003, he got a jolt, a boost to his soul like no other. It was a line of love stretching from Iraq to outer space, then to a ground receiver and eventually to Bagdad, Kentucky. The cyberspace warrior got to talk to his mom from his fighting hole in Iraq.

On April Fool's Day, Sean nearly became an April fool. He very nearly got shot by one of his own squad. He recounted the incident in his journal: *April 1. Packed up and loaded everything on the seven-ton. As we were sitting there waiting to move out, S, my point man in my fire team, shot his M-16 off. It was about 3 inches away from my A-gunner's foot. When it first went off, I thought S shot her in the foot. I yelled at S to give me his rifle and at the same time, looking to see if anyone got hurt. The bullet went straight through the metal floor. Early that day I had taken out the sandbags that were there so we would have more room in the truck. If I had left them there, the bullet would have bounced off the floor into someone.* Sean left out of his journal part of the story. After grabbing the rifle away from point man S, he pulled his hand back to punch him. Before he could deck the shooter, Sean's sergeant stepped in. Nerves were raw, and the last thing CSSB-10 or Sean's squad needed was for one of their own to shoot one of their own.

Day thirteen of the war was lucky thirteen in a couple of respects. Sean survived a friendly fire bullet from his own point man, and Army PFC Jessica Lynch was rescued by special operations forces. PFC Lynch's unit was attacked on March 23rd after the convoy they were traveling in took a wrong turn and drove directly into enemy fire. Under normal circumstances, Sean would have enjoyed the first day of April, playing pranks on his fellow Marines. But not this April Fool's Day. The 1st Marine Division was extremely busy conducting raids on a number of villages throughout central Iraq. Where Division went, so went CSSB-10.

Sean continued his April Fool's Day journal entry detailing more close calls. The close calls—whether by raining mortar shells, or from a friendly explosive ordnance disposal unit, or by his own Marine truck buddies—were starting to add up: *We drove north most of the day until we got to the airstrip that we were supposed to guard. When we first got there, a C-130 that was landing almost hit our truck. After that, a Cobra helicopter almost landed on the second truck behind us. Our tire was slashed by the spikes in the ground around the airstrip. We had to drive through a swamp to get to the airstrip. Our truck almost flipped over.* It was night when Sean's truck got to the airstrip. In addition to the Cobra helicopter that nearly landed on a nearby truck, Sean watched other Cobras through his night-vision goggles. Three more landed near his own truck. He could see the static electricity whipping around their rotor blades. At one point, the blades were only a few feet from the truck. It was a surreal sight, but the entire trip Sean had taken up to this point was surreal. Now he hunkered down with the rest of his squad to perform their new detail: *After getting to the northernmost point of the airstrip, we were told that there wasn't anyone guarding it since they made it a day ago.*

As Sean's unit set up on the airstrip to provide security, two tanks were passing by. Sean saw a Marine in the middle of the road about to get run over by the tanks. Sean yelled to him: "Get the hell out of the road!" He came running over to Sean demanding his name and rank. He was a Warrant Officer and did not appreciate being yelled at by a Private. Sean just stood there and took it. He probably saved the man's life, so getting an earful from him now didn't really matter that much. All that mattered out here was staying alive, even if a private had to yell at a Warrant Officer. Sean knew that; the Warrant Officer didn't.

At the airstrip, the troops of Sean's truck set up two .50 caliber machine guns and a Mark 19 automatic grenade launcher. Then another accident occurred: *As everyone got their gear to go guard the airstrip, an unmanned aircraft was taxiing for take off. At the end of the airstrip is a bridge. They converted a roadway into this airfield. The unmanned aircraft flew right into the side of the bridge, almost 20 feet away from us. Our seven-ton was parked underneath the bridge. We were lucky it didn't explode ... no one was hurt, but a 2-million-dollar piece of equipment was broken. The rest of the night was uneventful.* Sean and the Marines of his CSSB-10 unit had been leapfrogging with Division since they left Kuwait. Kuwait seemed a long time ago, but in fact, he left Kuwaiti soil only two weeks earlier. After a dozen days like he had been through, an uneventful rest of the night was all a Marine could really hope for. Uneventful was good. It meant no one died. It meant no one got hurt. But things would change soon.

By the second of April, coalition ground forces were knocking on Baghdad's door. Forces from the southwest and southeast had fought sandstorms, suicide bombers, the threat of chemical weapons, and the best army divisions Saddam could throw at them, and were now within thirty miles of the main goal. The tactics of war continued to bend away from the rules and toward a terrorist style of fighting. While the coalition forces tried to respect cultural objects, Iraqi forces occupied one of the most sacred of such objects, the Ali Mosque in An Najaf, using it as a combat center to fire upon coalition troops. On the second of April, over 1,900 coalition air sorties were flown. The majority of these were flown in support of advancing ground forces. Bombing resumed in Baghdad and Mosul. The Baghdad Division, defending Al Kut, southeast of Baghdad, was cut to ribbons by the 1st Marine Expeditionary Force. The Marines were closing in on Baghdad from the southeast, just as the Army's 3rd Infantry Division was closing in from the southwest. The Mesopotamia strategy was coming together.

It was just an average day in the war for Sean: *April 2. Black Hawk helicopter landed about 20 feet from our fighting hole, knocking our cami* [camouflage] *netting over. One helo took off and buzzed right over us. Another helo just landed behind us. They kick up sand and rocks whenever they take off or land. There are a lot of hajji people around here. I heard one singing earlier today. The pilots gave us some soda and candy to apologize for all the stuff they have done to us today. We are supposed to move out in 48 hours.* Sean barely knew where he was at any given moment. He knew they were driving north. He knew that Baghdad was the eventual goal. But under the circumstances of the near nonstop drive to Baghdad, he never had time to stop and check exactly how far he was from Baghdad. But on this date, his close contact with a Black Hawk helicopter pilot gave him a chance to look at a map. The pilot showed him that he was less than a hundred miles from Baghdad. He would never make it. The last entry in his war journal read: *April 3. Moving farther north round 1200 Zulu. Right now we are 76 miles south of Baghdad. Going to RP 20. Last night saw a lot of bombing, mortar, artillery, rockets ... being fired off. Quite a night through NVGs* [night vision goggles].

Soon after this final entry, Sean would become a statistic. As a matter of fact, he would become two statistics. For a few frantic minutes, he would be reported as missing. Then he would fall into the category of the injured. For the short time he was among the missing, his parents would lose faith in the people charged with letting them know what happened to their son. When the military officials later could not even tell them the extent of Sean's injuries, it would only make matters worse. The truth was that Sean S. Cassedy was almost killed on the battlefield, approximately seventy miles from Baghdad, Iraq, and nearly 6,500 miles from Bagdad, Kentucky.

Sean built MRE bombs.

Sean's squad found a pup from one of the mongrel packs and made it their mascot. They named him Duke E. Nukie.

operation Enduring Freedom

17th
We didn't know but on this day we
prepared our gear and trucks for departure.

18th Bombing campain started. We slept
all night on a 7-ton... Freezing cold
that night.

19th Drove to the staging area, changed
into MOPP suit. Moved to RP 2, Bombing
still going. Night time we could see the
light from the bombing against the clouds.
Provided security for RP2.

20th still at RP2 providing security.
Bombing still going. We could hear
division in front of us fighting.

21st Moved to RP7, crossed the road into
the oil fields. The landscape looked like
something out of hell. Supposed to
regroup with the rest of our platoon here.
Saw alot of death and destruction caused
by us. Once we got to RP7 we all slept
the whole night. Division provided security.

He began the journal with these three underlined words:
<u>Operation</u> <u>Enduring</u> <u>Freedom</u>.

They picked out a large seven-ton truck that would be their squad's home for all of the war that Sean would see.

The array of vehicles in the convoy was a mix of old and new.

...he thought to himself, 'I am in combat.'

As he stood in a field of death an Iraqi shepherd calmly tended his sheep amid the fires, the destruction, and the burning oil wells.

A sandstorm moved in during the night...Couldn't see my hand in front of my face.

Battles raged near the cities of Hindiyah and Hilla.

Chapter 9

Facing Down Death

... AND A TIME TO HEAL
Ecclesiastes 3:1

When it happened, Sean already had a bad feeling. He had seen a lot in the past day or two. Choppers nearly landed on top of his unit. A C-130 landed on a makeshift airstrip Sean's outfit was charged with defending and barely missed one of the trucks in Sean's convoy. His seven-ton truck nearly overturned in a swampy patch near that same runway. A tire blew out on the airstrip's metal joints, but, thankfully, it was self-inflating and re-inflated almost instantly. Then, when Sean's unit was told to move on north toward Baghdad, now a mere seventy miles away, an elite Marine unit took over airstrip security. It didn't add up. Strange things were happening. A Predator drone crashed on takeoff into the bridge Sean's truck was using for a hangar. The road north was filled with dust and smoke, and the villagers themselves didn't seem right.

So when it happened, Sean had a premonition about the face of the driver whose huge vehicle headed for Sean's truck. He had that look. It was the look Sean had learned so very quickly in his two weeks in Iraq. The gigantic logistics vehicle system, or LVS, moved directly toward Sean's corner of the truck. Sean heard the distinctive noise of metal colliding with metal. He heard brakes squealing like two great beasts going through their final agonizing death throes. He heard the sound of several huge engines, apparently vehicles of his convoy, still running after the collision. But most of all, through the blinding dust, he remembered the driver's face. And the driver's face seemed to be screwed to his instruments, and then it seemed to be frozen. Frozen out of life. It was the face of death bearing down on Sean.

There is a phrase that is sometimes used to describe the confusion that takes place during conflict. It has become more of a popular notion than a theoretical concept. It is the fog of war. Classic warfare thinkers used it in a much more limited way. The fog of war was used to express the unpredictable factors that just show up in battle. The fog is the literal fog or bad weather or any hazard that interferes with the execution of the war plan. More popularly, the media uses the phrase to describe almost any confusion

199

in war. Private Cassedy was about to enter a confusing cloud of smoke, dust, and gunfire that very nearly took his life. After his last journal entry, he helped pack up their seven-ton truck and headed north.

Sean's unit was being relieved by Marine Force Reconnaissance. To Sean, this was very odd, considering the elite nature of Force Recon. That unit was like a special ops unit, its troops specially trained for unique and extremely challenging insertion missions. The Marines of Force Recon are the real snake-eaters of the Corps. They specialize in underwater reconnaissance and deep penetration into an enemy's territory. Their roots go back to the landing force that stormed Iwo Jima, a force that Sean's grandfather was a part of. Their motto—swift, silent, deadly—says it all. So Sean had to wonder what kind of territory this was, and why the converted airstrip he guarded was taken over by the best of the Marines' best. April 3rd began on this bizarre note for Sean. Private Cassedy and his Marines loaded up and headed north. Their truck had been recently repaired from the tire damage done at the airstrip they were assigned to guard. Everything appeared fine.

The Force Reconnaissance replacements bothered him. He didn't exactly know why. But when his seven-ton truck left the airstrip, he had an uneasy feeling, the kind of gnawing feeling a combat troop tries to avoid. He didn't want to think it, but something was telling him his time might be up. In a sense it was. Several weeks after it happened, after being evacuated from the combat zone, Sean tried to piece together what happened. His notes, not journal entries, follow:

April 3, 2003. Everything was good, or so I thought. We had just driven past a small village full of people. They stood on the edge of the road, with some cheering us on, while others just stood there watching us. It made us a little nervous. We sat in a defensive position in the back of our truck. All weapons pointed outboard. We drove and then dust was all around us. We could not see a thing. We started to take some mortar fire and small arms fire from the right. We had been ambushed. Everyone in the back of the truck was yelling for info on what was going on and what we were supposed to do.

A fuel truck appeared out of the dust to our left, hitting the several packs of gear that hung on the outside of our truck. The driver moved further to the right. The Humvee in front of us was stopped. We didn't realize that he was stopped. We hit the side of the Humvee, knocking all our packs off the truck.

The packs he mentioned were the rucksacks of battle gear each Marine carried. Each one contained a load of about fifty pounds. To maximize space on the bed of the seven-ton truck, these packs were hung over the side of the truck, using the quick release latches to fasten them in place. His notes continue: *As the driver slowed down our seven-ton, I looked back when I heard a noise. Out of the dust appeared an LVS that was following us. This LVS weighed nearly seventy tons. It was pulling a trailer full of Marines and another trailer full of gear and ammo. I could see the driver's face trying hard to concentrate on the dials of his control panel. He knew at that moment that he was going to hit us. Everything started to go in slow motion. He was going to hit the same corner I was sitting in. I wasn't really afraid or upset. Strangely, I was calm. Everyone in the truck was yelling. I watched as the LVS hit my corner of the truck. Just before the truck hit me, I remember seeing the underside of it. I saw tires and the driver's face, which was really screwed up from the hit. His face told me he must have been killed. His blood was everywhere. I got knocked out of my truck from the collision. I was told later that the two trucks locked together and dragged one another a hundred meters. The next thing I actually remembered was being on the ground about to go into shock. Sgt. H. told me later that I was trying to cut myself out of the wreck with my K-bar. My legs were stuck underneath the tailgate, which was bent directly over them. My SAW's barrel had been bent as well. It was sitting on my lap.*

Just as quickly as the collision occurred, several Marines, uninjured by the crash, jumped into position. They had trained for rapid deployment like this while in Kuwait. They assumed a 360-degree defensive position, surrounding the site and pointing their weapons outward so every possible angle was covered. Before nearly passing out from his injuries, Sean saw three Humvees nearby. One had been clipped by the vehicles that collided. One was an ambulance vehicle, and the other one was just there. The lucky part of the incident, if there was a lucky part, was that the two main vehicles, Sean's truck and the LVS, had collided in a way that immediately forced both vehicles off the road. The convoy was extremely long and did not have to stop. Had things happened just a little differently, a chain reaction might have taken out a lot more vehicles.

When death explodes before us, it is always for the last time. Sean learned this the hardest way possible, from the driver of the LVS: *When I came to, I was in a field lying there, my body shaking from the shock. Marines were all over the place trying to see who had been hurt. Sgt. H. and another Marine were trying to revive the driver of the LVS. But it was too late for him. He was dead. Two Marines were trying to get me in a stable condition, cutting off my chem. suit and boots. Before I went to war, I placed my dog tag in the lace of my left boot. I placed my girlfriend's dog tag in my right boot. They took both tags out now and placed them in my right hand. I made a fist around them. I wasn't about to lose them. I was in a lot of pain. I could not feel anything from the waist down. I thought I was never going to walk again. I looked down at my legs. There was blood all over, and my right leg was swollen to twice its normal size. My legs had been crushed, and I had been shot in the right inner thigh. The doc came over to me and splinted my leg and put a bandage over the gunshot wound. They gave me morphine. Once it took hold, I was no longer feeling any pain. I calmly watched everything going on around me. They called for a medevac flight. The bird arrived about twenty minutes later. I was put aboard and arrived at Camp Viper (RP 24). The docs there patched me up some more and prepared me for another trip. This time, I was transported to another hospital in Iraq.*

This began Sean's trip out of the war zone. For him, as long as he could safely make it out of the war zone, it was over. The war to topple Saddam would continue. It would culminate in the capture of Baghdad. The images of the end of major combat would include several instances of Iraqi crowds pulling down statues of Saddam. They would include the dressed up bodies of Saddam's sons. They would even include a speech by President Bush on May 2nd aboard the *U.S.S. Abraham Lincoln* announcing the end of major combat operations in Iraq. A banner hung on the aircraft carrier announcing mission accomplished would ignite a political controversy when it became clear that the endgame in Iraq had a long way to go, and American military casualties continued.

But for Sean, it was over on April 3rd. In a way, the ambush, the crushed leg, and the bullet in his thigh may have been what saved him. He never reached Baghdad. Who can say what awaited him further up the road or inside the capital itself? Coalition forces have been under fire since the end of major combat operations, dying with alarming frequency. The enemy after the fall of Baghdad became like the Vietcong in Vietnam, an unseen, stealth enemy. This invisible enemy uses roadside bombs, detonating when coalition forces pass by. It uses shoulder-fired missiles launched from the middle of nowhere at coalition helicopters. But in the immediate aftermath of the LVS collision with Sean's legs, Linn and Carol Cassedy's son got to go home, and best of all, he got to return home alive.

The entire Cassedy family back in Kentucky was watching the war unfold with millions of other Americans. Embedded journalism had radically changed the way something as graphic as war fighting was covered. Watching this war was more like watching one of the trendy reality television programs. It was the ultimate survivor show, and Sean was one of over one hundred thousand participants trying not to be voted off the planet. This war's media coverage was radically different from that of the First Gulf War, when news blackouts were the rule. In Gulf War I, ground combat operations lasted just over four days, earning for that conflict the title of the Hundred-Hour War. Media coverage was severely restricted. By contrast, major ground combat in Sean's war lasted five times as long, twenty-one versus four days, and the Pentagon provided access directly to the front with the embedded journalist system.

But for the brothers and sisters and mothers and fathers of the troops fighting, it was a gut-wrenching experience. Sean's older sister, Heather, went to work every day in Frankfort, Kentucky, trying her best to stay focused on her job. But Sean was constantly on her mind. Sean had first warned the family about the possibility of going abroad in November 2002. Heather didn't think much about it then. The sabers were rattling, but it did not sink in that going abroad might mean going to Iraq to fight and maybe die. It began to finally hit home around Christmastime 2002. That's when Sean broke the news to his family he was headed to Kuwait. When his time for deployment came, Heather was glued to the television news coverage of troops leaving San Diego for the Gulf, trying to catch a glimpse of her brother. When he left in February, Heather did everything she could to keep up with his whereabouts.

On March 12th, just one week before he would begin his journey toward Baghdad, Heather received an e-mail from Sean. Sean told her that his unit was about to go. He meant cross over, out of the transitional territory into the actual war zone. Past the lod, or line of departure. The ups and downs of hearing from Sean and hearing the news of war would exact a toll on Heather. At the time the President declared to the world that the invasion had begun, she was seven months pregnant. The fear of Sean dying in Iraq scared Heather a great deal. Once the combat media coverage began, all she could think about was the very real possibility that she would never see her brother alive again, that he would never see the child she was now carrying. He would never enjoy being Uncle Sean.

Like many Americans, Heather became a war news junkie. She did her job at the office to the best of her ability. But whenever she could, she would go to the office law library where a television tuned to war coverage played almost continuously. She would look for David Bloom, one of the embedded NBC reporters. To Heather, Bloom always seemed to be where the action was. He traveled in a specially modified M88 tank retriever, a vehicle that quickly became known as the Bloommobile. He was often seen covered from head to toe in the desert dust of his travels, his hair almost white from the dust. But even Heather's favorite reporter died in this war. While traveling with the Army's 3rd Infantry Division, the thirty-nine-year-old Bloom died suddenly on April 6th, just three days after Sean's injuries occurred. Heather kept a close eye on the movements of the 1st Marine Expeditionary Force, figuring the many journalists traveling with that unit would have the best view of the war Sean was actually fighting. When she left work and went home, she watched more television coverage until she went to bed.

In the middle of the war, on March 29th, the Cassedy family was shocked by what they heard from the front. Sean's father was outside with all of Sean's brothers and sisters. Only Heather was missing. She lived with her husband some miles away from the farm. Linn was busy cutting a tree down with his power saw. The kids were there to watch and talk. That's when Sean's mother got the call. Attached to their main phone was a computer with a program that worked like caller ID, and the screen flashed something unbelievable: Baghdad, Iraq! It was Sean calling from his fighting hole. The howitzer shell launched by his mother on February 18th, when she told BBC interviewers about French dilettantes and about French obstructionism, had somehow landed on Sean's position. Of all of the coincidences Sean had ever experienced, meeting a French television crew in the middle of combat after his mother had attacked the French through the BBC was the most unlikely one of all. But Sean actually got something good from this French connection. He got to use the crew's satellite phone for twenty minutes. It had to be one of the most incredible wartime calls of all time.

During the 1983 invasion of Grenada, an Army paratrooper reportedly used a payphone to call in Navy air support to his beleaguered position. Twenty years later, a Marine private somewhere south of Baghdad, Iraq, was phoning home to somewhere outside of Bagdad, Kentucky, while in the middle of a war. When she answered the phone, Sean's mother thought it was some cruel joke. When she finally realized she was talking to her own son, she raced outside screaming like a crazy person for the rest of the family. Then they all gathered around the phone as Sean spent his precious twenty minutes trying to tell them as much as he could about what he had been going through. He told them that he was okay. He said that he had seen some fierce fighting. He recalled for them the close call of the previous Saturday night, approximately one week earlier, when enemy mortar shells nearly hit his platoon's position. And he told his mom what all good sons tell their moms, even under the most extreme conditions, that he was eating just fine. He did not mention that at times his platoon was carefully rationing their food and water. He also failed to mention his real opinion of the MRE chow he was eating. He also greatly exaggerated how much sleep he was getting, assuring her that he got four hours every night.

It was a telephone call for the ages. It was like those last calls made at Camp Pendleton just prior to deploying, but with a few sobering differences. This call was much more like a last call than the deployment call. His Pendleton call was made in anticipation of war; this call came from a fighting hole in the middle of war. At Pendleton, what might have happened—the tragic end that might have resulted—was then just a possibility. Here, Sean was telling his family about how he cheated death, and when the call was over, death still had the advantage because his combat time was not up.

Sean told his mother that he kept pictures of the family in his pocket. He also told her that he carried Tiffany's picture, too. What he did not say in the short time he had, but what anyone could have safely guessed, was that he thought about Tiffany nearly every day. It was the act of someone who was facing death all along the way. Thinking of her was like invoking a magical power to overcome the tension from the fear of being hurt or killed in Iraq. The face of death he saw everywhere could only be counterbalanced by the face of Tiffany.

He said a lot in the few minutes he had. His voice was very hoarse from literally eating sand from the great storm of just three days before. Even with his awful voice, he talked on, packing as much in the allotted time as he could. He spoke of the big gun he was handling, his awesome SAW, and how the sandstorms caused everyone in his platoon to constantly clean their weapons. By the 29th, coalition forces were closing in on Baghdad, and Sean indicated his outfit was headed there. For security reasons, he could not offer any details as to his own location.

It was as if the French were responding to Carol Cassedy's BBC comments and wanted to show her that these alleged dilettantes could do something nice for her family. Of course, this was not the case. But one of France's television journalist crews had just happened upon the son of one of France's leading Bagdad, Kentucky, critics. After using up his twenty minutes on the satellite phone, Sean agreed to answer questions of the crew. He was asked how he felt about the anti-war protesters. Sean gave an honest and intelligent reply. He said that he and his fellow troops were fighting for freedom and that included the freedom to protest.

If this call on March 29th represented the high point for the Cassedy family during the war, they were only five days away from being sunk to the bottom of the sea in terms of human emotions. When Sean saw the face of death on April 3rd, when he himself was covered in blood, when his legs were intertwined with the metal of two huge vehicles, the long way home had begun. For him, the uncertainty of the war was replaced by the certainty that his days fighting this war had ended. But his family had anything but certainty. For them, getting news from the front was just as chaotic as the fog of war Sean experienced during the collision. The first call came on April 4, at 12:30 AM Bagdad, Kentucky, time. A Marine Gunnery Sergeant called to report that Sean had been in an accident outside of Baghdad.

This could not have come at a worse time for the Cassedys. The war coverage was just then reporting that Saddam International Airport was under siege by coalition forces. On the day before this call, elements of the Army's 3rd Infantry Division took control of part of the airport. Not long before this, Marines had decimated the Baghdad Division of the Republican Guard. The ferocity of the fighting seemed to increase markedly as the coalition's noose around Baghdad got tighter. By April 4th, Sean's family had reached a false sense of confidence. The news reports told them that final victory was within grasp. Sean's phone call from the fighting hole convinced them that it was just a matter of a few days before they would be getting regular calls from their son, calls from the capital itself. That's why when a Marine Gunnery Sergeant called the family in Kentucky, all of the lights seemed to go out. Especially when he told them these frightening words: "We do not know the extent of his injuries or his location."

The family was devastated. Sean had become a statistic. But most distressing of all, they did not know which column he was in: missing, wounded, captured, or, most feared of all, *killed*. The phone call only fed their fears. They were now like dozens of other families across the United States, shocked by the fortunes of war. The media had reported this war very accurately for the most part. Embedded journalists indeed proved to be the lens to the battlefront, and it certainly seemed that much of the coverage was real-time, or very close to being real-time, reporting. But something was missing. The big picture often left the families of the injured behind. There was no great rush to stop and freeze-frame the hurt and pain of those Americans whose loved ones were being shot and shelled in this war. Now the Cassedys became one of these forgotten families.

Sean's sister, Heather, took the awful news that something had happened to her brother very hard. She woke up on April 4th early to do her pregnancy aerobics. The early morning news reported that U.S. forces were within a few miles of Saddam International Airport. She thought about Sean and the troops he was with. If there is something called a big sister's intuition, Heather had it that morning as she left for work. She had a feeling that something over there was wrong. Her parents knew about Sean being injured for hours, but they wanted their pregnant daughter to sleep the night before they told her. Heather checked the news again when she got to the office. Her husband, Brian, a computer specialist in the same office she worked in, called her from his office one floor above hers and asked her to come up. Something was wrong. It was very wrong. When Heather got to her husband's office, he told her that her mother had left a message on his cell phone. Sean had been injured. During the next several hours, Sean's pregnant older sister cried until the tears wouldn't come out anymore. The hurt was still there, but she literally cried her eyes out. The information about Sean was vague. It left the door open for the unthinkable. But Heather thought it anyway. She couldn't help herself. She could not get it out of her head that her brother might be dead. It would take another call from her parents to make her understand that things really weren't so bad.

For the seeming eternity of the next two hours after the Gunny's call, Linn and Carol Cassedy agonized under the same heavy weight as Heather, thinking their son would not come home alive. For the life of him, Linn did not know why somebody in the Marine Corps with such a lack of information would even make this call. He was worried, but he was also mad. When the Gunny gave him the news, Linn pressed him for details, for an explanation, even asking him just what kind of call this was supposed to be. The Gunny simply had no answers.

As he stewed over the call that sent the entire family into a panic, the phone rang again. At 2:30 AM, a young man phoned the Cassedys and told them things were much better than they had thought. It was Private Sean S. Cassedy! He was safe. He was in the hands of friendly forces. He told his parents by satellite phone that he had been shot in the leg. He told them also that his legs were crushed. He didn't really know how it happened. He said he thought he was still in Iraq. The news was as startling and welcoming as the first call had been devastating. The family had gone on a roller coaster ride of emotions. What would this war do to them? From the calls they received after Sean's call, things began to become clearer, and Sean's journey to Baghdad began to transform into a very long road home to Bagdad, Kentucky. As his seriously injured son spoke to him, Sean's dad tried to get him to keep talking. He could tell Sean was speaking under the influence of medication. He was talking all over the map. Some of it didn't make sense. Sean spoke of hundreds of enemy killed. He could not seem to focus or answer a straight question, but that didn't matter because Linn and Carol and the rest of the Cassedy household now had direct evidence that Sean was alive. He was not in enemy hands. He was not blown to pieces. He was not an awful statistic. He did not fall into one of the terrible categories. He was not missing in action, not captured, and thank God, he was not killed. A seven-ton weight had not only been lifted off their son during a tragic collision, at least seven tons of worry had been lifted off the family's shoulders. It took a while, but eventually Heather got the word, and she too rejoiced in the news. The uncle-to-be was alive.

The same Gunnery Sergeant who first called them called again at 5:30 AM. This call came still on the fourth of April. It had only been five hours since the first call sent the Cassedy family into a tailspin. Amazingly, he had nothing new to report. It was not for another thirty-six hours that the family heard through official channels that Sean was removed from the war zone and was in Kuwait. A Marine Captain called them at 5:30 PM on the 5th of April to tell them this. He also told them that Sean would most likely be sent to Germany for treatment. The family was learning that the fog of leaving war meant that official calls only confused them. Piecing it all together, the news was not that bad. From Sean, they knew he was alive. From the Gunny and now the Captain, they understood he was on his way for more medical treatment. But they still had no way of knowing how bad his injuries were and how their son was hurt.

Despite the confusion and worry, Linn Cassedy decided to launch his own Operation Returning Son. Not satisfied with the flow of information he was getting from official channels, he contacted a military support group. Through the support group, Linn was able to locate a casualty officer in Kuwait. Through this source, Linn was able to track down Sean. The result was spectacular. Soon after the casualty officer found out Sean's whereabouts in Kuwait, Linn received the most wonderful e-mail imaginable. It informed the family that their son was recuperating from his injuries in Kuwait. More than that, there was an attachment to the e-mail. It was a photograph of Sean lying in a hospital bed. The caption to the photo said it all: "Doing fine in Kuwait."

Sean's route home from the combat area was as unpredictable as his journey toward Baghdad. Immediately after being injured, he was flown to Camp Viper, also dubbed RP 24, still inside Iraq. Here, inside a Mobile Army Surgical Hospital, or M.A.S.H. unit, he and several others who had been injured in the same collision received emergency medical treatment. Sean was heavily medicated, so he never knew for sure where he was or even how many times he was moved after the collision. He only had a hazy understanding that one of his stops was inside a medical tent. He was waiting for a helicopter to take him out of the area to somewhere behind the lines. While there, he found himself surrounded by his own troops, many of whom were much more seriously injured than him. He also heard the screams of a badly wounded Iraqi soldier lying in the middle of American wounded. It was the last thing in the world Sean had expected. It seemed completely unreal. The Iraqi troop was obviously in great pain and kept yelling something in his native tongue. A Marine lying next to Sean offered to put him out of his misery. Sean was moved by helicopter to yet another medical unit in Iraq.

It was at the second site that Sean called his family and gave them some very sketchy details of what happened. By the time he reached this location, he was beginning to think his legs were permanently damaged and that he would be returning home paralyzed for life. The injuries made it look that way. The painkillers probably dulled his ability to feel anything in his mangled legs. But he kept these horrible thoughts to himself, never mentioning them to his family when he spoke with them. He was eventually evacuated to Kuwait, where the famous e-mail with photo attachment came from. He had spent nearly two days in Iraq after being injured. It had been a very confusing two days. His injuries and the medications had clouded his ability to think and recall clearly. But Sean did remember one thing crystal clear, or, more accurately, Tiffany clear. During the entire time he was evacuated for medical treatment, Tiffany's dog tag remained firmly clenched in his right fist. Nothing could pry it loose.

From Kuwait, Sean was sent to the U.S. Naval Station Rota, located outside the port city of Cadiz on the southern end of Spain that meets the Atlantic Ocean. He was never sent to Germany. That bit of information from official channels was simply wrong. Rota provides support services for the U.S. Navy's Sixth Fleet. The base has a relatively complete naval hospital. Sean's flight to Rota was a long and unpleasant eleven hours. He arrived totally exhausted and in great pain. He shared a hospital ward with men returning, like him, from Iraq. Some of them he knew. He felt connected to them all through a common military bond and by blood drawn from the same war. He spent a week with them in the ward. It was a week that affected him like no other time in his life, except for the time he spent fighting in Iraq. It began to sink in after the doctors gave him great news. They told him there did not appear to be any permanent damage to his legs. They estimated that he would be off crutches within two months. After hearing this, it hit him. He looked around and saw wounded who were much worse off than he was. One poor Corporal was covered from head to toe with bandages. The gruesome details of his wounds were hidden, but Sean knew it had to be very, very serious. This Corporal was constantly calling the nurse, maybe trying to maintain earthly contact as long as he could. A second wounded Marine had lost his leg. He kept up a conversation with Sean, openly giving the younger Marine free advice. Sean knew that he was talking nonsense. He was so traumatized by his last battle, his tongue just kept rolling and Sean politely kept listening. He saw some men in very bad shape who he was certain would not leave the ward alive. He would eventually go home to the States on crutches, but he saw men who had lost legs. Sean vowed to himself never to forget this special group of brothers and never to dwell on his own problems. Compared to the maimed and dying, he had no problems.

Back home, Sean's parents were desperate to hear from him. Sean's dad contacted the editor of the *Stars & Stripes*, the newspaper known as the GI's newspaper. The editor contacted the public affairs officer at Rota, who sent Linn Cassedy an e-mail. Linn replied and asked for the phone number to the hospital so he could call his son. The reply was frustrating. The hospital did not have complete telephone service. It was equipped for making calls to the outside world on a collect basis, but it could not receive calls from the States. Linn was stymied, but not for long. He e-mailed very simple instructions to the Rota public affairs officer. They were then passed on to the Marine liaison officer at Rota to pass on to his injured son: "Sean, phone home!" Sean followed these orders to the letter. The call was billed at the rate of eight dollars a minute. It was a small price to pay to hear from Sean and finally get the details of his injuries.

The Cassedy family learned what many families learned during this conflict. Communication from official sources directly to the families of injured service members was far from perfect. During Sean's entire ordeal, from the moment he was evacuated to Kuwait City until he landed fatigued and hurting in Spain, the Cassedys never got an official clarification of what happened to him. It is one of the costs of war. It may have something to do with the fact that over one hundred thousand families were worrying about their troop sons and daughters. At some point, the bureaucracy set up to handle the flow of information simply breaks down. In the end, after several days of wondering, Sean and his family made contact and figured everything out on their own.

Eventually, Sean flew back to the world and began his recuperation. His feelings on the flight back were mixed, if not full of contradictions. He had survived a war. He had done what he was told to do. In some small way, he kept his word to the 9/11 victims and fought a tyrant's army. That was all good. But there was plenty of bad. He had been beaten up by the war. His body ached from his injuries. He lost over forty pounds. He was returning on crutches. Most of all, he worried about Tiffany. How would Tiffany react to all of this? Would she even want to see him again? She last saw him when he was at the peak of fitness. Now he was scarred and weak. As he began to worry about himself, the pain of the others, the more seriously injured, and the dead stopped him from any further self-pity. Men who fought the same war visited him with screams and frozen stares. They were there on the road to Baghdad. They were there in the M.A.S.H. tent. They lay nearby in the ward at Rota. One of them in particular always seemed to be there. It was the driver's face, the driver of the logistics vehicle system that collided with Sean's corner of the war. That face never seemed to go away.

A handful of media accounts were written about the incident of April 3rd that had taken Sean Cassedy out of combat in Iraq and ended a young man's life. Some accounts described a sandstorm, suggesting that the death and injury occurred as a result of poor visibility. Sean disputes this. He recalls only a hazy day with sand occasionally kicking up, but he does not recall a storm. A doctor told him there was a hole in his thigh, and it looked like a bullet hole. Someone else told him long after he left Iraq that the driver of the LVS also had a gunshot wound in his body. Sean believes that the convoy was ambushed. He learned something that his father had learned years earlier in Vietnam: Sometimes you cannot see the enemy even when he's right on top of you; sometimes conditions prevent you from even knowing when enemy soldiers are all around you. Linn went through a similar experience in Vietnam as Vietnamese men jumped on his small re-supply convoy traveling from Danang to Hue. These men threw boxes of food and ammo off the trucks. Linn reacted like he was trained to act, opening fire. To him and the men of his convoy, the intruders were Vietcong. To Sean, his convoy had driven into an ambush.

The news reports of Sean's incident accurately reported a collision occurred and that it involved an LVS. The collision was reported to have taken place east of Ash Shahin, Iraq. The focus of nearly every account was on the driver who died. Like Sean, he was twenty years old and he came from a small rural community. He was a Marine Private First Class from Camp Pendleton. He played on his high school football team. He liked to lift weights. He helped with farm chores on a farm where his family raised pigs and steers. He came face to face with a fellow Marine on April 3rd, and he died in the service of his country. An article in his hometown newspaper poignantly described how the family learned of his death. The article quoted the young man's stepfather, and his words were simple but telling: "We heard the dogs barking and then the knock on the door." Someone in the house saw three Marines in their white saucer hats and realized immediately the news was bad. The young Marine who died east of Ash Shahin, Iraq, had simple dreams. Like Sean, he was greatly moved by the attacks of September 11, 2001. He wanted one day to become a police officer or firefighter. His mother remembered her son's soft heart and ever-present smile. Now he was gone forever.

Sean's small-town world collided quite literally with another Marine's west Texas world on April 3, 2003. He spent the last moments of a fellow Marine's life on this earth locked in a death grip. Sean was helpless in preventing the driver's death. All he could do was watch him struggle over his instruments to the very end. There were so many things about his fifteen days in the war that made Sean appreciate life so much more. But on his final day in the war, he had only one teacher.

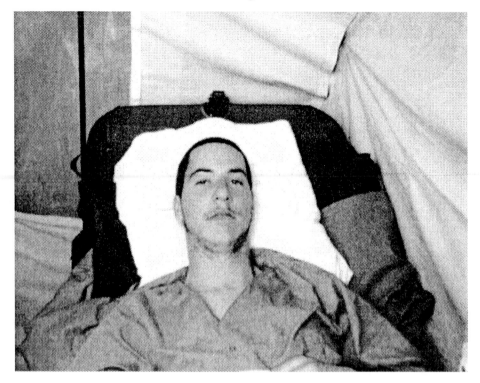

Doing fine in Kuwait.

<u>Chapter 10</u>

Coming Home: Returning Son, 1971

O CAPTAIN! MY CAPTAIN! OUR FEARFUL TRIP IS DONE!
THE SHIP HAS WEATHER'D EVERY RACK, THE PRIZE WE SOUGHT IS WON,
THE PORT IS NEAR, THE BELLS I HEAR, THE PEOPLE ALL EXULTING.
Walt Whitman, O Captain! My Captain!

The letter was the model of efficiency:

Greetings:
You are hereby ordered for induction into the Armed Forces of the
United States and to report on Tuesday April 16, 1968, at 06:30 AM.

Linn Cassedy had just returned from Switzerland where he spent what would have been his junior year in college. He had gone abroad to expand his horizons. He was moved to search more deeply, to seek out a program of study that gave him a more philosophical view toward his college education. He wanted not only to study philosophy but the meaning of his own existence. The L'Abri Fellowship of Huemoz, Switzerland, was founded for people like Linn. At the same time, he wanted the practical although somewhat exotic experience of working with his hands in a foreign land, and he got that working in the vineyards of Switzerland. But by remaining out of a U.S. college to study abroad, Linn lost something very important. He lost his student deferment status from the draft. He received his draft notice as he was returning to school in California.

It is a great irony that the head of Sean's family was sent to Vietnam for trying so hard to find a path to God. Before his trip to Switzerland, Linn had been seriously considering entering a theological seminary. But when he heard Dr. Francis Schaeffer deliver a lecture on how God could be known, his life was changed forever. Schaeffer founded L'Abri in 1955 so that people like Linn would have a place to find answers to questions about Christianity and God. The name comes from the French word for shelter. Linn was inspired by the lecture and sought out Dr. Schaeffer immediately afterwards. From this brief contact, Linn traveled to Switzerland and studied directly under Schaeffer. His journey abroad provided him with the spiritual resolve that would help him get through Vietnam, and that would even help him instill a peace of mind in Sean as he prepared for war in Iraq.

The draftees of Linn's day played a version of double Russian roulette. First, there was the induction room. Half of the inductees in Linn's room would be sent into the United States Army. The other half would be Marines. Linn was in the Marine half of his room. Second, he could choose between signing up for two years or four. Linn could sign up for two and join the infantry, or he could sign up for the longer term and head into the aviation branch. At the time, he had no idea which road was safer. He had no idea of the endgame. As it turned out, it did not matter. But at the time, he had no way of knowing that the Vietnam War would result in so many deaths, that it would end with nearly 60,000 Americans killed in action. No one knew. No one could have estimated that the final cost of the war he would be ordered to be a part of would see 304,000 troops from his country wounded, with over half of the total classified as seriously wounded.

Linn did not have any after-action report to guide him. While casualty figures were being reported, there was no way for a young man in the middle of it all to truly appreciate just how lethal the trend really was. For Sean and the war in Iraq, Americans were killed in relatively small numbers, both during the assault on Baghdad and in the immediate aftermath of the president's declaration on the aircraft carrier that major combat operations had ended. But on Linn's battlefield, the numbers were staggering beyond comprehension. It was a war with nearly exponential leaps in casualty figures for American GIs dying in Vietnam. In 1966, approximately 5,000 died there. In 1967, the figure exceeded 9,000. By the time Linn was drafted, over 14,000 laid down their lives on a foreign battlefield far from home. The number of killed would peak in 1968 and fall off each year after that. Newly elected President Nixon would fulfill a campaign promise to Vietnamize the fighting by assigning more and more of it to the South Vietnamese. But Linn Cassedy entered at precisely the moment when the shark's jaw was open the widest.

The grapevine convinced him that the infantry in Vietnam was a much riskier proposition, so he signed up for the longer term as an aviation troop. He did not fly the planes, and he did not perform maintenance on them. His job was to locate critical parts that kept them flying. Like his son, Linn had gone to Parris Island. He also was a computer geek of his era, even though the machines of Linn's day would be considered dinosaurs compared to the ones Sean customized for clients. Linn used key punch cards to communicate with his computer, not the sophisticated menu-based operating system of his son's day. But his work-a-day job in the Corps was always secondary to job one in a combat zone, and that was fighting. To enhance his combat role even more, Linn Cassedy was sent to language school at El Toro Marine Corps Air Station and trained in Vietnamese. Graduating at the end of August 1969, Linn went to Vietnam qualified in computers and weapons and as an interrogator for captured Vietcong.

As the plane taking Linn Cassedy to Vietnam approached his permanent duty assignment at Danang Air Base in late 1970, it was greeted with a small fireworks display. It was a very sobering welcome to the war for Linn in the form of night flares sent up to light the sky to reveal enemy troops bent on bringing down the plane. There were also mortar rounds and a few surface-to-air-missile, or SAM, exhaust trails that told Linn this was the real thing. It was a moment similar to Sean's own sudden realization that he was actually in war, fighting, defending, killing, and hopefully surviving. Just a few miles into Iraq, Sean had thought to himself, "I am in combat." His dad had the same sharp slap as he landed in Vietnam.

Linn was assigned to Marine Aircraft Group 16. Like Sean, he was not a career grunt, but a non-grunt specialist with grunt combat duties. He used the much less refined computer network of his day to find the aircraft parts that kept his F-4 Phantom fighter squadron flying. The F-4 was the fighter workhorse for the Navy, Marines, and Air Force in Vietnam. Linn also performed perimeter security around his base, guarding it against intruders. In addition, his unit would ferry much-needed supplies to troops in the field by either small truck convoys or with helicopters. Linn took his turn in one of the more dangerous duties in Vietnam: night patrol. Whatever the mission required, he did it. It did not matter if he arrived in country trained to do it or not. It did not matter how dirty it was. He would learn the true Marine credo was to do any job, no matter how awful, under the worst of conditions, with the least amount of training, manpower, and equipment.

To say Linn was at the front would be a misnomer. There was no true front in Vietnam. Unlike Sean's well-defined battle zone, Vietnam pitted unconventional warfare, so-called guerrilla warfare by the Victcong, against the world's most powerful conventional military force. The Vietcong were insurgents organized by the Communist government of North Vietnam to take over South Vietnam. They joined forces with elements of the regular North Vietnamese Army and fought at times and in places of their choosing. North Vietnam denied having its regular army or even its infiltrating insurgents in South Vietnam. Instead, they claimed the people of South Vietnam were rising up against their oppressors in a great civil war. U.S. forces could never be sure whether they were opposing local insurgents, infiltrators, or North Vietnamese regulars.

The enemy they did oppose freely attacked its target, whether that was concentrations of South Vietnamese troops, Americans, or even civilians suspected of supporting the U.S. forces. U.S. forces in Vietnam fought against the world's first stealth weapons. These were the Vietcong themselves, soldiers who blended into the landscape as effectively as a stealth bomber avoided enemy radar. They became the trees, the bushes, and virtually any feature of the terrain they fought from. They became so skillful at merging with the landscape that a new chemical weapon had to be developed to unmask them. Between 1962 and 1971, Agent Orange, originally created as a weed killer, blanketed large areas of Vietnam, defoliating trees and destroying green underbrush that could hide the enemy.

Vietnam is a story that some Americans don't remember at all and others recall as a very bad experience but with very little detail. The French had occupied the country for decades before the Second World War, but this control was interrupted when Japan captured vast regions of Southeast Asia. Vietnam fell into a morass after the defeat of Japan by the Allies. Communist leader Ho Chi Minh wanted to seize control, but so did the French. After efforts at sharing control of the territory failed, Vietnam's first modern war against the West began. The French fought the Vietminh forces of Ho Chi Minh for nine years and lost close to 95,000 colonial French troops in the war. The turning point came at the battle of Dien Bien Phu, when approximately three thousand French troops were killed. With this defeat, the conditions were set for a partitioning of the country. This crushing end to a dominant Western power's influence was, if not a forecast of things to come, at least a dark foreboding for U.S. involvement in Vietnam.

In 1954, President Eisenhower warned that the fall of Vietnam (Indochina) was like a domino falling in Southeast Asia, suggesting that Communism would take over other countries of the region. Thus began the domino theory of the spread of Communism. This theory would become the political theme for the next three administrations after Eisenhower's. According to the theory, the national security of the United States itself depended upon stopping the first domino from falling, thus preventing a chain reaction of Communism in the entire region. In Sean's war, national security was tied to the threat posed by Saddam's weapons of mass destruction. Whether it was the domino theory or the weapons of mass destruction theory, the American people were asked to support a government ordering young men and women into combat.

The real start of the U.S. buildup in Vietnam began several years before Linn ever arrived. The defeated French and the Communist government led by Ho Chi Minh reached an accord in Geneva in 1954 that allowed two Vietnams to coexist, a Communist North and a Capitalist South. But by the late 1950s, Ho Chi Minh embarked on a campaign of infiltration, sending his guerilla fighters south to aid the Communists already trying to overthrow the government there. Soon after his election in 1960, President John F. Kennedy sent one hundred military advisors and four hundred troops to South Vietnam. The number of troops grew to eleven thousand by 1962. On November 1, 1963, the president of South Vietnam was assassinated, reportedly with tacit U.S. approval. Three weeks later, President John F. Kennedy was assassinated.

The primary escalation of the U.S. involvement would take place during the presidency of Lyndon B. Johnson. He would earn a reputation of micromanaging the war from the White House. But he had staked his name on two other wars, the war on poverty and the war against racism. In a March 1964 message to Congress, he outlined his plans to fight the first war with the creation of a job corps and expanded educational opportunities for the needy. In July of the same year, he signed into law the Civil Rights Act of 1964, which among other things prohibited job discrimination against black Americans. Somehow all three wars would collide in Vietnam.

Based upon a tenuous claim by the president that North Vietnamese had attacked United States naval vessels in international waters, men like Linn Cassedy would be drafted to defend against the spread of Communism. He was defending against the fall of dominoes. In August 1964, the Gulf of Tonkin resolution authorized the president "all necessary measures to repel any armed attack against the forces of the United States and to prevent further aggression." This single joint resolution of Congress opened the floodgates for sending hundreds of thousands of American soldiers to Vietnam. It is almost unbelievable that the executive and legislative branches could arrive at a piece of paper based upon one allegation of one attack against the world's mightiest navy that would change the lives of so many people.

By the time Linn reported for induction into the service on April 16, 1968, the country was reeling over the assassination of Martin Luther King, Jr. twelve days earlier. And before Linn ever finished boot camp, one of the outspoken critics of the war, Senator Bobby Kennedy, was also assassinated just as it looked like he was headed for victory as the Democratic nominee for president in 1968.

When Linn went to Vietnam, troop morale was on a downward spiral. No one seemed to be able to explain why so many Americans had to go so far to fight this war. More than that, no one in or out of the theater of battle could explain precisely what victory was. Was it winning territory? Was it winning provincial capitals? Or was it eliminating the Vietcong from South Vietnam altogether? Winning a war when winning itself could not be defined against an enemy that kept disappearing into the countryside became an exercise in futility. The voices of protesters grew so loud that Linn could hear them as he served in the war zone. Racial tensions between black and white troops flared. Many blacks felt disenfranchised. A year before he was assassinated, Bobby Kennedy criticized the national draft system during a televised discussion with California Governor Ronald Reagan. Kennedy argued that the draft system was responsible for the unusually high number of blacks being sent to Vietnam because the system discriminated against the poor.

Linn witnessed firsthand racial tensions that sometimes exploded in bar fights in Vietnam. He watched one fight erupt between whites and blacks only to be settled by an outsider. The peacemaker was a small Korean

Marine. He was small, but he was also a black belt in karate. Linn watched him drop over a dozen of the brawlers before they knew what hit them.

The typical grunt, white or black, was a draftee forced to fight under the most extreme of conditions imaginable. There was no defining moment like Pearl Harbor or 9/11, only the constant criticism over the reasons for going to war and over the way the young, the poor, and the blacks were singled out to shoulder the brunt of the combat. Linn had become part of a war whose ending was becoming almost predictable. His homecoming would be his own personal timestamp on that end.

The troops of Linn's war were young men who could not get into college and attain the deferred status. Or they were young men who got into college but, like Linn, lost their deferment for one reason or another. They were young men who did not want to face a five-year jail sentence for refusing to be drafted. They were men who did not want to go into self-exile to Canada. Those who did would be offered a conditional amnesty in 1974 by President Gerald Ford, the same year he granted an unconditional pardon to President Nixon. No matter the motivation or absence of motivation, these were all, for the most part, young men. Vietnam was combat by young men, but thousands of women also served there. Linn and the rest of the men who went to Vietnam shared one very important thing with Sean and the men and women who invaded Iraq: Once in uniform and once on the battlefield, their options ended.

The heart and soul of the draft system was the category of men between the ages of eighteen and twenty-six. Nearly two million men were inducted through the Selective Service System between 1964 and 1972. Drug problems in the theater of combat grew. Relations between black troops and white troops deteriorated. Relations between officers and enlisted troops generally reflected declining troop morale, which led to declining discipline, which led to even worse morale, which led to even worse discipline. When twenty-three-year-old Linn Cassedy got there in 1970, these problems were rampant. A bizarre officer-elimination practice had evolved called fragging. The target was an unpopular officer, sometimes a completely inexperienced one looking to make a name for himself at his men's expense. His enemy, who was also one of his own troops, would roll a fragmentation grenade into his hooch to eliminate the green lieutenant. There are no accurate statistics on fragging, but one report estimates ninety men were killed in fragging cases between 1969 and 1972. The same report estimates that eight hundred were wounded as a result of fragging attacks. The war in Iraq would include a modern-day version of fragging at Camp Pennsylvania, Kuwait.

Linn did not see any fragging incidents during the ten months he spent in Vietnam. But he had his own episodes with inexperienced officers. After completing nine months of his ten-month tour, he was assigned to perimeter security duty. By this time, he was a hardened veteran of this war. A monsoon rain was howling all around him. No one was allowed inside the perimeter unless they answered a challenge with the correct password. Linn was armed with a .45 semiautomatic sidearm and his service rifle. The wind was nearly blowing him away when he noticed someone approach his position. He called for the password. Through the wind and the rain, he could not make out the reply, so to be certain, he pointed his rifle in the intruder's face and told him to lie flat on the ground in a spread-eagle position. Then he leaned down so his face was touching the man's face, yelling through the storm for the password. The intruder turned out to be a young second lieutenant who was now absolutely fuming. He fumbled around, and somehow through his sheer anger at Linn, he managed to give the password, and Linn let him up. The lieutenant spent the next several minutes dressing down Linn, telling him in vivid detail how much trouble the enlisted man was now in. Linn never heard from him again.

Linn also experienced a grenade incident with a lieutenant, but not a fragging incident. A second lieutenant in highly starched green fatigues approached Linn's squad with what he said was some fantastic new technology. It was a chain-driven grenade launcher. He explained to Linn's squad that he needed to field-test it. He told them it could fire fifteen grenades in rapid succession. But there was a catch. The grenades that would be loaded into the launcher had to have their pins removed first. This did not set well with the squad. They took the lieutenant's toy and told him they would test it in the morning. That night, they had an explosive ordnance guy blow it to pieces. The next morning, they told the lieutenant that a grenade had gotten hung up in it, and it exploded by accident. They never heard from the lieutenant again.

The reasons for low morale were many. Drafted black troops went there after one of the most prominent leaders among African-Americans, Martin Luther King, Jr., was assassinated. White troops were also largely draftees. The system favored those who could afford to stay in college and those with connections who could pull the right strings. The residue of this system was a fighting force of draftees. The cream rose to the top and out of danger. Draftees were sent to fight against falling dominoes. When Sean stepped across the lod into Iraq, he knew so many more things than his father knew when he landed at Danang. Sean knew the rules of engagement, and these rules told him he could win. He knew that his squad and his CSSB-10 unit would support another Marine unit using sound military tactics that would allow them to move methodically toward their primary goal, the capture of the Iraqi capital. For Linn and the Marines he fought beside, the ROE was a mishmash of rules that no one really understood. The mission was always blurred. The endgame was absolutely beyond comprehension.

Drug abuse was just one offshoot of the declining morale. Linn avoided the temptation. He was one of the truly lucky men who went to Nam and served a full tour without getting killed, wounded, or scarred by drug use. He did drink. He and his fellow Marines even devised a concoction consisting of all available booze of whatever kind dumped into a huge trashcan. They called the resulting explosive drink the Hairy Buffalo.

Death came in a variety of ways in Vietnam and sometimes in the most unlikely way. The death of a friend of Linn's exemplified this. His friend was a Warrant Officer who flew one of the helicopters assigned to the same squadron Linn was in. He had risen through the enlisted ranks to become an officer and pilot. Linn thought very highly of him. One day, as he took off from Danang, his helicopter crashed into the Gulf of Tonkin. It looked like a survivable crash, but when they pulled Linn's friend out of the chopper, he was dead. He had no bullet wounds. He had two small marks on his neck. The base medics concluded that he was bitten by a sea snake, and the snake's venom killed him. Linn watched as Marines blanketed the area of the crash with concussion mortars to eliminate the venomous snakes.

His son would fight inside a vast desert. Foliage would not be a problem. Rain would come, especially when the sandstorm hit, and many elements of the coalition heading to Baghdad would be stopped in their tracks. In Linn's war, the tropical climate and the lush jungle battlefield meant a constant war within a war against insects, snakes, and rats as large as dogs. Yet, like his son did with MRE missiles in Kuwait and windstorm-surfing with ponchos in Iraq, Linn found ways to break the deadly seriousness of war. Linn and some friends built their own crude version of a Predator drone at Danang Air Base, Vietnam. They constructed a huge kite from crates and parachute cloth, anchoring the string to a mop bucket. The unmanned aerial vehicle flew so high that the control tower thought it posed a threat when it could not be identified. The string to the mop bucket was promptly cut.

On certain missions, Linn was the NCOIC, or Non-Commissioned Officer In Charge. Sean was part of a fire team in Iraq. His father was sometimes in charge of his own fire team in Vietnam. During a re-supply mission to Hue, Linn came face to face with the stealth enemy. Hue was located about seventy-five miles north of his home base at Danang. Linn's squad had to get food and ammo to U.S. troops near Hue and were traveling in a small convoy loaded down with the needed supplies. They were traveling on a crude dirt road filled with large holes, which they had filled with water. As Linn's unit approached a small Vietnamese hamlet, the local people began moving water buffalo into their path. The Americans had just crossed over a bridge when Linn noticed a small building on his left. They had entered a kill zone. The building, the bridge, and the water buffalo worked together to form a triangle of death. There was no way to make a quick retreat. Linn's unit was too far from any base to call in for help. Instead, the squad began to bunch up, and armed men jumped out of the bush and onto the trucks. Then they began throwing the supplies off the trucks. Linn and his truck driver opened fire. After a brief exchange of fire, the supply convoy was able to move forward, past the now-frightened water buffalo, barely escaping what might have been total disaster.

The convoy continued on to Hue and completed its re-supply mission minus the supplies the Vietcong had thrown off the trucks. After surviving the harrowing trip, Linn reported the incident to his immediate commander. The captain told Linn that since he was the NCO in charge, he was responsible for the lost cargo. He intended to dock Linn's pay for the losses. It was as if Vietnam was a fantasy world all its own, and normal rules simply did not apply. Armed men attacked his convoy, so Linn was expected to pay. Linn told the captain he could do what he wanted, including charging Linn for the losses. Nothing was ever done to Linn.

During another engagement, his compound was under a heavy enemy rocket attack. A rocket hit a jet fuel storage tank, causing a tremendous explosion. Linn escaped injury, but then faced a new attack when the Vietcong began to lob hand grenades. One landed squarely at Linn's feet. Had it exploded, Sean's story would never have happened. The grenade did not explode.

Linn's time in Vietnam was not easy. He went on many re-supply missions throughout Vietnam during his tour. He survived several close calls. The entire experience left him feeling lucky but not charmed. He was not immune from death or injury, despite having escaped both in a very dangerous combat zone. But his experiences in Vietnam would help him become a better father. His story of survival became part of the family legacy of making it through tough times. He drew upon this legacy when he sought to comfort Sean as Sean received his orders. He could tell his son with a straight face, "I went to war, and I came back. You will come back, too."

Linn served a full tour—ten months in Vietnam—experiencing all of the discomforts of not being at home. During Christmas 1970, he saw a USO show featuring the legendary Bob Hope. Maybe USO tours are anachronistic today. If Sean's war is the sign of the times, and complex technology translates into lightning-swift results, then USO shows may be a thing of the past. But being stuck in a war zone for ten months meant that any little piece of Americana a GI could see and hear was a very welcome respite from the dirty task at hand.

Linn did not mind the two- or three-week delays, and sometimes longer, in getting mail from his family in the States. He was from the pinball and snail mail generation, not a cyberspace warrior like his son, who could communicate instantly from the war zone with e-mails and satellite phones. Despite the slowness in getting to Vietnam, mail from the world never lost its morale-building significance. The letters Linn got were little pieces of home. Whether bringing good news or not-so-good news, they nonetheless brought him news. They connected him with the people he loved. The anti-war protests did not matter as much as who did what in his family back home. When Mom or Dad wrote a letter, it was like taking a painkiller. It didn't last long, but it relieved the awful pain of loneliness. There was beer and whiskey and other things, but maybe the most powerful painkiller for Linn was mail call.

Ten months in a combat zone is an incredibly long time to be away from what you're used to. It's an incredibly long time to live inside an intentional zone where so many people are trying their best to kill you. Some GIs kept short-time calendars once they got down to a month or less left on their tour. Linn never started one. Instead, he focused his energy and excitement on the R & R promised to long-timers. Once they reached a certain point in their tour, they were entitled to a rest and recuperation period, a short vacation outside of Vietnam. Linn got his break after reaching nine months of service in country. He flew to Sydney, Australia, where he got re-acquainted with the real world. He enjoyed his time there a great deal, and nearly too much. He almost missed his plane ride back. He woke up late after spending his last night in civilization and realized everyone going back to Vietnam had already left for the plane. Linn paid a taxi driver to speed to the plane. He made it with only minutes to spare. Someone told him after he got on board that, had he missed his flight, he would have had to pay for the next flight back.

Linn survived his tour. He survived the combat action and reached something that every GI in Vietnam dreamed of reaching: DEROS, or Date of Expected Return from Overseas. He was going back to the world. He made it to the day when he would board a Freedom Bird back to the United States. This time, he would not be late. Just as Linn was about to board his freedom flight home, the airfield came under enemy mortar and rocket attack. His plane took off without him. Most of the planes at Danang took off to avoid being hit. They stayed in Japan until things calmed down. This diversion delayed Linn's much-anticipated departure by four days. He was billeted in a small bunker off the runway to await the return of the Freedom Bird. It was as if he entered Vietnam with an armed welcome, and he had to go out the same way he came in.

Danang was a special place of departure in Vietnam. It was a central point of collection for America's most revered cargo—those who died in action. Danang was where the pallets were loaded with black plastic body bags. Linn Cassedy saw them. Linn observed firsthand expired human life piled unceremoniously on wooden pallets and then loaded aboard a C-141 Starlifter or C-5A Galaxy. He saw them up close and frequently. Linn got to ride back alive, and that's where his guilt began. His son performed corpse duty in Iraq and thought how much better it was to be the one who carried. When Sean traveled back to the world, he too felt the guilt of leaving a war zone much better off than other Marines and other coalition forces who would not return in one piece or who would not return alive. That's where his guilt began.

Linn's freedom flight flew from Danang to Tokyo and then to Okinawa. His final plane ride took him to March Air Force Base, California. He really did not know what to expect. He was a draftee and a very proud

Marine. He had gone through all of the tough Marine training his country asked him to go through. He had fought for his honor against an unjust charge and had won at his court-martial. Then he followed his country's orders into the war zone of Vietnam. Now he was going home. Mission accomplished. Fears overcome. Bullets and explosions avoided. The sights, sounds, and smells of his stay in Vietnam were all deeply embedded in his body and mind.

As his plane landed at March Air Force Base, he honestly did not know what awaited him on the other side of the airplane door. He moved down the aisle with the nervous excitement that a homecoming brings. The plane was full of returning Vietnam troops, and everybody was excited. The letdown that he and the others would experience had something to do with their expectations. After what they had been through, they all shared a fantasy that there were people on the other side of that door just as excited about their coming home as they were. There must be people who understood their sacrifice out there. It was the difference between what the returnees expected and the reality of the situation that made coming home so hard.

The door opened, and the inside of the terminal came into full view. At seven o'clock in the morning, a dead silence greeted Linn as he deplaned. There were no people waiting to greet Linn Cassedy—none at all. The only image burned into Linn's mind is coming home to an empty airport and seeing the cleaning crew on the other side of the airplane departure door. There were no well wishers from the local community throwing flowers his way as he stepped out of the plane. There were no parents proudly hoisting children on shoulders to catch a glimpse of the returning combat veterans. There was no delegation from the city, no marching band, and no high school pom-pom girls. It did not matter that this planeload of men had dodged bullets, mortar attacks, rocket attacks, and booby traps. It did not matter that they lived in hooches built inside compounds where giant rats ran free. Linn's memory was just of a few men and women assigned to polish the floor, vacuum the carpets, and empty the trash.

He called his parents soon after getting off the plane. He woke them up. It was seven in the morning on the West Coast, but only 4 AM where they were on the East Coast. They did the best they could to make him feel welcome. But even his own parents seemed to miss the boat. They didn't really understand that he had been to hell and back. The empty airport and the empty phone call would forever stay with Linn. It would change him.

It would shape what he would do when his own son went off to war and when he returned. When Sean was taken out of combat by the collision of April third, Linn put out the word to his family. No matter when a call came through, no matter what time of day or night, all Cassedys were under strict orders to make Sean feel needed and to show him how much they loved him. This order was obeyed to the letter.

The planeload of Marines left the terminal and boarded buses that took them to barracks at Marine Corps Air Station El Toro, near Santa Ana, California. Nothing awaited them there either, not even a debriefing. The military itself didn't seem interested in what they had been through. Things only got worse when Linn was granted town liberty and he heard the whispers from the folks he had fought for. What he heard being said about Marines like him who fought in Vietnam was not pleasant. It was insulting. It was a low point in the life of Linn Cassedy. But it was one that he would learn from. It was a very negative experience that made him understand better than anyone else that young men who are ordered into battle should never come home like he did. His son would say something that Sean felt deeply as he came home from Iraq, but it also applied to Linn's homecoming. Sean told reporters, "They prepare you well for war, but not how to come home." Linn was stung by the burning truth of his young son's words.

Danang Marine Air Base, Vietnam.

F-4 Phantom Danang.

During a re-supply mission to Hue, Linn came face to face with the stealth enemy.

During Christmas, 1970 he saw a USO show featuring the legendary Bob Hope.

Greetings...

FROM OUR HOME TO YOURS!

Rob, Bill, Linn
Danang, Vietnam
Christmas 1970

Despite the slowness in getting to Vietnam, mail from the world never lost its morale building significance.

Waiting to board the freedom bird. Linn is in the middle.

<u>Chapter 11</u>

Returning Sun, 2003

When I consider life and its few years—
a wisp of fog betwixt us and the sun,
a call to battle, and the battle done
ere the last echo dies within our ears;
... I wonder at the idleness of tears
From Tears by Lizette Woodworth Reese

It is the uniform that makes our hearts yearn. It is the storied history that now includes the follow-on to the famous line "let's roll" with names like Basra, Al-Najaf, An Nasiriyah, Umm Qasr, and Baghdad that makes our knees weak. When a father greets a son, his voice cracks with pride. When a returning son first sees his mother and he blurts out almost instinctively, "Mom!" When the crowd greets him at the airport—all exulting—Marines in full dress uniform are there and eyes are filled with tears. Sean carried with him all of the answers to all of the questions of why Marines makes us feel that way. Just a very young man ordered to do a very large job, risking his life in the bargain and taking someone else's life when necessary. We told him to do that. We gave him the uniform, the gun, and the orders. Democracy hired Sean Cassedy to place it all on the line. And when he walks down the street or when he comes home from war, the very least we can do is to show our pride. Pride in our hearts and through our tears.

Sean's welcome home began before he ever began the long trip back to the States. It began with the expressions of love and care from family members, from friends, and from complete strangers. When he was safe, when he was removed from the battlefield, seriously injured but alive, Sean's homecoming began when he read the e-mails sent to his somewhereinkuwait. com address. He had not been able to open his e-mail account while fighting inside Iraq. The blackout prevented that. The war prevented it. But there was something magical about cyberspace. Real words representing sincere feelings and emotions were sent, and, even though Sean could not open and read them, they hung there, frozen in time, waiting for the blackout to lift. All the recipient had to do was survive!

As he and thirteen others of his squad crossed over from Kuwait to Iraq, a close family friend sent Sean one of these flash-frozen e-mails. It was dated the twentieth of March.

Sean,

We've been praying for you and the rest of the guys. Now it's time to kick ass! We love you. By the way, what's with the story on this chick [Tiffany] *your mom and dad have told us about? Drop us a line if you can. God is with you.*

Heather wrote to him the next day:

Sean,

Hello! How are you? Well, I know a lot has been going on for you. We saw on the news that your unit crossed over and is on the way to Baghdad. Mom and Dad have been e-mailing me every day, and we have been talking on the phone a lot. It is amazing the technology that the news media has now ... We have been praying for you as well as the other troops. There have been a lot of prayer services here at home at various churches ... I pray for you and Tiffany. We love you, and everyone back here at home is very proud of you. God Bless America.

Sean's cousin Nick from Hopkins, Minnesota, sent an e-mail on March 24th:

Hey,

I just wanted to write and say what's up. I hope you are all doing okay out there. I just talked to your grandmother [Nana Erkenbrack], *and she said your spirits were high. I hear the weather is sunny and sandy out there ... I'm kinda at a loss for words. I know you can't send out e-mails, but if you wanna write me back and let me know how you're doing, feel free. Talk to you later, man. Tell the unit to kick some ass.*

Nick wrote Sean at the same time that Sean and his assistant SAW gunner faced off, machine gun versus digging tool, nearly creating a friendly fire incident of their own.

It is nearly impossible to explain the difference in attitudes between the way Vietnam veterans were treated when they left the country and returned after war, and the way veterans from the invasion of Iraq were treated. Maybe friends and relatives in 2003 could separate themselves from the international debate. Maybe they weren't swayed by the war's popularity or lack thereof. Whatever it was, Sean could feel the love and care when he left for war, and he could feel the same when he came back.

A good friend of Sean's parents also e-mailed Sean. She was the owner of a farm in Payneville, Kentucky, a small community located about a hundred miles from Bagdad. She wrote to Sean on March 26th, offering a simple but touching expression of gratitude: "Thanks to all your fellow service people." She volunteered to write to "anyone who does not have someone to correspond with." She told Sean that her own son-in-law was an Army scout and was leaving for Kuwait, then exclaimed, "The greenhouse is just about ready ... planting time is here!" The next day, she wrote to Sean wondering if it was okay to send Christian material to an Islamic country: "One of our concerns is if we could send literature or devotionals from our church. Some questioned if it was okay, given the country you are in." She also reminded Sean of her previous commitment: "I will send letters in your package directed to *troop.* Could you pass them along to people you think are needing someone from home to talk to? I know you are being a great warrior there, not only for our country but for God."

On the thirtieth, just four days before Sean's legs would be crushed between the LVS and Sean's own seven-ton truck, Sean's uncle wrote to him. The fighting reported by the press was constant and ferocious. The outcome after just ten days of the invasion was still far from certain. His uncle's e-mail conveyed the concern many Americans must have been feeling about the safety of loved ones serving in Iraq. His uncle warned Sean to be "careful in your present endeavor" and to be "constantly aware of your surroundings." He told his nephew that his "safety and well-being" were in the forefront of the family's prayers. He closed with: "Stay warm and drive safe." It was an odd thought considering where Sean was and what he was doing. But it still got to the heart of the matter. It communicated the real concern: *Don't die on us, Sean! You're too young, and we love you too much!*

Sean's dad wrote to him on April 5th, or two days after Sean's injuries occurred. It was not really a suspended message, frozen in cyberspace waiting for Sean to finish combat. This one was his first post-injury e-mail. "We talked with Tiffany this afternoon and told her your situation, and your mother also told her you love her and miss her." In fact, Linn had passed on to Tiffany that Sean said he loved her. At the end of this message were the names of the entire Cassedy family.

The last e-mail sent to him before Sean began the long journey back to Bagdad, Kentucky, came from a stranger. In fact, it even began with: "Hello, Sean! You probably don't recognize who I am." It was sent on April 7th by a friend of a friend. "We continue to fight for you back here." She mentioned the ongoing debate about the war and how many people in the country were opposed to it. She assured Sean that there were many more that supported the war. "You all are so brave to fight for freedom. I really admire you. Every time the news comes on, they talk about the 1st Marine Division. And I try to keep up on who's where and if everyone is okay. I know that your guardian angel is watching over you. And you will be home soon." She was right about Sean's guardian angel. She had written her e-mail four days after his injuries. She was also right about his returning home, but it would not be so soon, and the journey would be a strange one. She told Sean that she was anxiously waiting to see if her fiancé was going to be deployed. He was in the Army's 10th Mountain Division.

Sean was one of the lucky ones. He was sent into a battle zone filled with deadly surprises. He entered the fog of war and took part in the exhaustion and confusion of fighting other men bent on killing him. And he survived. Though not unscathed, he was able to say that he made it back from war. Like his father, he was going home alive. Like his mother's father, a Marine who survived World War II and Korea, Sean was another returning son.

The time Sean spent getting medical treatment was divided between an unknown period moving around Iraq, a few days behind the lines in Kuwait, and some grim days in a hospital ward at U.S. Naval Station Rota, Spain. He learned at each place just how lucky he was. He heard the screams of an Iraqi wounded prisoner as he was first treated in Iraq. But it was at Rota where he saw his brothers in arms scarred permanently with gruesome wounds of the war he just left. The experience of it all—of the blitzkrieg toward Baghdad, of the bodies he saw and buried in Iraq, and of seeing the seriously wounded among his own brothers—would soon manifest itself. Almost immediately, he became sensitive to light. He also developed flashbacks that returned him to Iraq.

His father developed similar symptoms from his time in Vietnam. Sean learned the hard way just how much his father was affected by war. During his childhood days in Southern California, an incident happened that sent a clear message to all of the children. Sean decided one day to show his father that he could get the drop on him. He literally climbed the walls of their house and somehow was able to assume a spread-eagle position high up above a doorway, almost against the ceiling of the house. When his dad came through the doorway, Sean leaped on him. Instantly, Linn was back in Vietnam. Before Sean had any time to react, his father assumed the squat attack position he was taught and delivered a blow toward the center of Sean's chest. Sean was not hurt, but for the first time he realized that his father had some of Vietnam left inside. The children learned never to sneak up on Dad.

The first time Sean suffered a flashback, he was safe and sound in Camp Pendleton, still recuperating from his injuries. He was in the barracks sleeping in his own bed. The stitches holding his crushed legs together were still fresh. Some friends had tied balloons to the four posts of his bunk to welcome him home. But when Sean awoke in the middle of the night, all he could see were four Iraqi soldiers surrounding him. He grabbed a lamp and began beating the balloons until he came to his senses.

There was no rhyme or reason to Sean's actual homecoming to Kentucky. In fact, it only came about as a result of luck, fatherly devotion, and the strength of character of a very young pilot. Sean had departed Rota, Spain, not for his home, but for his home unit—back to Camp Pendleton, California. He was nobody special, just one of the thousands ordered into combat on the first of spring 2003. If the e-mails sent into cyberspace were a prelude to Sean's real homecoming, there was no one in the Marine Corps willing to make a homecoming to Kentucky happen. Until he was released by the doctors, he was staying put in his barracks in California. After that, it would be up to him to find a way home.

The Cassedy family learned the hard way that the same military with slick television recruiting ads was largely unskillful when it came to the endgame. Linn and Carol first saw this when they could not get a straight answer about Sean's whereabouts or the extent of his injuries. They also saw it when they realized that a Marine who was nearly killed in Iraq was sent back to recuperate in his barracks. Once back in the States, Sean was just another Marine, and all of the pent-up worry inside the Cassedy household in Bagdad, Kentucky, did not seem to matter. Two parents had been kept on the edge of their seats, first being told that Sean was missing. Four sisters and two brothers had watched the war on television, and at the very moment when fierce fighting was going on around Baghdad, the word came through that their brother was seriously hurt. But the very most they could get from Sean's superiors was permission for him to go on leave once he was medically cleared to travel, assuming he could afford it!

Sean was effectively broke on his private's pay, and his family in Bagdad was suffering the same bad economic times as many others during early 2003. Arranging for a ticket on short notice was a costly event. There was no way for the Cassedys to predict twenty-one days in advance when their son would be injured and when official channels would finally release him, let alone when they could buy an affordable plane ticket. So Linn began to tap into the Marine support group he was a part of.

He first contacted some pilots who worked for United Parcel Service, asking if there was any way Sean could catch a hop on a UPS plane from Southern California to Kentucky. That's when he learned about the rule. The rule stated that only UPS employees could ride on UPS planes. He doubled his efforts to put the word out that his injured son wanted to come home. Through every possible connection over the Internet and through his military channels, Linn spread the word.

The initial results seemed promising. A pilot flying for Delta answered the call. He lived in LaGrange, Kentucky, and was based out of Los Angeles. It seemed too good to be true. It was. Despite his best efforts, the pilot could not persuade his managers to let Sean ride home free. Linn would not be defeated. Next, he turned to the postmistress of Bagdad,

Kentucky. Her cousin lived in Sacramento and flew Lear jets. That too fell through. That's when a sharp young man appeared on the radar screen. Through some friends of Linn and Carol's, friends who lived down the road in Shelbyville, a laid-off pilot became their last best hope to get Sean home. His name was Nathan Reed.

Nathan was just twenty-four years old. He grew up wanting to fly for the United States Marine Corps. Before ever joining the service, he learned to fly at Bowman Field, a small commercial airport a few miles from Louisville. Bowman Field has its own unique character and proud tradition. Dating back to 1919, it was Kentucky's first commercial airport. World War I aviators inspired its namesake, Abram Bowman, and the field hosted pilot training for decades to come. Famed aviators from Charles Lindbergh to World War I ace Eddie Rickenbacker made stops at Bowman Field. In 1943, glider pilot combat training began. And Nathan Reed earned his wings there, too.

Reed joined the Marine Corps immediately after graduating from college. But he ran into an old military problem. Hurry up and wait! The Corps told him that he would have to wait at least a year before he could be considered for pilot training. Nathan could not wait and resigned his commission. Instead, he took a job flying for Continental Airlines. But one of the offshoots of 9/11 was that far fewer Americans wanted to fly. Nathan was one of many airline pilots laid off. So, Nathan had to take the best available job, and he did. He went from a Marine aviator wannabe and Continental Airline pilot to a man working for a small company in Shelbyville, Kentucky. On Saturday, April 19th, when things looked bleak for getting Sean home any time soon, Nathan Reed responded to Linn Cassedy's query, telling Linn he would take the case.

This twenty-four-year-old dynamo persuaded the management at Continental Airlines that Sean was a very worthy cause. To the airline's credit, Nathan was given company authorization to fly in his pilot's uniform from Louisville to San Diego to make the pickup. He did not fly the plane, but with the proper uniform and credentials, he was acknowledged as a Continental crewmember entitled to travel on a Continental plane. He was allowed to sit in the jump seat used for just this purpose.

Operation Returning Son commenced one day before Easter. Timing was critical. Linn learned that Sean would not be given a medical release to travel until three days after Easter Day. He was still on crutches and even having difficulty making it down to the chow hall to eat. The Marines of his barracks at Camp Pendleton were all given a four-day pass to enjoy the Easter holidays. When Linn learned of this and he realized that his own injured son couldn't take advantage of it, his resolve to get his son home became an obsession. Privately, he resolved something else. Sean would be met by more than the cleaning crew.

Before Sean ever left California, his parents were making plans for his homecoming. With the help of a close family friend in Bagdad, Louisville television networks, including NBC affiliate WAVE TV and ABC's WHAS TV, were contacted with the news that a hometown boy injured in Iraq was coming home to Kentucky for the first time since being medically evacuated from the war zone.

On April 22nd, Sean received medical clearance to travel, so Nathan Reed left Louisville at 6 PM on the same day. He arrived in San Diego at 10 PM. He arranged for Sean to stay at the hotel where Continental flight crews stayed. He treated Sean like an honorary crewmember. Sean and Nathan stayed up all night talking, and at 7:30 the next morning, they boarded a flight to Fort Worth. Sean kept his family informed of the progress of his journey home by cell phone. Sean's dad relayed the information to local television crews. Something good was about to happen. In the aftermath of what Sean had gone through and with the war in Iraq still going on, the return of an injured Kentuckian was the news of the day. Linn phoned the television crews when Sean informed him of his change of planes in Fort Worth. News trucks were dispatched and *Sean-watch* began.

One problem threatened a smooth return. Even with his flight uniform and ID card, Nathan could only manage to obtain standby status for Sean on the flight from Fort Worth to Louisville. No one had expected this. The Cassedys of Bagdad were told of the very real possibility that the return would be indefinitely delayed. They waited anxiously to hear if they made the flight. Then it happened. Linn got the call from Nathan. Nathan confirmed that both men were safely aboard the flight and on their way to Louisville.

Linn timed his trip to Louisville International Airport so he would be able to arrive well in advance of Sean's landing. He and a very large entourage of family, friends, and Marines arrived hours early. But that didn't matter. Sean was coming home. On the way to the airport, Linn got several calls from the media. Carol had given an interview earlier in the day to the Louisville radio station WHAS announcing her son's return, and that seemed to spawn a flood of media inquiries. The flood was now deluging Linn as he drove. Each call seemed to generate more questions. He was soon in overload as he drove the family to the airport. Senior Drill Instructor Carol made him pull over so she could drive and he could talk.

The sun was shining brightly on April 23, 2003. It was just three days after Easter, and Sean was coming home. It was home to Kentucky. His legs were healing. On the day he arrived in Kentucky, he was strong enough to walk without crutches. His strength came from the good progress he had made recuperating. But it also came from his vow to the less fortunate. One young man died before his very eyes. Several more Marines at Rota had horrible wounds from the war with Iraq. For all of them, he would try to walk unaided. He would not let his own injuries garner pity.

As Sean deplaned at the Louisville International Airport, he had that same feeling of expectation that his father had over thirty years earlier. He had no idea what awaited him on the other side of the airplane door. As he made his way through the walkway chute connecting his plane to the waiting area inside, he heard the sound of cheers, first a few then a steadily increasing drone of cheers. He had come into view of the friends, family, and media people gathered to welcome him home. There was a quick chain reaction of yells, as a couple of people caught sight of Sean, and then everyone began to unload their feelings with cheering.

His two sisters Sarah and Hannah were first to reach him. They exchanged hugs. His dad was next, followed closely by Heather, big with child. At some point, Sean caught sight of his mother, and his instant response was to cry out, "Mom." It sounded like it came from a third grader. She clutched her son and then presented him with a bouquet of flowers.

Off to one side were three smartly uniformed Marines. One of these was Sean's recruiter. Drill Instructor Linn had called him and told him it would really be great if he and his two sidekicks could be there when Sean arrived. His response was, "How high?" When a Marine asks a fellow Marine if he could attend his Marine son's homecoming, this is not really a request. It is a courtesy notice. Marines simply don't refuse under these circumstances. Sean paid careful attention to the small Marine detail there to greet him. He had to talk to a lot of people. He had to say a few words now and then to show those who showed up how grateful he was that they came. But he never lost sight of the three Marines. Periodically, he turned their way to make small talk with these special brothers of his. It was just a part of being one of them.

Nathan Reed seemed to appear out of nowhere, standing just behind Sean and looking handsome in his Continental Airlines uniform, a security badge hanging down from his belt. Sean kept the promise he made to himself and walked without crutches. It was not an easy thing to pull off. His injuries had not completely healed. His limp was noticeable. He would spend a long time on his feet at the airport and then another long spell on his feet in Shelbyville. He made a point of greeting as many people at the airport as he could. One snapshot at the airport that was captured on the video his family recorded really captured the emotional essence of the moment. Sean was seen bending down to speak with a woman in a wheelchair. A large mural on the opposite wall displayed five very happy children. The handicapped woman clutched a tiny American flag. It was a brief moment that spoke volumes.

Sean spent his first few minutes in the airport talking to anybody he met, shaking hands, and hugging family and friends. It wasn't really a time for long speeches. It was Sean's time. These were exciting moments but also simple ones. He wanted to enjoy it. He wanted to feel the moment and enjoy the air of his own state. It was his air, and it was air that did not reek of war or sting his face with sand. He mentioned to a reporter that he felt so good looking out of the plane as it flew over Kentucky seeing how green the state looked. A reporter asked Sean point blank how he felt at the very moment of his arrival. Sean did not hesitate. He said the feeling was bittersweet. He explained that in coming home he had left his brothers back in Iraq, meaning his fellow platoon members. So, while coming home was wonderful, it made him think about them, the ones still fighting, and how they could not enjoy what he was then enjoying.

Another reporter asked Sean what was the first thing he wanted to do when he got back home. He didn't mention his favorite food. He didn't say he wanted to go fishing or go out with friends. He seemed to be wearing some of the war on his face as he said: "I just want to go on a long walk and be by myself for a while." Sean spoke to the airport crowd a few minutes later: "I'm really glad to be home. I'm glad to be alive. I'm glad to be back in my country." His arrival at Louisville International received heavy television coverage.

Linn Cassedy had told reporters as much as he knew about how Sean had been injured. But the problem was that the Marine Corps itself did not know what happened. For the several months following the April 3rd collision, the entire episode was classified as a non-hostile accident pending further investigation. It occurred as coalition forces approached Baghdad and its airport. Sean himself was not a good source. He could remember the events leading up to the incident, but once the collision crushed his legs and he found himself in a field being administered morphine, he was in and out of consciousness. So the news accounts of Sean's end of combat varied widely. One television report accurately characterized Sean as "one local injured Marine" but then said his Humvee had come under attack. Sean was not in a Humvee. Another news channel reported his injuries as a result of a firefight at the Baghdad International Airport against the Iraqi Republican Guard forces. Yet another station said Sean was wounded near Baghdad when the vehicle he was riding in collided with a tank, and he was shot by Republican Guard troops. Another report repeated the part about colliding with a tank but added that the injury to Sean's leg came from another collision with a "multi-ton armored vehicle."

The truth is that no one knew exactly what happened, including the participant himself, Sean S. Cassedy. His story happened when other stories were circulating. Just a few days before Sean's incident, it was reported that two Marines were killed as they slept when their own vehicles ran over them. Sorting out precise details of each injury and death was like trying to photograph a rushing river. Things moved too fast, and no one was stopping the war to offer any details.

Sean's return to Kentucky was front-page news in the local Shelbyville paper on April 23rd. "In the desert darkness, Sean Cassedy's Marine unit made its way toward Baghdad ..." began the account by the *Shelbyville Sentinel-News*. The article described an ambush that occurred fifteen miles from Baghdad. The homecoming plans of that day were previewed. Key Kentuckians who helped make the trip home and the celebration possible were identified, including State Representative Brad Montell, local bank president Billie Wade, and State Senator Gary Tapp. Also mentioned as part of this distinguished group was Mr. Nathan Reed. Representative Montell was quoted as telling everybody to bring a welcome-home sign. The article ended with a few words from Linn Cassedy recalling his own homecoming:

"I remember coming back from Vietnam, and I remember there was nobody there."

As the county seat, Shelbyville was picked to lead the celebration of Sean's homecoming. With a population of approximately ten thousand, it is a small Kentucky city, but still many times larger than Sean's hometown of Bagdad. Sean traveled with his family in their SUV from the Louisville airport to Shelbyville. Everyone was packed into the Suburban. This was all seven Cassedy children, Mom and Dad, and Heather's husband, Brian. Brian served as the cameraman for the trip from the airport to Shelbyville. He kept his camcorder rolling nonstop all along the route. Linn drove, and Sean rode shotgun next to his dad. After the beautiful reception at the airport, Sean had little idea what lay ahead.

It was an incredibly clear, blue sky that greeted the Cassedy family as they headed east on Interstate 64 toward Shelbyville. The ground was covered in beautiful early spring grass. Some trees had a coating of young leaves, while others were still rather barren. Sean tried to lead the conversation in the SUV, knowing he was the guest of honor. Everyone in the family was dying for news of what he saw and did in Iraq. He told them about the unusual things leading up to his injuries. He mentioned the iron spikes that caused his seven-ton truck's tires to blow. He told them about the Predator drone that crashed before his very eyes. Just as he was recounting these things, his dad tuned in the local Shelbyville news on the radio. It was news about Iraq, so he turned it up for everyone to hear. The newscaster said that Saddam's chief intelligence officer had just surrendered. He indicated that this could be critical in learning the whereabouts of Saddam himself and of those elusive weapons of mass destruction. Next, he reported that Iraqi protesters in southern Iraq had blocked coalition forces as they were about to cross the Tigris River.

After this international news, something incredible happened. Sean had been on the ground in Kentucky for less than two hours. He had already been welcomed by a small but enthusiastic group of supporters. Somehow, one of the reporters who covered his airport welcome had already filed a report with the radio station the family was listening to in the Suburban. The news broadcast from the local Shelbyville station turned from what was happening in Iraq to the local news of that day. Amazingly, Sean was listening to news about Sean! In fact, Sean listened to sound bytes of him speaking at the airport. His comments on how returning home left him with mixed emotions aired: "Bittersweet from the fact that my brothers are still in Iraq fighting the war, and I'm enjoying all of this." The cyberspace kid did it again.

They had just passed a sign indicating that Shelbyville was just another eight miles ahead when Sean got a call from Tiffany on a cell phone. The rest of the Cassedys made small talk with one another as Sean tried his best to speak to the woman he loved inside the close quarters of the SUV. He told her about the things happening to him that day and arranged to call her later that night. As the Suburban pulled off the interstate and onto the road into Shelbyville, Sean ended the call with, "I love you, too." He later told a reporter that he had spent many nights in Kuwait and Iraq thinking about proposing to Tiffany.

On the outskirts of Shelbyville, Linn pulled into the Wal-Mart parking lot and rendezvoused with four waiting police vehicles. Sean got out for a minute or two to greet the officers. Then the full Cassedy vehicle fell in behind two police vehicles and ahead of two others. Sean was now part of another armed convoy, but this one traveled in all friendly territory. The flashing lights and blaring sirens stopped traffic, and Sean sat in amazement through it all. The whole family reacted to the small but flashy escort with loud cheers inside their Suburban. Heather and her younger sisters remarked over and over again how incredible it all seemed.

The little but very loud caravan started at one end of Shelbyville, traveled down the main drag into the city's center, then out the other end, making a sharp right turn just past the McDonald's. A couple of miles past this was the finish line at the Shelbyville Fire and Rescue Station Number 2.

As the vehicles pulled away from the rendezvous with the police at Wal-Mart, the first of several specially prepared business signs appeared. Linn knew all about them, but Sean did not have a clue. Linn excitedly told his son to look at Pizza Hut. Instead of the special of the day, the marquee announced, "Welcome Home, Sean Cassedy!" Still on the outskirts of town, the Ethington Building Supply marquee read, "Support Our Troops." A few hundred yards further and Sean saw "Welcome Home, Sean Cassedy" in front of the Top Cut hair salon. He was nearly in shock. The whole town was thinking about him. Heather broke in as if Sean might miss them, "Look, Sean, at the Tumbleweed. Look over there at the Dairy Queen!" Both restaurants had "Welcome home, Sean" signs. The Sean Express passed a row of houses, eventually arriving at the city's center. Shelbyville is an old but very beautiful Kentucky city. The sirens seemed to catch everyone on the street by surprise. Before too long, the convoy was on the other side of Shelbyville heading out, and more signs welcoming Sean appeared in front of Papa John's, Colvin's Auto Sales, and McDonald's. The city fathers had arranged for over a dozen Shelbyville businesses to display the signs.

The small group of vehicles made a right turn just past the McDonald's and traveled another couple of miles until the local fire station came into view. Sean was again surprised, this time by the loud, cheering crowd waiting for him. He saw people holding American flags of different sizes. As the Cassedy SUV drove up to the crowd, sunshine was streaming over the people. Everybody waiting at the fire station seemed to be locked together in the excitement of the moment. It was the same kind of cheering he experienced at the airport. There was an almost indescribable enthusiasm to the sound. But it really could be not described. For the second time on this first day of his return home, Sean heard the sound of unbridled patriotic fervor. He heard yells that told him these local people really cared for him and they really appreciated what he did.

The local printing company had produced a large banner stretched across the entrance to the firehouse:

WELCOME HOME, SEAN CASSEDY
WE APPRECIATE YOUR SACRIFICE
THANK YOU AND BEST WISHES

It was a wonderful sight. The side of the firehouse had a large American flag draped over it. Little children were hoisted on the shoulders of those who brought them to this joyous celebration of one man. Just as soon as Sean left the vehicle, he began shaking hands and hugging people in the crowd. His limp was pronounced, and the extended time on his feet at the airport was taking a toll on him. Without a microphone, he told the crowd that he was at a loss for words, but he took the time to thank them. A couple of minutes later, someone handed him a microphone, and he told the crowd he would always remember this day.

Several city officials took turns with a wireless microphone praising Private Sean S. Cassedy. He was presented a special citation passed by the Kentucky House of Representatives and another from the state Senate.

Mayor Tom Hardesty of Shelbyville read a proclamation making Wednesday, April 23rd, Sean Cassedy Day in Shelbyville. After the speeches, Sean was again handed the microphone. He was nearly speechless and offered just a few more words of thanks. He introduced his father, pointing out that he, too, was a veteran, a Vietnam veteran. Linn graciously thanked everyone, singling out the efforts of Shelbyville native Nathan Reed in getting Sean home. Carol Cassedy said a few words and asked the crowd to recognize three other Marines: Staff Sergeants Peterson, Matthews, and McDew. Peterson and McDew were part of the recruiting team that recruited Sean. SSgt Matthews belonged to the Marine Corps public relations unit out of Louisville. They were Sean's loyal Marine detail self-appointed to greet him at the airport.

That evening and the next day, television news included video footage from the Shelbyville homecoming. Faces in the crowd were asked their feelings about Sean. One man, identified on the video footage simply as a veteran, put it very plainly: "He's a serviceman. That's what's best about him." He spoke of a special bond that connected all men and women in uniform. There was also a small sound byte from Nathan Reed that aired without any explanation at all. Unless you had been part of the Returning Son team assigned to bring Sean home, his words would have floated right by. But Sean's family knew. Nathan spoke into the camera and said, "Anytime you have a Marine that's in need, you know, somebody ought to go help him." The Cassedys knew what he was talking about and so did every Marine listening.

Despite his injuries and all of the fatigue built up from the travel and the homecoming crowds at the airport and in Shelbyville, Sean could not sleep. He stayed up all night his first night home. He could not stop talking with his family. They did not want him to. He wanted to tell them everything that happened, and they wanted to show him that they appreciated it all. They also wanted to show him that they loved him all the more for what he did. In Kuwait, before he jumped off into war, Sean got his feelings out through e-mails. In Iraq, he recorded his life in his daily journal. Now, free from the threat of the intentional world, he still wanted to get it out. He wanted to tell them all what it was like so they could begin to understand it all. They were hanging on his every word. It was a far cry from his father's return.

His actual time home was short. He was too much in love with Tiffany not to be thinking of her constantly. He had spent endless nights in Kuwait and in Iraq praying for the day when he could propose to her. Now that day had come. He had survived, and there was nothing stopping him except money. He could afford to drive to where she was, in New Jersey, and then propose. But his injured legs had not healed enough to allow him to drive. He called on the one Marine resource he could always call upon. He asked his father to drive him to New Jersey, to Fort Dix where Tiffany was. It was a doubly painful trek. It was like the cross-country bus ride he had taken to prove his love to her. Now he was going on a seven-hundred-mile trip to ask her to marry him. Father and son hit the road. Sean's legs acted up during the trip. But he also experienced another pain. It was the pain of his father's pinball-generation driving. Linn was a speed-limit driver. Sean had gone to hell and back. He was a mere nine hours away from arranging for his future. He was about to nail down the answer to one of the three big questions the Cassedy children were taught as home schoolers, and his father was extending the trip by another two hours with his slow driving. It was a good trip, but there were moments the two Marines were at each other's throats.

Two days after his homecoming in Shelbyville, the *Sentinel-News* ran an article recapping Sean's return. The article quoted Sean as saying he would remember his homecoming the rest of his life. What a difference a war makes. His father remembered his own homecoming for over thirty years, but for a completely different reason. The article mentioned the ribbing Sean took in Iraq from his fellow Marines when they learned he came from Bagdad. As they got closer to Baghdad, they would tell Sean he was almost home. He was and he wasn't. As he got closer to the capital of Iraq, a collision happened that did in fact give him his ticket back to Bagdad, Kentucky.

Things were different. The buildup to this war was different. The country had changed. It was the difference between phantom enemy attacks in the Gulf of Tonkin and 3,000 dead civilians, murdered on the home front in less than two hours. A new national attitude seemed to embrace the old adage that life was simply too short. Even if weapons of mass destruction proved to be elusive, even if Saddam and bin Laden were not connected, the wounds of September 11th were still being felt. The new attitude said that when America sent its sons and daughters to fight, the very least Americans could do was welcome them home with open arms.

This was the attitude that saw a small Kentucky community turn out so enthusiastically when one of its own came home from a war. It was an attitude hammered from tragedy. Firefighters who never questioned the need to go inside the doomed buildings on September 11th helped forge the attitude. Airline passengers who woke up to a bright summer day only to die at the hands of terrorists helped shape it, too. Millions of Americans watched the terrorist tragedy puzzle unfold before them. They saw after-the-fact video footage of the lunar landscape inside the twin towers that became the tomb of our known soldiers of police and firefighters. They listened to cell phone calls from Flight 93 of the last desperate moments of passengers trying to say "I love you" in the face of certain death. All of this changed the way many Americans thought about young men and women going off to war—any war.

Sean's father's return from Vietnam happened thirty-two years before Sean's return. But it was really thirty-two million light years away, somewhere out there in deep space, past Neptune and past Pluto. The lessons of Vietnam can't be forgotten. Don't fight a war you have not decided to win. Lessons of the past are sometimes ignored. The country's first president warned in his farewell address against excessive foreign entanglements. The thirty-fourth president warned in his farewell address against an ever-growing military industrial complex. But the lessons of 9/11 are still fresh. When we send our warriors off to fight, we must be ready to welcome them back. This is nothing new to the folks of tiny Bagdad, Kentucky. They have a tradition of revering those who serve in the military.

When a veteran of a foreign war comes home to a small country town, it means so much because it touches so many. The local pastor of Bagdad's Baptist church explained it this way: "They know they're our own flesh and blood." He was referring to the whole town when he said "they know." He was talking about military men and women heading off to war when he said "they're our own flesh and blood." This was the farm pond theory of returning soldiers. Throw just one small pebble into a tiny pond and the entire pond feels it. When just one veteran is hurt or dies, every family in town feels the ripple effect. Sean knew that firsthand, and he knew it from a spirit who would always walk with him, a great teacher…the brave driver of the LVS.

Over one hundred thousand American military members were involved in the capture of Baghdad and the defeat of Saddam's army. Each one had a family. Each one had a hometown. A few came from well-to-do families. Most did not. No matter what their background, they were each sent to risk their lives in the name of their country. They did that. All of them. And they got down to a level of existence that non-combatants can only imagine. Some of them like Sean had to overcome a rocky military start only to go on to face an enemy intent on killing them. They raced through a foreign desert. They were caked with sand and beaten down by the climate. They slept either in tents or in holes dug out of the desert sand. They were packed like sardines inside foul-smelling trucks. They ate MREs, and every day and every night they dealt with one real problem, the job of staying alive.

War is not really about who is right or wrong. The troops on the ground don't think that way. They just understand fighting and surviving. It really isn't about which countries are right or wrong. War is always a bad solution because it means people must die. But the alternative may be worse, especially if innocent people will die unless murderers are stopped. Sherman said it was hell. When we order men and women into combat, the impersonal government, the entity, the institution that issues those orders must take responsibility. The Sean Cassedys of the world cannot come back to an empty airport. War may be ill advised. War may be the complete wrong thing to do. But the men and women told to wage it have no choice. They fight or die, and tragically sometimes they do both.

To this day, no one knows exactly what happened on April 3, 2003, just seventy miles south of Baghdad. Sean isn't sure himself. He is only certain that he went on a short trip through hell that day. He doesn't consider himself a hero in any way. Despite his ups and downs in the Marine Corps, Sean remains a dedicated Marine. He is the product of the best training the United States can offer. He was hammered into a SAW gunner, and he performed his duties in Iraq well.

In September 2003, a television military analyst said of the morale of U.S. troops in Iraq: "They are professional troops. They will do what we *ask* of them." But what he said was not technically accurate. Within the military, despite what critics may say or do, no matter where we send them, U.S. troops will do what they are *ordered* to do, not what they're asked to do.

On June 4, 2003, Sean's older sister, Heather, gave birth to Brooke Elizabeth Johnston in Louisville, Kentucky. A month later, Sean Cassedy married Tiffany Fitzgerald. Sean's wounds had substantially healed. After a tumultuous two years in the world's most potent military machine, he continued his service in the Marine Corps. He was allowed to go back into the computer specialty he was so skilled in. The court-martial seemed a million miles away except for the scar it left on his record. When President Clinton left office, he pardoned several convicted felons. Sean Cassedy continues to fight for his honor in a world that pardons high crimes, but lets the military record of a war veteran remain tarnished.

Tiffany Fitzgerald Cassedy is the newest American warrior, a kind that no one could have foreseen. She is the reservist who has been converted by military necessity into a full-time soldier. She is no longer a weekend warrior. Her life has been unexpectedly altered in a major way. Because of U.S. commitments in Iraq, Afghanistan, and throughout the world, National Guard and Reserve units across the country are being called up for longer and longer tours of duty. Men and women with fully established civilian careers have to leave their jobs and their families to satisfy the military needs of the country. On February 18, 2004, Tiffany deployed with her Army unit to Iraq as part of the Quartermaster Corps.

Sean is living proof of the craziness of war. He was sent to Iraq after a court-martial stripped him of his rank and took away a great job. After being injured on the road to Baghdad, he was able to resume his computer specialty. Once his injuries had completely healed, the specialty that he fought so hard for became a ticket back to the intentional world of Iraq. In February 2004, a critical shortage of computer specialists led the Corps to order Sean back to Iraq. He was offered a grand choice. He could deploy to Iraq immediately and spend approximately six months deployed to Baghdad, or he could wait until the summer of 2004 and then spend a ten-month tour in Iraq. Sean chose to go right away. On March 2, 2004, Private First Class Sean Cassedy left for his second tour in Iraq. He is assigned as a data systems analyst administrator with a medical unit.

POSTSCRIPT: E-MAILS FROM THE WORLD'S LARGEST SANDBOX

Husband and wife are now located with their respective services just a few miles apart in the Fallujah area. On March 27, 2004, Sean sent an e-mail to his family. He offered a unique twist to the notion of the happily married couple, describing married life for two members of the American military stationed near one another in a war zone. He also noted that he still deals with the face of death:

I hope this e-mail finds you all well. Tiffany and I are doing well. Things have been really busy here. A lot goes on where I work. I've already seen quite a few deaths. In fact, you might have heard about the major and sergeant that got killed by a mortar. They were in the Army. That mortar hit about twenty feet from where I now work. But all is well. Life is treating us well. It sure is great that Tiff is here. It adds a little stress, but it is worth it. Let everyone know that we are well and miss you all. I'll try to call soon. Sean out.

In June, 2004 Sean wrote that the temperatures were in the 110-113 degree range. As a result, physical training was reduced from six times a week to three. The exercise regimen included flag football, ping pong, volley ball, and horseshoes. He noted that in early June *only* two incoming rounds fell near his location. He wrote: "Being bored is a very good thing for us." He also sent birthday greetings to his beautiful little niece, Brooke Elizabeth, who was about to turn one year old. Sean had yet to spend any time with her. War got in the way. Little things for stateside Americans meant all the difference in the world to Sean. He wrote that his unit received the ultimate privilege for a Marine in Iraq--one hour at a swimming pool. For that short time, Sean said he forgot he was even in Iraq.

In July, Sean's sandbox e-mail told everyone back home that the love of his life, his wife, Tiffany, was leaving his immediate area. He told of how blessed he felt he was to be able to be so close to her for even the few months they were stationed just minutes apart. He also noted with a little sadness that he would not be there when she celebrated her twenty-first birthday. He would turn twenty-three on his next birthday.

Sean had come full circle. He was back in combat mode. Instead of worrying about what Tiffany was doing back home, now he had to worry if she was safe in Iraq. That's the way Sean's life went. It was filled with ups and downs. It was filled with death. But most of all, it was filled with living. His father was already thinking about his son's next homecoming.

At some point Sean caught sight of his mother and his instant response was to cry out, 'Mom.'

Off to one side were three smartly uniformed Marines.

Nathan Reed seemed to appear out of nowhere.

...while coming home was wonderful, it made him think about the ones still fighting...

The local printing company had produced a large banner stretched across the entrance of the Firehouse.

THE SENATE
OF THE
COMMONWEALTH OF KENTUCKY

To All To Whom These Presents Shall Come, Greetings:

Know ye that

Sean Cassedy

is recognized and honored for his brave and courageous service as a member of the U.S. Marine Corps who was recently wounded outside the city of Baghdad, Iraq, while serving in support of Operation Iraqi Freedom. Inasmuch as this outstanding Kentucky citizen is a highly-skilled member of the United States Armed Forces who is prepared to boldly and skillfully do what is necessary to maintain peace and preserve freedom in the world, Sean Cassedy, a native of Bagdad, Kentucky, is congratulated for the great honor and pride that he brings to his community and to this Commonwealth by his efforts in this critical endeavor; is extended sincerest best wishes that he may return home safely and under the flag of victory; and,

on the motion of

Senator Gary Tapp

is hereby deemed by this honorable body most worthy of its recognition.

Done at Frankfort, Kentucky, this twenty-third day of April, in the year two thousand and three.

_____
President of the Senate

_____
Member of the Senate

Kentucky Senate's recognition of Sean Cassedy.

THE HOUSE OF REPRESENTATIVES

OF THE

COMMONWEALTH OF KENTUCKY

The House of Representatives of the Commonwealth of Kentucky hereby pays ardent tribute to

Sean Cassedy

of Bagdad, Shelby County, Kentucky, in recognition of his military service as a member of the United States Marine Corps while stationed in Iraq in support of Operation Iraqi Freedom. The entire membership of this honorable body is honored to join Representative Brad Montell in saluting this exceptional individual, who was wounded in battle outside of Baghdad, Iraq, for both the courage he has exhibited and the sacrifices he has made while serving his fellow man. For inasmuch as this valiant citizen has given much to gain victory and ensure freedom, he has brought great honor to his family, friends, and all citizens of this great Commonwealth. It is with solemn pride that this distinguished body honors Sean Cassedy for the dignity he has enabled us to maintain in this Commonwealth and Nation and extends expressions of deepest gratitude for his contributions as a courageous member of the United States Armed Forces.

Done in Frankfort, Kentucky, this twenty-third day of April, in the year two thousand and three.

Speaker, House of Representatives

Member, House of Representatives

Kentucky House of Representatives recognition.

City of Shelbyville
Incorporated 1792

Proclamation

WHEREAS: Our soldiers believe in the concept of freedom for this and all nations; and

WHEREAS: They are willing to leave their families and travel half way around the world to proudly fight for that freedom; and

WHEREAS: One of those soldiers, Sean Cassedy, who was willing to risk his life and health for a humanitarian cause, has returned home to Bagdad, Kentucky, after being injured while serving in Operation Iraqi Freedom,

NOW THEREFORE, I, Thomas L. Hardesty, Mayor of Shelbyville, do hereby proclaim Wednesday, April 23, as:

SEAN CASSEDY

day in the City of Shelbyville, and do commend this observance to all of our citizens.

MAYOR: Thomas L. Hardesty
Dated this the 23rd day of April 2003

Sean Cassedy Day.

Additional Memories of Sean in War and Peace

Special airport flag brigade.

Lil Sis flag brigade.

Heather's homemade welcome home sign.

Waiting for brother to come home.

Waiting for war.

Sean on the highway of death and destruction.

Sean's motley crew.

Home sweet home in the back of a smelly old truck.

Two returning sons flanked by mom and dad.

Oil field fires were lit to confuse coalition forces.

Epilogue

In the aftermath of what many perceived to be a strikingly quick military victory, the world continues to analyze this war. Many critics have questioned the need to stay in Iraq in light of the continued U.S. casualties. The invasion officially began on March 20, 2003. Sixteen months later some 900 American military members had died, with approximately 75% of these listed as combat deaths. In a combat environment, whether victory is declared or not, the one thing that remains constant is that casualties will grow with time. Unlike Europe after World War II, the rejoicing over being liberated from a tyrant has been replaced by disdain over being occupied by a superpower. It is virtually impossible to accurately measure how widespread that feeling is among Iraqis. Questions have been raised over the motives of the Bush administration in starting this war. Some argue that the Iraqi operation has diluted the war on terrorism and that removing a secular dictator has done nothing to stop religious extremists like Osama bin Laden. Still others believe the war in Iraq and the occupation of Iraq by America have alienated many countries against the United States.

When the world learned that American soldiers abused Iraqi prisoners at Abu Ghraib, a group of terrorists filmed the beheading of Nick Berg. They claimed it was in retaliation for the abuses. The difference between American military members caught abusing enemy combatants, and terrorists committing murder is vast. The American GIs must face a legal process designed to punish the criminal violations. Terrorists are not lawful combatants. They do not fight according to the rules. They are criminals aligned with no country's government. They take the law into their own hands and commit criminal atrocities against the innocent. They represent a return to piracy and lawlessness. The rules on war and peace continue to change. Player Killers now roam the earth looking for victims. But they are real killers, not virtual ones.

The rules have changed. Traditional rules of warfare have been modified to meet non-traditional enemies. A Justice Department legal memo from 2002, and a Pentagon Working Group memo issued two weeks before the invasion of Iraq, both suggested that prisoner interrogations could be much more "aggressive" and still comply with the international law outlawing torture. The prisoner abuses and the news of these "torture memos" may have unleashed a wave of terrorist atrocities. A vicious random player killer's version of the golden rule is operating. Innocent, helpless victims. The photographs of American Army soldiers abusing Iraqi prisoners at Abu Ghraib prison produced a reaction from alleged Al Qaeda sources. "We will treat American hostages like you treated Iraqi prisoners." That was the message. It did not matter that Al Qaeda represented no country. It did not matter that its members were terrorists operating outside of treaties, outside of the customary rules of war, and outside of the law altogether. Reciprocity was threatened and retaliation was exacted in a most shocking and brutal way.

Nick Berg's beheading in Iraq followed Daniel Pearl's beheading in Pakistan. So the savagery existed before the invasion of Iraq ever happened. Paul Johnson, a Lockheed-Martin employee and another innocent civilian, was murdered after Mr. Berg in the same ruthless manner in Saudi Arabia. Al Qaeda operatives in Saudi Arabia claimed responsibility. The atrocities are not confined to Americans. A South Korean civilian employee, Kim Sun-Il, was taken hostage and beheaded in late June, 2004. A murderous genie has been let loose, and there are very few options available to stop an enemy who obeys no rules at all.

Countries never want to appear to give in to the criminal category known as terrorists. But that general rule saw exceptions in 2004. On March 11, 2004, over two thousand innocent Spanish commuters became casualties when terrorist bombs exploded, in an attack that killed 191 and injured over 2,000. The brutal attack occurred just days before the country's national election. With a population of just over forty million, the assault was on a scale comparable to the 9/11 attacks on the United States. Political observers felt the attack was the single most important factor that the pro-American party in power was voted out. As a result, Spain eventually withdrew its troops from Iraq.

In July 2004, when terrorists threatened to behead a civilian Filipino hostage, the government of the Philippines agreed to terrorist demands to withdraw its contingent of fifty-one humanitarian workers. The President of the Philippines explained the withdrawal by saying, "I cannot apologize for being a protector of my people." Terrorists played a numbers game with two countries and won. But who won? Who were the two countries responding to? They weren't dealing with any government or country, because no nation publicly recognizes terrorists. They weren't dealing with any legitimate group at all. They agreed to leave Iraq to stop the death of their own citizens.

But which devil they struck their bargain with no one really knows for certain. Despite the loss of military support from two countries, as of July, 2004, over thirty countries besides the United States were providing military troops in Iraq, although many of these offered relatively small contributions compared to the U.S. and Great Britain.

One year after the President landed on the U.S.S. Abraham Lincoln to announce the end to major combat operations in Iraq, coalition forces were fighting a major insurgency. American military deaths had passed the 750 mark with the death toll for the first four months of 2004 alone exceeding 250. But for all of the criticism and in the face of the staggering number of deaths, one truth remained: Military men and women have to fight no matter how unpopular the war.

War is hell. No one understands General Sherman's warning better than newly promoted Lance Corporal Sean S. Cassedy. Sean was injured in the war. The official report calls the incident that caused his injuries a non-hostile accident. But whether it was an ambush, as Sean thinks it was, or a major collision caused by other factors, Sean carries with him a set of numbers. Of the forty or so men and women in his platoon, thirteen were injured and one was killed on April 3, 2003. In reviewing the casualty accounts of this war, parents will not be relieved or worried by the way their loved one died. They simply know a son or a daughter died. They died while examining explosives. They died when their vehicle fell into a ravine. They died manning security checkpoints. They died in helicopter crashes throughout Iraq. They drowned crossing canals. They died during accidental discharges of weapons. They died of sudden illnesses and from rocket-propelled grenades. To the loved ones of those who died, they died serving their country. After Vietnam and during the war in Iraq, some have claimed that American troops died in vain. Causes may be wrong. Policies may be terribly wrong. Presidents can make serious mistakes. But the men and women who die in combat doing what they were told to do never die in vain. Never. As Linn Cassedy would say, "End of discussion!"

Sean was in the first wave of the invasion in 2003. He returned to Iraq during what many people feared was the absolute most dangerous time, the months leading up to the transfer of sovereignty to the Iraqis at the end of June, 2004. He is scheduled to serve his country in Iraq for several months after the transfer. That post-transfer period has become the new "absolute most dangerous time."

In some ways Sean and his father are mirrors for one another. Linn Cassedy can look into his son's face and see his own life. He can see his Marine days coming back to life through Sean. And Sean can look into his father's eyes and realize that he must take the best and worst of his dad's experiences and learn from them. Sean's parents taught him to explore life's processes by searching for the answer to three questions: Where will you spend eternity? What will be your life's work? Who will be your life's partner? Sean's faith in God is rock solid, so he strives for a heavenly eternity. Despite the many crucibles he has passed through, including a very humiliating court-martial, he still looks upon the Corps as a career, and as his life's work. And his wife, Tiffany, is the most beautiful answer to question three that he could ever dream of.

Sean's country is also searching for answers to some very basic questions. It too must look in the mirror and make sure that it never forgets the good and the bad experiences of that past. What are the real goals in Iraq? Are the military missions clear? Do the people we seek to liberate understand freedom the way we do? National soul searching goes on in the face of many deaths. You never know really know that death is a teacher…

About The Author

Dennis W. Shepherd is a lawyer and a retired Air Force lieutenant colonel. As an enlisted Russian linguist he flew aboard reconnaissance missions that targeted the former Soviet Union, North Korea, Cuba, and North Vietnam. This included eighteen combat support missions over Vietnam and Thailand during the Vietnam War. As an Air Force JAG he served as a prosecutor and defense counsel before becoming an international law specialist and Law of War expert. He and his wife, Sudar, have been together since 1974. They have one son, Shane, and two grandsons, Jared and Kyle. The Shepherds make their home in Lexington, Kentucky.

Printed in the United States
24625LVS00005B/166

9 781418 424589